Lucretius and Modernity

The New Antiquity

Edited by Matthew S. Santirocco

Over the past two decades, our understanding of the ancient world has been dramatically transformed as classicists and other scholars of antiquity have moved beyond traditional geographical, chronological, and methodological boundaries to focus on new topics and different questions. By providing a major venue for further cutting-edge scholarship, *The New Antiquity* will reflect, shape, and participate in this transformation. The series will focus on the literature, history, thought, and material culture of not only ancient Europe, but also Egypt, the Middle East, and the Far East. With an emphasis also on the reception of the ancient world into later periods, *The New Antiquity* will reveal how present concerns can be brilliantly illuminated by this new understanding of the past.

MATTHEW S. SANTIROCCO is Senior Vice Provost for Undergraduate Academic Affairs at New York University, where he is Professor of Classics and Angelo J. Ranieri Director of Ancient Studies, and served for many years as Seryl Kushner Dean of the College of Arts and Science. He taught previously at the University of Pennsylvania, Columbia, Brown, Emory, and Pittsburgh. He is the former editor of the APA Monograph series, *American Classical Studies* and the journal *Classical World*. His publications include a book on Horace, as well as several edited volumes and many articles. In 2009, he was elected a Fellow of the American Academy of Arts and Sciences and is currently Assistant Secretary of the Academy for Humanities and Social Sciences.

Published by Palgrave Macmillan:

Horace and Housman by Richard Gaskin
Combat Trauma and the Ancient Greeks edited by Peter Meineck and David Konstan
Lucretius and Modernity: Epicurean Encounters Across Time and Disciplines edited by Jacques Lezra and Liza Blake

Lucretius and Modernity

Epicurean Encounters Across Time and Disciplines

Edited by
Jacques Lezra
and
Liza Blake

LUCRETIUS AND MODERNITY

First published 2016 by
PALGRAVE MACMILLAN

The authors have asserted their rights to be identified as the authors of this work in accordance with the Copyright, Designs and Patents Act 1988.

Palgrave Macmillan in the UK is an imprint of Macmillan Publishers Limited, registered in England, company number 785998, of Houndmills, Basingstoke, Hampshire, RG21 6XS.

Palgrave Macmillan in the US is a division of Nature America, Inc., One New York Plaza, Suite 4500, New York, NY 10004-1562.

Palgrave Macmillan is the global academic imprint of the above companies and has companies and representatives throughout the world.

Hardback ISBN: 978–1–137–58199–0
Paperback ISBN: 978–1–137–59189–0
E-PUB ISBN: 978–1–137–56655–3
E-PDF ISBN: 978–1–137–56657–7
DOI: 10.1057/9781137566577

Distribution in the UK, Europe and the rest of the world is by Palgrave Macmillan®, a division of Macmillan Publishers Limited, registered in England, company number 785998, of Houndmills, Basingstoke, Hampshire RG21 6XS.

Library of Congress Cataloging-in-Publication Data

Lucretius and modernity : Epicurean encounters across time and disciplines / edited by Jacques Lezra and Liza Blake.
    pages cm—(The new antiquity)
    ISBN 978–1–137–58199–0 (hardcover : alk. paper)—
    ISBN 978–1–137–59189–0 (pbk. : alk. paper)
    1. Lucretius Carus, Titus—Criticism and interpretation. 2. Lucretius Carus, Titus—Influence. 3. Epicureans (Greek philosophy) I. Lezra, Jacques, 1960– II. Blake, Liza, 1984– III. Series: New antiquity.
PA6484.L854 2016
187—dc23   2015030189

A catalogue record for the book is available from the British Library.

CONTENTS

Part IV   Following Lucretius

ACKNOWLEDGMENTS

The chapters collected in this book were read, in earlier form, at "Lucretius and Modernity," a conference held at New York University (NYU) in the fall of 2011. The conference was the Annual Ranieri Colloquium in Ancient Studies, sponsored by NYU's Center for Ancient Studies. Cosponsors included NYU's Departments of Comparative Literature, Classics, French, and Philosophy; the Humanities Initiative; the Gallatin Fund: Classics and the Contemporary World; the Program in Poetics and Theory; and the Medieval and Renaissance Center. We gratefully acknowledge the support of each of these cosponsors, with special thanks to the Center for Ancient Studies.

Introduction

JACQUES LEZRA AND LIZA BLAKE

Lucretius and Modernity

"Lucretius reaches the mainstream": thus, rather dolefully, Gordon Campbell titles his 2007 review of the *Oxford Readings in Classical Studies: Lucretius* and *Cambridge Companion to Lucretius* collections.[1] It is 2016 now; two millennia after the work was drafted, the long shadow cast by Lucretius's *De Rerum Natura* (*DRN*; before 50 CE) falls across the "mainstream" disciplines of philosophy, literary history and criticism, religious studies, classics, political philosophy, the history of science, and others. How do we account for the work's *modernity*, if that is indeed what it is? Or perhaps for its arresting resistance to every effort to line it up with a period's preoccupations—whether we have in mind the time of its composition; its rediscovery; its first, scandalized reception; its persistence as a Gothic, philosophical monster haunting the attics of the Enlightenment; its uncomfortable flirtation with critiques of determinism; its reentry into academic conversation in the late twentieth century? What does *DRN* mean to *us*? "Suave, mari magno," we read at the opening of the second Book (2.1–2), "turbantibus aequora ventis / e terra magnum alterius spectare laborem" [Pleasant it is, when on the great sea the winds trouble the waters, to gaze from shore about another's great tribulation], but nowhere do we find firm ground, ourselves, from which to contemplate serenely the tossing seas of Lucretius's reception: we are always also aboard, always carried along in and on the poem.[2]

"Lucretius reaches the mainstream." Does he, though? Has he? And if so, what happens to the "mainstream" on his arrival?

There is no doubt that over the past two decades interest in *DRN* has grown dramatically in academic fields and beyond. Hidden Epicurean influences on well-known writers have come to light; the decline of a school or of an orthodoxy has left room for a return to Lucretius, and to the Epicurean tradition more broadly—as with the eclipse of normative materialisms in philosophy and politics. Contemporary physics has found in the ancient atomist tradition a strange and evocative mirror.[3] The Lucretian *declinatio*, the minimal and unpredictable swerve of atoms that the poem's Book 2 describes, provides a poetical precursor to debates regarding physical causation, moral responsibility, and their possible relation.[4] The place of Lucretius's poetics in the development of modern poetic genres, techniques, and themes has come into sharp focus; the strange resurgence of creationism in the United States is found to revive complexly the old counterarguments that Lucretius's poem provides, many years avant la lettre; political philosophers have identified what Louis Althusser called a "subterranean current" in the materialist tradition, flowing from Epicurus through Spinoza and Marx and to Deleuze, propelled by Lucretius's great poem.[5] Stephen Greenblatt's popular account of the poem's rediscovery by Poggio Bracciolini, and of its reception in early modernity, has won a Pulitzer Prize and the National Book Award in the United States.[6] His subtitle is diagnostic: "How the World Became Modern." Outside the walls of the academy and within, though in different ways, the American twenty-first century seeks, and finds in the comic-heroic, fairy-tale-ish story of *DRN*'s survival, the story of its *becoming*.

When we refer to a work or to an author's "modernity" we have in mind at least three things.

First, works or writers are "modern" in a flatly chronological sense when they write in the era generally called "modern": the era of print culture, of the emergent nation-state, of secular conceptions of association and identity, of interiority, of the scientific method. We call "modernity" what we recognize as *our* period, and which we usually designate as beginning in "early modernity." "We" here means scholars, critics, and a general public that accepts a normative, Burckhardtian, or Weberian historiography, and imagines the European human animal to have suffered a period of darkness after antiquity, from which it is reborn when Petrarch ascends Mt. Ventoux and finds his past in the classics; or when Gutenberg revolutionizes the mode of textual production and of distribution; or, as in Greenblatt's account, when Poggio Bracciolini comes upon the manuscript of *DRN*.[7] Even within this book you will find "modernity" variously defined: Phillip Mitsis's chapter, for example, begins by arguing that for the discipline of the history of philosophy, "modernity" begins with Cartesian philosophy.[8] In this strict chronological sense, Lucretius is not, cannot possibly be, modern, living as he did centuries before "modernity" in any definition began.

"Modernity," in this first usage, usually signals a step out of obscurantism, dogma, "enchantment," or mythology, out of the rote performance of identities and into a world and a worldview in which method, interiority, subjectivity, and an emergent sense of autonomy emerge to replace these older ways of being. The step is a historical event: modernity arrives *at* a moment, and we can judge it to have arrived *from* a moment—our own—indebted to it for (among other things) the capacity to identify modernity's arrival. Needless to say, this prejudicial understanding of "modernity"—which is inseparable from value-judgments explicit (those "dark ages" before "modernity" cleared out cankered, walled-in, cobwebbed thinking) and implicit (there are quasi-Hegelian developmental and teleological metaphors at work in historiography: a period may be "early," "middle," or "late"; it may reach "maturity"; it may be a moment when societies leave infancy and *acquire a voice*, as in Kant's famous description of the Enlightenment)—in no way squares with what scholars of earlier periods have shown to be true.[9] Some of the clearest and most cogent critiques of the negative effects of this polemical modernity were collected in a cluster of miniature book-review essays in the journal *Exemplaria*, essays that reconsider Greenblatt's argument about the world becoming modern by means of Lucretius from scientific, historical, book-historical, literary-historical, affective, secular, and ideological perspectives.[10]

Second, works and writers may be "modern," too, when it seems *as if* they belong to our period, as we understand it—belong to it stylistically, conceptually, or thematically. Here the governing concern is to understand how different times come to see Lucretius's poem as modern, where "modern" means something like "contemporary."[11] The "modernity" of these older "modern" writers, or works, is not a matter of *when* they wrote, but of *how,* or of *what* they wrote; they are in these respects our contemporaries. Apuleius's ironies are not only precursors to the novel, this mode of defining modernity might opine: they speak as much to our day-to-day experience as Bulgakov's *Master and Margarita*, or Mann's narratives, or Bolaño's. Chronology and "modernity," in this way of defining "modernity," will prove antagonistic, or quite separate, concepts.

Finally, a writer or a work may be "modern" (or have a relation to modernity) when a later writer has based his or her "modern" work (now in either of the first two senses) on an earlier one: we might say that under this definition of modernity, we are speaking of something like Lucretius *in* modernity.[12] Among classicists, this reception history is often treated separately from the study of the poem itself. For example, Gillespie and Hardie's *Cambridge Companion* breaks its Table of Contents into two sections, "Antiquity" and "Reception," the latter collecting essays that treat how Lucretius was taken up and reworked in different centuries and countries. A number of the chapters in this book operate by this understanding of modernity, seeing how and why Lucretius's poem moves into different times, disciplines, and authors.

Matters get slippery very quickly, of course—a chronologically "modern" writer may write deliberately classicizing, premodern works; our understanding of what makes our "modern" era "modern" may differ (one critical school's "modernity" in this sense is another's archaism, or yet another's postmodernity). An author may be inconsistent, and appear out of time with him or herself: Lucretius, for example, may seem modern because of his secular impulses but non-modern because of his antiquated scientific beliefs (as Joseph Farrell argues in this book). Someone may well be my "contemporary" but not yours, though you and I live at the same time. In his chapter in this book, David Konstan points out that someone I consider my contemporary might be so not because he or she is modern but because he or she is *post*modern. One may go as far as Bruno Latour and declare that *We Have Never Been Modern*, or may follow the lead of Brooke Holmes in this book and think about nonlinear models of time and history in which concepts like "modernity" cease to have a clear meaning.[13] Lucretius himself—the poem itself, rather—makes matters harder for us still. (It helps not at all—indeed, quite the contrary—to observe that the tendency to make things hard for its readers and audience on this point is one of *DRN*'s most recognizably "modern" features.)

Lucretius as non-modern; Lucretius as modernity; Lucretius as modern; Lucretius in modernity. Modernity as period; as historical causation; as a-temporal, untimely connections; as a set of traits that define a way of thinking, writing, or acting in the modern world. There is a mixture, then, in this book, of two issues that are usually separate, or addressed separately: that of periodization, and that of reception studies. Each raises difficult methodological questions: under periodization, we must decide whether and then how to separate historical periods, what attributes belong to which period, and which authors or thinkers or artists belong where. In reception studies, if we accept that classical texts are resolutely classical, ancient rather than modern, then we must decide how to conceptualize the interaction between classical past and modern present. Are these texts and thinkers our contemporaries, mutating and almost living beings, changing with each century in response to new environments? Or are they texts of an ancient moment, whose potentiality to be used or misused by future centuries depends more on the ingenuity of future centuries than it does on any individual text itself?[14] Our chapters cut across both of these grains: they recognize that the distinction between how we conceive of periods and how we conceive of reception is itself *both* a characteristic of a period (ours, perhaps), *and* a mode of reception. Some of the chapters ask, polemically, what is at stake in classifying—or refusing to classify—Lucretius as "modern" (see especially Farrell and Konstan), while others use the question of classification to rethink temporality or reception itself (Holmes, Montag, Gigandet), or to rethink how Lucretius's travels through later centuries might warp the history of philosophy (Wilson, Mitsis, Lezra), the history of poetry (Hardie), the history of politics (Kavanagh), etc.

Modernity and Modality

DRN pays a great deal of attention, not to "modernity," of course (that term's lexical history begins considerably later), but to "modality," its kin semantically and relative etymologically. Philosophy, as it is known in the West, takes shape around questions that Lucretius's poem also seeks to address: What shapes and what things are possible in nature, what outcomes, what causes? Of the possible ways of formulating statements about such things and their coming-into-being and going-out-of-existence at one or another time, which work best? Which are more truthful? How do conditions of enunciation and comprehension modify—modulate, *modalize*—such statements? The answers that *DRN* provides, however, swerve violently from the dominant metaphysical tradition. The poem's sense of what it means to "live," to "live at the same time" as another person, to live in time or in a time; and of what it might mean to appear *as if* one were something or other (to appear, say, to treat themes that resemble those that worry a "modern" writer, our contemporary); and more generally, what it might mean for one thing to *appear* at all, *to another*—these are all highly controversial. Moreover, the poem itself is, in an important way, a *mode* and a *modification* of, a *modulation* upon, a tradition. Lucretius's poem shows its readers, or the audience hearing the poem read, the currency of Epicurus's thought: for that reason Epicurus's *modernity* is the result, the product, the intended or the unintentional effect, of Lucretius's poem.[15] Indeed, as concerns the history of philosophy, *DRN* is the definitive example of how a chronologically distant work can be made contemporary. The central conceptual claim: that contemporaneity is *fashioned*; it is a *product*, not a "natural" state of affairs; contemporaneity is not part of the nature of things.

The poem fashions contemporaneity and "modernity" in various ways. We recognize, for instance, how carefully the poem establishes how it makes claims: the edges, drawn sharply in modernity, between pedagogical language, persuasion, and constative speech are constantly, and deliberately, crossed and marred. "Perspicere ut possis res gestas funditus omnis," writes Lucretius:

> non ita uti corpus per se constare neque esse
> nec ratione cluere eadem qua constet inane,
> sed magis ut merito possis eventa vocare
> corporis atque loci, res in quo quaeque gerantur. (1.478–82)

In Rouse's slow translation, this is:

> So that you may perceive that things done never at all consist or exist in themselves as body does, nor are said to exist in the same way as void; but rather you may properly call them accidents [*eventa*] of body, and of the place in which the things are severally done.

"Possis eventa vocare / corporis atque loci:" you *may* call things done, *res gestas*, "accidents" (*eventa*), with a greater degree of merit (*magis ut merito*) than if you called them by another name, or thought of them as existing in themselves, as body does, or void. The verse instructs Memmius, not in what can be said to be *true*, but in how one *may speak*, with greater or less merit. "Memmius," it says, "you may call something done an event, and the event of calling, *vocare*, may be called, with greater merit than if you used a different word, 'accidental' or event-al." To speak about things done, about *res gestas*, is to do something too, so the poem, a thing done, an act, a song, is an accident or an event supervenient to something else, a location or a body. Time, then, is a mode of matter, an accident, a supervenience. For that reason, being-in-time, or judging that events coincide temporally, or that so-and-so or this-or-that event or work are simultaneous, or "contemporaneous" or "modern," are judgments concerning a modality, made or sung in a medium that is itself material.

The poem carries this *modalization* of its themes and techniques through with the most searching, unsettling thoroughness and self-consciousness. At one level, for instance, Lucretius's physics sings how matter acquires a boundary, a measure, a quantity, one-ness, body, a *modus*—and then loses it. At the same place in the poem that *DRN* reflects upon how matter, subject to *foedera naturae* or pacts of nature, can be represented, it also reflects upon how it, the poem itself, fashions sound and sense poetically out of the elemental matter, letters and words, that the poet handles. Take the discussion of *simulacra* in Book 4, ll. 30ff. This is no doubt among the poem's most famous, and perhaps the strangest, efforts to press a materialist outlook to its consequences: *esse ea quae rerum simulacra vocamus*, "there exist what we call *images* of things," where "images" translates *simulacra*, given in the next line as *membranae* or thin films.[16] In both *simulacra* and *membranae*, ὑμήν (*hymen*) is probably the term Lucretius is seeking to render, as preserved in the Epicurean inscription of Diogenes of Oneonada.[17] Look: *simulacra*, membranes of things, their *hymen* or one of them, touch us. At every instant every thing casts off its thin film for another's eye to catch: the shells of things trouble the air constantly. And Lucretius's verse then touches us as well, bearing to our imagination on his letters a film of that forest of floating films; and now these words you are reading add another: alike, materially kin, but distinct. These films you are reading now are temporally related, but not coincident, since the *simulacrum* is the membrane of a body at a moment.

DRN is indeed a *simulacrum* of *natura* at a moment, and of the *simulacrum* of nature provided by Epicurus. Being also a material image, it follows the *foedera naturae* it depicts: that there will be sudden, spontaneous variation and event whenever there is body, void, and movement. Every analogy the poem provides regarding its material operation is thus *like* a membrane it casts off from itself, and it *is also* such a membrane, and hence separate, materially as well as temporally, from itself. Highly fashioned, reasoned modes of the poem's matter, these reflexive moments also swerve violently from Lucretius's text—according to a rule the poem lays out for its readers and audience. The poem understands itself immanently, but it represents itself exoterically. As to the *content* of such analogies—the register of alphabetical similes to itself that the poem unfolds, the marvelous pedagogical simulacra it offers for natural elements and for its own workings—here something unexpected and uncontrollable happens as well, as if in accord with the *natural* rule of *declinatio*, the unexpected swerve that occurs "at times quite uncertain and [in] uncertain places" (2.218–19).

The definitive alphabetical analogy (throughout, but first at 1.196–98: "So...you may more readily believe many bodies to be common to many things, as we see letters [*verbis elementa*] to be common to words, than that anything can exist without first-beginnings") states, as it were, theoretically, explicitly, its technique, what the poem seeks to *do*, and *how* it will accomplish it. The analogy, inasmuch as it is a poetic statement *in* the poem regarding *how* the poem makes statements poetically, in poetic matter, is a mode of the poem's matter, of its *elementa*. Hence the paradoxical standing of the poem's reflexive, metadiscursive moments: as *modes* of the poem, they are *like* the poem, *like* what happens at the poem's elemental level. But to that extent and also necessarily, they are unlike it, in the way that the simulacrum is like the original, and indeed is materially *part* of the original, but exists distinctly from it, and always only records a past moment of the existence of the original—the moment at which the original shed its membrane, its film, its *hymen*.

And note: *similitude, simulacreity*, if such barbarism can be countenanced, is a reflexive relation. I am like my brother, but this also means that he is like me; an atom is like a mote of dust, and a letter is like an atom, and a poem composed of words made up of letters is like the things in nature—and vice versa. "What a piece of work is a man!" Hamlet will exclaim. "How noble in reason, how infinite in faculty, in form and moving how express and admirable, in action how like an angel[!]"[18] Man is *like* an angel in action, but this means necessarily that an angel is *like* a man in action as well.[19] The pedagogical, illustrative moments in which the poem provides analogues for natural phenomena are *like* what the poem's discursive, "philosophical" exposition shows, as the poem is *like* the nature it sings—but natural things are like the poem as well, and the "philosophical" exposition in *DRN* is like the poetic and pedagogical analogues it spins off like membranes. On this unsettling description, natural things are like thin material film spun from the matter of the poem, and the "philosophical" exposition in *DRN* is also the thin *hymen* of its metadiscursive, poetical analogues. Membranes of membranes; films of films. Throughout, the philosophical principle of identity is in question, but so is the poem's coherence. *DRN* is, and is not, contemporaneous with itself; it is, and is not, part of itself; it is fashioned coherently, and swerves, at uncertain times and places, from its fashion. It is a *simulacrum* of nature, which is its *simulacrum* too.

DRN's Disciplines

At the heart of *DRN*'s threatening attraction to scholars lies the poem's paradoxical modalization of its medium, theme, and moment. We bring

Lucretius to us—to the "mainstream," to our time, to the conventions and protocols of a specific discipline—as a way of escaping the verse's radicalism. As the poet seems indeed to reach the mainstream, the number and variety of scholarly publications on his work and influence have increased correspondingly. What is notable is the continued compartmentalization of scholarly approaches. Despite the poem's increased influence and visibility, very little resembling a cross-disciplinary conversation regarding *DRN* has taken place. Marked philological advances—spurred in part by scholarship on the Epicurean tradition—have not found echoes in the interpretation of the poem's poetics; the use that political philosophy (and philosophy *tout court*) has made of the poem barely acknowledges that the work is, indeed, *a poem;* with very few exceptions, the poem's physics and its poetics are treated separately.[20] Classicists engage the poem in a disciplinary context removed from contemporary literary critics; continental historians of science who follow the work of Michel Serres largely bypass the treatment of the poem to be found in departments of philosophy in the United States. Historians of Epicureanism treat *DRN* as an event in one history, and students and scholars of the classical epic treat it as an event in another.

This scattering of approaches is diagnostic, as is the stress on the poem's "modernity." Both speak at once to the evolution of academic disciplines, which frequently run in parallel rather than convergent or conversing tracks, and to the specific shape and content of Lucretius's poem. One of the great, persistent oddities of *DRN* is indeed what we should call its systematic incoherence, and this oddity feeds the scattered way the poem can be read at one and the same time. By "systematic incoherence" we mean a number of peculiarities in the poem, which seem to work at different levels but hand in hand. What to make, first, of the poem's seeming contradictions? How to reconcile, for example, the goal of achieving Lucretian *suavitas* or Epicurean katastematic pleasure (καταστηματικὴν—think of the observer at the shipwreck, in the lines from Book 2 cited above), on one hand, and the tragic vision of plague and desolation on which the poem ends (6.1138–286), on the other? The controversy these closing lines provoke remains unabated. Does the dismal ending stem from the poet's despair? Or from his characterization, from the balanced Epicurean position the poem advocates, of the fate of the fearful, the unenlightened, of those whose moral sickness will be figured as physical morbidity? It is a matter of life and death—and of the possible life or death of the Lucretian tradition, which can be consigned to the ash-bin of lunatic, suicidal ravings on one reading (Jerome, about Lucretius: he was "driven mad by a love-potion and, having composed in the intervals of his insanity several books which Cicero afterwards corrected, committed suicide"[21]), or, on another, to the exalted tradition of moral philosophy that paints "the prospect of salvation and of a heaven on earth... [that] shines with a brighter and stronger light on account of this dark and hellish picture of what life is like without the guidance of Epicurus," as W. H. D. Rouse's note has it.[22] What to make of the poem's addressee? Is Memmius, the dense pupil, a proper stand-in for the poem's reader? Will we learn? Did he? And the invocation—in what way is the mythological register on which the poem opens ("Aeneadum genetrix," "alma Venus") compatible with its strict critique of religion (1.62–80 and throughout)?[23] In what way is the extraordinary crafted-ness of the verse, the deliberate formalism with which it picks up and acts out the philosophical theses it expounds, compatible with the centrality of aleatory processes in those theses?

It is not improper to imagine these controversies regarding *DRN* as the effects of a system at work in the poem—loose, disaggregated, but a system after all, a set of rules (think here of the rules of nature, *foedera naturae*; we would be drawing an analogy to *foedera* or *regulae scribendi*, rules of writing) according to which the poem produces contradictions and impasses that require of its readers unforeseen interpretive and philological swerves, *declinationes* that bring different interpreters up against the protocols they are living and applying, sometimes unthinkingly. The less coherent the response at any moment to *DRN*, the less conventionalized, the less easily *collectivized*, the better a society—minimally, grammatically, "we"—will have been reading the work.

Perhaps it is this remarkable double condition, of diagnostician as well as agent of systematic incoherence, operating at so many levels and in so many different discursive registers, that brings *DRN* into "the mainstream" today. We bring the poem to us, we have said, as a way of taming the verse's radicalism, but we do it at our peril. No academic discipline in the humanities—not philosophy, literary studies and literary history, classics, philology—can comfortably lay claim to a systematic organization that might protect it from derogation, defunding, or from an attack on political or economic grounds. None but the blind can still dream that the contradictions between the smooth globalization of economic market paradigms, the striated, pockmarked, and disaggregated fields of human culture, and the ephemeral and resisting nature of things, subject to the depredations of both and finally so threatening to both, can be systematically or coherently addressed, let alone resolved. There is no shore from which to watch, gently, distantly, as our societies and our universities toss and drown. We cannot lay claim to the disinterest and *suavitas* that the poem both presses on and denies its readers. *DRN* is a poem for our time, then, in the precise measure that it discloses to us at every step, and at every level, the incoherence of our experience of natural time and the contingency and fragility of our claims upon a collective experience ("our time"). It is a poem for our academic time, for the incoherent and fictitious time of the academy, as well as for the chaotic, plagued time in which the human animal strives suicidally to bring things—their natures and their ecologies—under the sway of laws of interpretation, extraction, manufacture, distribution, and consumption.

Lucretius and Modernity: Clusters, Themes, Chapters

The chapters in this book are organized into four main clusters, each of which takes a different approach to tackling the question of what kind of work "and" might play in connecting the words, or concepts, "Lucretius" and "Modernity." Our first cluster, "What Is Modern about Lucretius?," is perhaps the most polemic. In it Brooke Holmes, Joseph Farrell, and David Konstan explore what, if anything, is particularly "modern" about Lucretius himself, focusing the question primarily through the lens of modern science. The three chapters, together, question the "modernity" at stake in our collective title *Lucretius and Modernity* by arguing against the usefulness of "modern" and "modernity" as key terms, whether or not they see Lucretian science as contemporary in some way with our own. In the second cluster, "What Is Lucretian about Modernity?," Catherine Wilson and Thomas Kavanagh take up the question of Lucretius's political modernity. Their chapters demonstrate the important and often radically conflicting political and philosophical uses of Epicureanism in Enlightenment and post-Enlightenment France. Our third cluster, "Lucretian Figures of Modernity: Freedom, Cause, Truth," explores philosophical engagements with Lucretius's poem. Phillip Mitsis, Jacques Lezra, and Katja Maria Vogt not only track engagements with key modern philosophers (including Locke and Marx), but also each explore a concept that figures centrally in modern philosophical debates. In the final cluster, "Following Lucretius," Warren Montag, Alain Gigandet, and Philip Hardie trace encounters by later writers (Spinoza, Strauss, Renaissance poets) with the texture of Lucretius's poem. These writers follow Lucretius in the sense of coming behind him, but they also follow Lucretian *vestigia* or traces to new and often unexpected places.

The chapters also speak to one another across the groupings and clusters, connected by threads of common interest and concern. One question that cuts across the book is that of reception, especially the reception of the "classics" by modernity; this is theorized most explicitly in Holmes's chapter and the first cluster but is also at stake in Mitsis's chapter. Wilson's chapter examines Lucretius in Enlightenment Europe, but is explicitly concerned with his reception among philosophers, and for that reason ties in with the third cluster on Lucretius's philosophical modernity. A shared interest in the varied reception in philosophy of Lucretius's swerve brings Montag into an encounter with Mitsis and Lezra. The first cluster's exploration of Lucretius's scienticity resonates well with Vogt's chapter on the Epicurean claim for the truth of sense perceptions. Key themes of science, philosophy, rationality, and politics unite all the chapters, weaving their ideas and arguments together. Each of the book's 11 chapters is described in more detail below; together, they present a nuanced, skeptical, passionate, historically sensitive, and complicated account of what is at stake when we claim Lucretius for modernity—or what *has been* at stake across the intervening centuries between Lucretius's poem and our own present(s).

Brooke Holmes's "Michel Serres's Non-modern Lucretius: Manifold Reason and the Temporality of Reception" engages with Michel Serres's reading in *The Birth of Physics*, in which he argues that the discoveries and interests of modern physics—with its emphases on fluid mechanics, turbulence, and flux—shows that Lucretius was "right" about his physics. Holmes argues that the most valuable contribution of Serres's argument is not so much its claim for Lucretius as a modern physicist, but how the Lucretian physics that Serres discusses allows us to rethink temporality—the temporality with which we think about something like "reception," but also the untimeliness of Lucretius's poem itself. Holmes reviews the different models and theories of temporality at work in Serres's study, including topological time (in which time has folds, tears, and crumples like a handkerchief), time as isomorphic with matter, and cyclical history. The various models all rely, Holmes argues, on Serres's understanding of liquid, nonlinear, turbulent history. She then uses the understanding of reception that flows from this liquid history as a lever to rethink the reception of classical texts and ideas more broadly. Current models of reception combat ideas of texts as timeless by anchoring them in the historical period that receives or encounters them; Serres's understanding of temporality, Holmes argues, allows us to see how Lucretius's poem in particular allows classicists to think reception studies.

Joseph Farrell's "Lucretius and the Symptomatology of Modernism" reviews a few arenas in which Lucretius is frequently said to be modern—science, rationalism, and atheism—and shows how Lucretius, when examined in these arenas, is decidedly not modern (or, perhaps, as Serres would have it, not "right"). In the context of ancient science, for example, Lucretius looks non-modern when compared to ancient astronomers who attempted to quantify and mathematize their observations about the universe, or to Aristarchus, whose heliocentric view of the universe, as Farrell puts it, makes "modern astonomy...a direct descendant of its ancient ancestor in a way that is certainly not true of atomic physics." Lucretius is antiquated, Farrell argues, not only from our perspective but also from his own time; rather than incorporate the latest scientific ideas into his poem, Lucretius brought forward Epicurean ideas in their entirety, something that Farrell compares to "evangelical fundamentalism." As a result, Farrell concludes that Lucretius is far less modern than other ancient authors—a claim best made when "modernity" serves as a descriptive, chronological claim rather than one of praise.

David Konstan's "Lucretius the Physicist and Modern Science," like Farrell's chapter, calls into question whether "modernity" is internally coherent as a concept that might neatly and disinterestedly divide historical periods from one another. In particular, he examines other examples of "modernity" (in discussions of novels and of perspectival painting), in which a genre or form is defined as "modern" in order to imply "an unambiguous advance" rather than one fashion among others in the history of narrative or art. Newtonian physics, likewise, Konstan argues, has defined modernity and modern physics in a narrow way that excludes the mathematical and physical ideas of Epicurean philosophy from inclusion in a "modern" canon. Against these teleological models, Konstan reexamines the mathematical and geometrical concept of the Epicurean minima, arguing that Epicurean and Lucretian ideas of quasi-infinity align well with recent developments in post-Newtonian physics and mathematics. The chapter as a whole implies that "modernity" is not the most useful concept by which we might judge Lucretius, and Konstan ends with a proposal that is as much aesthetic as polemic: "Perhaps we can say, then, that Epicurean atomism is to modern physics as *Don Quixote* is to postmodern fiction: a flourish of creative freedom from a time before a single model came to dominate the field and that found an echo only when that model gave way to rival structures of thought."

Catherine Wilson's "The Presence of Lucretius in Eighteenth-Century French and German Philosophy" begins by reviewing the state of scholarship about Lucretian philosophy in the eighteenth century; some conventional understandings of Lucretius's influence need to be reconsidered, while other seldom-noticed or studied aspects deserve more attention. In particular, she discusses the different parts of Lucretius's poem that interested eighteenth-century audiences, including those sections focusing on origins: the origins of species, of societies, and of religion. To demonstrate this new focus, Wilson examines the work of the Comte de Buffon, a French naturalist who published a number of works in the eighteenth century that took up these central Lucretian and Epicurean themes. She also examines the role that eighteenth-century pessimistic readings of Epicurean philosophy, by Buffon and others, played in Kant's turn to critical philosophy. In the end she concludes that if we are to consider the seventeenth century as thoroughly Epicurean, we should also, in light of her argument, see the eighteenth century, at least in its moral and political philosophy, as having a "distinctly Lucretian stamp."

Thomas M. Kavanagh's "Epicureanism across the French Revolution" begins by giving a historical argument, showing how the Epicurean philosophy that had been so popular during the French Enlightenment came to be replaced with a Stoic understanding of Republican virtue. Epicurean pleasure, with its emphasis on individual, sensual pleasures exchanged among others, came to be replaced during and after the Revolution by a "civic happiness." As Kavanagh puts it: "Pleasure was grounded in the senses; happiness would flow from the congruence of all with the common good as dictated by the General Will." In light of these historical developments, Kavanagh turns to *The Physiology of Taste*, a meditation on gastronomy published by Anthelme Brillat-Savarin in 1825. Brillat presented in his text, Kavanagh argues, a wide-ranging analysis of taste that traced taste in such disciplines as physiology, human anthropology, history, political and economic analysis, and more. More importantly, Brillat emphasizes the performative power of gastronomy, thereby creating a potential bridge between individual and shared Epicurean pleasures.

The emphasis on shared pleasures—and specifically the shared pleasures of taste—shows the political and ideological importance of Brillat's text, which proposes, as Kavanagh writes, "a new social contract," "a new and positive conviviality outside any General Will promising collective happiness."

Phillip Mitsis's "How Modern Is Freedom of the Will?" is a case study comparing the freedom of the will in Lucretius and John Locke; at stake in the study is the larger question of how we talk about Lucretius's modernity. Neither a proponent of Lucretius as the harbinger of the modern, nor an advocate for the idea that Lucretius is avowedly antimodern or premodern, Mitsis argues that the comparison between Lucretius and the unquestionably modern Locke forces us to rethink, as he puts it, "the unbridgeable conceptual divide between antiquity and modernity." Against traditional narratives in the history of philosophy that posit a radical break marked by Descartes and Cartesian philosophy, Mitsis proposes that the history of the philosophy of the will requires different topography, landmarks, and heroes. Mitsis then undertakes a meticulous comparison of Locke's and Lucretius's understanding of the question of the "freedom" of the will, showing in both, among other similarities, a combination of an understanding of voluntary action rooted in causal sequences but simultaneously, and importantly, an emphasis on the importance of the freedom of rational evaluation. After showing that it is more than possible that Locke's incorporation of Epicurean arguments came from the Epicurean philosophy of Gassendi, Mitsis concludes with a methodological argument about the history of philosophy; tracing detailed histories of certain concepts, especially materialist concepts, as Mitsis shows, allows us to read continuities across the divide that so often separates ancient from modern.

Jacques Lezra's "On the Nature of Marx's Things" is a study of the philosophical and aesthetic "uses" of Lucretius in Marx's early notebooks, compiled while he was pulling together notes for his doctoral dissertation. Lezra does a detailed reading of a Marxian epic simile, in which Petrarch is figured as a cold moralist clutching his coat and causing viewers to clutch their own coats in turn, and Lucretius is an acrobat causing viewers to forget themselves. Lezra then traces Marx's early Epicurean musings into his later questions about the relationship between things and thought. In particular, Marx's writing on the swerve, on the declination, or on the Hegelian "jump" from quantitative to qualitative relations, becomes, in Lezra's reading, about possibilities for writing the history of philosophy, and about the status of philosophy and its uncertain position (is it swirling above the world of things like the acrobat, or bringing the world of the acrobat and the world below into some kind of relation?). This leads, for Lezra, to a reading of the poem's poetics, to the traces of argument enacted at the level of the letter: Lezra shows that Marx learns from Lucretius's poem *contingency*, the swerves or discursive declinations that register both in the content and in the form of Lucretius's poem. At the end of the chapter Lezra gestures to a larger argument about "how Marx's early encounter with Lucretius will shape the nature of Marx's things."

Katja Maria Vogt's "All Sense-Perceptions Are True: Epicurean Responses to Skepticism and Relativism" examines Lucretians' bold epistemological claim that all sense perceptions are true, a claim that is mounted, she argues, as a defense primarily against skeptics and relativists. She reviews the variety of arguments that Lucretius mobilizes to support the claim that all sense perceptions are true. She begins by showing that Lucretius, and Epicurean philosophy more broadly, locates sense-perception in the sense-organs, not the mind, and shows that they are mere reporters of perceptual content (and therefore cannot alter sensation). She then shifts the debate about the nature of "truth" at stake in the claim that "all sense perceptions are true" to say that the truth is not propositional, and must go beyond the understanding of truth that is at work in a claim like "beliefs are true or false." Ultimately, she proposes that in order to understand Lucretius's claim that all sense perceptions are true we might understand it to be a claim that perception, like knowledge, is "factive"—that is to say, unerring, true by its very nature. However, she distinguishes the idea that perception is factive from the idea that perception is equivalent to knowledge; this distinction, she argues, disables the possible Platonic critique of relativism that might otherwise arise.

Warren Montag's "From Clinamen to Conatus: Deleuze, Lucretius, Spinoza" studies Deleuze's reading of Lucretius as it appears in an early essay on Lucretius and in that essay's later revision in the appendix to his *Logic of Sense*. Deleuze, Montag argues, reads Lucretius through Spinoza, mapping Spinoza's *conatus* onto Lucretius's *clinamen* and, in the process, arguing that "Lucretius may prove as acute a reader of the *Ethics* as Spinoza is of *The Nature of Things*." Deleuze's linking of clinamen and conatus rereads the Spinozan conatus as no longer exclusively relevant to animate matter only; this reading goes against the grain of many current readings of Book 3 of Spinoza's *Ethics*, which insist on seeing something like intention in the conatus. Montag shows that Deleuze's insight allows us to see that Spinoza's understanding of conatus is a mediated and reworked understanding of the Lucretian clinamen. Likewise, Deleuze's combination of Lucretius and Spinoza allows us to understand a larger point about causation in all three authors: Deleuze adds Spinoza to Lucretius, Montag states, "as if he could discern in these thinkers past the barest signs, not of destiny, nor even the future, but of a present still to be known."

Alain Gigandet's "Notes on Leo Strauss's 'Notes on Lucretius'" opens with the strong claim that, for Leo Strauss, reading Lucretius both introduces us to modernity properly defined and helps us understand "how problematic the concept happens to be." Gigandet gives a detailed account of Strauss's unusual encounter with *DRN*, which, among other things, placed great emphasis on Lucretius's *style*; his critique of religion, which Strauss thought was immanent throughout the poem and not just emergent in a few key passages; and its rhetorical structure, which, Strauss thought, was a systematic reworking of the opening hymn to Venus. Gigandet shows that Strauss's scattered and symptomatic way of reading Lucretius sought to show the ambiguity of religion and theology in the poem itself. Ultimately, Gigandet argues, Strauss believed Lucretius to be "doubly involved in the origins of the 'enlightened' modernity" in that he sees not only the outlines of secular modernity but also its practical downfalls. Gigandet ends with a reflection on the Strauss's own style, reflecting on the refusal of systematicity inherent in the "notes" in which he chose to publish his interpretation of Lucretius's poem. Underlying both his interpretation and his style, Gigandet argues, is Strauss's elitism.

Philip Hardie's "Reflections of Lucretius in Late Antique and Early Modern Biblical and Scientific Poetry: Providence and the Sublime" examines Christian writers who, despite having antimaterialist agendas and outlooks, turned to Lucretius's *DRN* in their own works. Hardie shows in great detail how Lucretius was systematically incorporated and absorbed into hexaemeral poetry, poetry that recounted the six days of creation as told in Genesis. Some of the accommodation of Lucretius happened because Lucretius had already been reworked by previous writers: for example, Ovid mixes Lucretian cosmogony into his own, and was in turn revised to seem continuous with Christian cosmogony. Hardie documents the extraordinary flexibility of mind and rhetoric required for poets with providentialist worldviews to fit Lucretius into their poetry, paying particular attention to the way Du Bartas folds Lucretian philosophy into his poetry. At the end of his chapter he traces the trope of the "sublime Lucretian image of Epicurus' flight of the mind through the void," showing how Christian poets at once figure it as rational overreaching and attempt to, nevertheless, incorporate it into their worldviews.

Notes

1. Gordon L. Campbell, "Lucretius Reaches the Mainstream," *Classical Review* 59:1 (2009): 115–17. Campbell's review covers both Monica R. Gale, ed., *Oxford Readings in Classical Studies: Lucretius* (Oxford: Oxford University Press, 2007) and Stuart Gillespie and Philip Hardie, eds., *The Cambridge Companion to Lucretius* (Cambridge: Cambridge University Press, 2007).
2. Lucretius, *De Rerum Natura*, trans. W. H. D. Rouse, rev. Martin Ferguson Smith (Cambridge, MA: Harvard University Press, 1992). Unless otherwise noted, both Latin quotations and translations are taken from this edition.
3. For more on this claim, see David Konstan's "Lucretius the Phycist and Modern Science" in this book.
4. See, for example, Michel Serres, *The Birth of Physics*, trans. Jack Hawkes, ed. David Webb (Manchester: Clinamen Press, 2000).
5. Louis Althusser, *Philosophy of the Encounter: Later Writings, 1978–1987*, ed. François Matheron and Oliver Corpet, trans. G. M. Goshgarian (New York: Verso, 2006).
6. Stephen Greenblatt, *The Swerve: How the World Became Modern* (New York: W. W. Norton, 2011).

7. For a nuanced way of discussing historical change and "revolution" while trying to avoid narratives of rupture, see, for example, Steven Shapin, who begins his book *The Scientific Revolution* with the following sentence: "There was no such thing as the Scientific Revolution, and this is a book about it" (Chicago, IL: University of Chicago Press, 1996), 1.

8. For a similar argument that the history of philosophy largely neglects philosophy before the seventeenth century, see also Kellie Robertson's "Medieval Materialism: A Manifesto," *Exemplaria* 22:2 (2010): 99–118. Robertson warns in the essay that Greenblatt's approach to Lucretius threatens to use philosophical materialism as a way of creating new barriers between the medieval and early modern periods, comparable to the kind of periodization that took place around theories about subjectivity current in the 1980s. As Robertson puts it, "The 'new Lucretianism' threatens to become the new 'new subjectivity'" (109).

9. While Greenblatt's book has recently received a great deal of attention, positive as well as negative, it should be noted that there are a number of recent book-length studies of the reception of Lucretius in early modern Europe that do *not* claim that Lucretius is a "modern" writer, or that he inaugurates modernity: see, for example, Gerard Passannante's *The Lucretian Renaissance: Philology and the Afterlife of Tradition* (Chicago, IL: Chicago University Press, 2011), which shows how early modern writers and thinkers used Lucretius's poem to rethink tradition and influence, and Alison Brown's *The Return of Lucretius to Renaissance Florence* (Cambridge, MA: Harvard Univesity Press, 2010), which gently teases apart heterodoxy from potentially anachronistic ideas of atheism or secularism. Brown's book also includes, in her fourth chapter, an important study of Machiavelli's manuscript of *DRN*. Jonathan Goldberg's *The Seeds of Things: Theorizing Sexuality and Materiality in Renaissance Representations* (New York: Fordham University Press, 2009) reads Renaissance texts that explore the philosophy of Lucretius; its claims are primarily theoretical and philosophical rather than historical. Ada Palmer's *Reading Lucretius in the Renaissance* (Cambridge, MA: Harvard University Press, 2014) came out too recently for us to incorporate into this introduction, but promises a detailed study of the humanist reception of Lucretius and Epicurean texts.

10. Tison Pugh et al., eds., "Book Review Forum: *The Swerve: How the World Became Modern*. By Stephen Greenblatt. W. W. Norton, 2011," Book Review Cluster, *Exemplaria: A Journal of Theory in Medieval and Renaissance Studies* 25:4 (2013): 313–70.

11. For a reflection that looks at and builds on Michel Serres's theories of temporality as a way of rethinking Lucretius's potential "contemporaneity," see Brooke Holmes's "Michel Serres's Non-modern Lucretius: Manifold Reason and the Temporality of Reception," in this book.

12. This, perhaps, is the guiding structure of the overview offered in Stuart Gillespie and Donald Mackenzie's "Lucretius and the Moderns," in *The Cambridge Companion to Lucretius*, ed. Stuart Gillespie and Philip Hardie, 306–24. See also, in a similar vein, the essays collected in Timothy J. Madigan and David B. Suits, eds., *Lucretius: His Continuing Influence and Contemporary Relevance* (Rochester, NY: RIT Press, 2011). More specific studies include Jonathan Kramnick's reading of Lucretius in his *Actions and Objects from Hobbes to Richardson* (Stanford, CA: Stanford University Press, 2010), esp. pp. 61–98, in which he argues that Lucretius's poem was deployed as a monist system that was used in the late seventeenth century to rethink concepts of mind, action, and causation against the Cartesian and Christian dualism that preceded it; Paddy Bullard's "Edmund Burke among the Poets: Milton, Lucretius and

the *Philosophical Enquiry*," in *The Science of Sensibility: Reading Burke's* Philosophical Enquiry, ed. Koen Vermeir and Michael Funk Deckard (New York: Springer, 2012), 247–63, which argues that Burke's sublime is Lucretian; Stuart Gillespie's "The Persistence of Translations: Lucretius in the Nineteenth Century," *English Translation and Classical Reception: Towards a New Literary History* (Malden, MA: Wiley-Blackwell, 2011), 150–62.

13. Bruno Latour, *We Have Never Been Modern*, trans. Catherine Porter (Cambridge, MA: Harvard University Press, 1993). In addition to Holmes's chapter in this book, the discipline of literary studies has recently addressed the untimely and queer temporality of texts in medieval and early modern Europe, as well as the temporality at work—for us and for older texts—both in contemporaneity and in being out of time. See, for example, Jacques Lezra's *Unspeakable Subjects: The Genealogy of the Event in Early Modern Europe* (Stanford, CA: Stanford University Press, 1997), Jonathan Gil Harris's *Untimely Matter in the Time of Shakespeare* (Philadelphia: University of Pennsylvania Press, 2009), and Carolyn Dinshaw's *How Soon Is Now? Medieval Texts, Amateur Readers, and the Queerness of Time* (Durham, NC: Duke University Press, 2012). See also Karla Mallette's musings on time and history in her "Ahead of the Swerve: From Anachronism to Complexity," in Pugh et al., "Book Review Forum," 359–62.

14. In fact, in "Why Stephen Greenblatt Is Wrong—And Why It Matters" (*The Los Angeles Review of Books*, December 1, 2012, Web, November 11, 2014), Jim Hinch argues that Greenblatt's book is in fact two books: one of religious polemic (the problematic part of the book) and, positively, one that offers "an engaging literary detective story about an intrepid Florentine bibliophile named Poggio Braccionlini…This *Swerve*, brimming with vivid evocations of Renaissance papal court machinations and a fascinating exploration of Lucretius's influence on luminaries ranging from Leonardo Da Vinci, to Galileo, to Thomas Jefferson, is wonderful." In other words, what is potentially redemptive about Greenblatt's narrative is how it contributes to a story of reception, despite the evils it does from the point of view of periodization.

15. For a related but different claim, see Joseph Farrell's "Lucretius and the Symptomatology of Modernism" in this book, which argues that Lucretius's strict adherence not to the doctrines of his own present but to those of Epicurus's time, in fact make both potentially *non*-modern. See also James Warren, "Lucretius and Greek Philosophy," in *The Cambridge Companion to Lucretius*, ed. Stuart Gillespie and Philip Hardie, 19–32.

16. Italics added.

17. Lucretius, *De Rerum Natura*, trans. Rouse, 4.31n.

18. William Shakespeare, *Hamlet*, ed. Stephen Greenblatt, in *The Norton Shakespeare: Based on the Oxford Edition*, ed. Stephen Greenblatt et al. (New York: W. W. Norton, 1997), 2.2.293–96.

19. The claim that more "perfect" beings—angels, gods—should not be compared to lesser beings is a mark, one might say, of theological anxiety regarding the logical reflexivity of the relation of similitude. Patristic theology, to Augustine's discomfort, is awash with efforts to show that man's Fall entailed a loss of *spiritual* "likeness" to God but the preservation of *imago dei*.

20. While Richard Minadeo's claim in his 1969 study *The Lyre of Science: Form and Meaning in Lucretius'* De Rerum Natura (Detroit: Wayne State University Press) that Lucretius is neglected as a poet ("The body of writing on *De Rerum Natura* which might reasonably be called literary criticism is small. Within it, no nearly thorough study of the work's positive art has ever been attempted."; p. 9) is no longer true, it is

true that such studies are often compartmentalized. For an exception to the general point about the separation of physics and poetics in readings of the poem, see Stephen Hinds, "Language at the Breaking Point: Lucretius 1.452," *The Classical Quarterly* N.S. 37:2 (1987): 450–53. For a slightly more impressionistic study with similar interests, see also Jonathan Pollock's *Déclinaisons: Le naturalisme poétique de Lucrèce à Lacan* (Paris: Editions Hermann, 2010).

21. The English translation from Jerome's *Chronica* is taken from W. H. D. Rouse, "Introduction," in *De Rerum Natura*, by Lucretius, trans. W. H. D. Rouse, rev. Martin Ferguson (Cambridge: Harvard University Press, 1992). On Lucretius's biography, see also Leofranc Holford-Strevens, "*Horror vacui* in Lucretian biography," *Leeds International Classical Studies* 1:1 (2002): 1–23; see also L. P. Wilkinson, "Lucretius and the Love-Philtre," *The Classical Review* 63:2 (1949): 47–48.

22. Lucretius, *De Rerum Natura*, trans. Rouse, 6.1139n.

23. For further comments on these inconsistencies, see also Joseph Farrell's chapter in this book, "Lucretius and the Symptomatology of Modernism," and Alain Gigandet's chapter in this book, "Notes on Leo Strauss's 'Notes on Lucretius.'"

PART 1

What Is Modern about Lucretius?

CHAPTER ONE

Michel Serres's Non-Modern Lucretius: Manifold Reason and the Temporality of Reception

BROOKE HOLMES

Michel Serres begins his 1977 study of Lucretius, *The Birth of Physics (La naissance de la physique)*, by stating a consensus: "Everyone knows, everyone concedes that atomic physics is an ancient doctrine but a contemporary discovery."[1] The ancient atomists, according to this consensus, for all their ambitions, pursued an ideology lacking in rigor, not a "science of the world."[2] It is therefore only fitting that Epicurean doctrine finds its most robust extant expression in a work of poetry—namely, the *De Rerum Natura (DRN)*—and fitting, too, that the poem has been entrusted to historians, philologists, and philosophers, rather than to physicists. And so one concludes that, despite its "intuitions" (to borrow Gaston Bachelard's term), ancient atomism is an artifact from a bygone era.

The diagnosis that Serres offers of ancient atomism's twentieth-century reception, which is almost synonymous with the reception of Lucretius, remains a fair one nearly 40 years on. Particularly in the Anglo-American world, interest in Lucretius the scientist (and ancient atomism as a science) was already starting to drop off in the eighteenth century; after a brief Lucretian renaissance in the late nineteenth and early twentieth century, it declined even more steeply over the course of the last century.[3] The rationale offered is simple. By the early twentieth century, the gulf between the *DRN* and modern physics had become just too great to bridge. Under such conditions, the most charitable and indeed the most reasonable response for a historian would seem to be to withhold judgment on the truth value of Epicurean claims altogether.[4]

The noncommittal strategy, however, is not the one that Serres himself seems to adopt. Far from conceding the obsolescence of ancient atomism as a science, he brazenly insists on its fundamental correctness: "Lucretius is right [*Lucrèce a raison*]. He accomplished the revolution being carried through by the sciences of today and which philosophy continues to neglect."[5] Elsewhere, Serres writes: "We can no longer read the atomist physics as a naïve phenomenology of things, it has rigorous support... A mathematical physics, close to the world and proven, in fact existed among the Greeks who were not supposed to have one. Traces of it abound in the *De Rerum Natura*."[6] The language of rigor, mathematics, and proof suggests that Serres wants to restore Lucretius to the very domain from which he has been so decisively excluded, namely, that of a science that hews "close to the world." In a series of five interviews with Bruno Latour conducted in 1991 (and published the following year), he refers approvingly to Jean Perrin who, in the early twentieth century, undertook experiments inspired by his reading of Lucretius.[7] And, in fact, in Serres's own reading of Lucretius, the Roman poet is advancing a physics of flow and turbulence that is fitted to the mathematics of Archimedes and validated by twentieth-century physics in its turn away from solids to fluids and from classical mechanics to chaos theory. Against readings of Lucretius grounded in literary criticism and cultural history, Serres reintroduces a framework of evaluation that to all appearances is unapologetic about truth in the sense of an alignment between theory and physical reality: Lucretius is right.

As it turns out, the pendulum does not swing so cleanly. Despite the rhetoric of validation from contemporary science and mathematics, Serres is not so much relocating Lucretius from the faculty of philology to the faculty of physics as he is disrupting and complicating the polarization of these two domains—precisely on the grounds of physics' claims to being right—in the name of philosophy. One of the instruments of this disruption is the double meaning of Serres's expression "Lucretius is right" in French. For the expression "*Lucrèce a raison*" means not simply "Lucretius is right" but also "Lucretius *has reason*." In his interviews with Latour, Serres describes the Lucretius book as part of a project to "restore to material judged irrational the respect owed to straight reason (*la droite raison*), even if it means redefining the latter."[8] I return to Serres's willingness to redefine reason at the end of the paper. But before doing so, I take up another crucial piece of his strategic negotiation of the traditional divide between the sciences and literature—namely, his negotiation of an equally powerful divide within the history of science between past and present, a negotiation that is enabled, but not exhausted, by a heterodox theory of nonlinear history.[9]

Serres famously illustrates his theory of nonlinear history in the interviews with Latour as a crumbled handkerchief. Take a handkerchief, he says, as if laid out flat to iron. Draw a circle, and you will easily see that some points are near, some far apart—Lucretius and Jean Perrin, for example. But if you crumple up the handkerchief and put it in your pocket, you create a different set of proximities. Those points that were once distant are now very close; they may even be superimposed on one another. Conversely, a strategic tear will estrange points that were once neighbors.[10] The manipulation of the handkerchief is a primer in topology.

For, Serres argues, time behaves for us in a topological manner, not in a linear fashion, as "classical" theories of time would have us believe.

A topological model of history does not just bring us closer to Lucretius by virtue of its unexpected folds. It actually emerges out of the reading that Serres offers of Lucretius in terms of the physics of flow and turbulence, on the one hand, and the isomorphism of time and matter, on the other. That is, what Serres memorably calls "liquid history" (*l'histoire liquide*) is a concept that explains why Lucretius sits on the threshold of our world in Lucretius's own terms.

My aim in this chapter is to take a closer look at Serres's model of history in order to better understand its consequences for the double claim that Lucretius is right and that Lucretius has reason. I begin by moving beyond the storied handkerchief model to explore the complicated dynamic between transhistorical proximity and temporal process in Serres's work on Lucretius. Serres, at times, seems to talk about Lucretius as though he arrived in the present via a kind of time travel. Here the topological model is most pronounced. At other times, however, Lucretius is the origin point of a series of what Serres calls "invariants" within history and, more specifically, within the span of time between us and antiquity. Rather than reconciling these two models, I want to think about what each of them does for our understanding of temporality and our sense of Lucretius as our contemporary.

For Serres, Lucretius's contemporaneity is, in fact, double.[11] If Lucretius is of our own time, it also matters to Serres that Lucretius is of his own time, too, that he is arriving among us from elsewhere, and that the elsewhere is a place that is not so much premodern as non-modern. Why it matters, though, is not immediately obvious. For Serres is not interested in the strangeness of the text in the way that a historian, committed to the complexities of historical difference, might be. Nor does he approach the poem as an object to be deciphered through philological investigation or even philosophical exegesis. The otherness of Lucretius is, rather, more elusive.

Nevertheless, it is the otherness of Lucretius as much as his dazzling contemporaneity with us that is the key to understanding why Lucretius matters to the present in Serres's view. The problem that is created when we begin to talk about Lucretius as right or wrong is not simply whether we can accept either claim. It is also what is at stake in making such claims. If all that mattered was giving a correct account of the world, history would never come into play: chaos theory, for example, is sufficient. So it cannot just be about discovering a useful theory. A traditional historian of science, alert to the distribution of credit and honor, might be concerned about giving Lucretius (and Democritus, Epicurus, and Archimedes) their due in the grand narrative of Western science. But Serres is no traditional historian of science (and not even a revisionist one, however much he professes an interest in restoring respect to texts written off as irrational). Nor does he have the least enthusiasm for the grand tradition of historical epistemology in French philosophy of science associated most in the twentieth century with Bachelard, and he thoroughly eschews, as we have seen, the linear model of progress such a tradition assumes. So what does it mean for Lucretius to be right according to a different mode of reason?

I come back to this question in the last section of the chapter, suggesting two lines of response. The first considers what Serres's model of time contributes not to our understanding of physics and the physical world but to our understanding of history and the very temporality of reception. The radical comparatism proposed by Serres is a challenge to the forms of historicism practiced by mainstream reception studies. As such, it serves as a provocation to our assumptions about linear time.

The second line of response puts pressure on the very notions of rightness and reason in order to see what makes Lucretius not so much correct but, as Nietzsche would say, untimely, arguing that what keeps the value of Lucretius from being exhausted by the duplication of his physics in chaos theory is precisely the untimeliness of his reason. As Serres says at one point in the Latour interviews: "The messenger always brings strange news; if not, he's nothing but a parrot."[12] Lucretius is "strangely" close to us in *The Birth of Physics*.[13] The strangeness of the *DRN* lies in part in the very fact that it is a poem. For Serres reads the refusal in the history and philosophy of science to engage the past as anything but a series of failures and successes judged by our own standards of rightness as a problem directly implicated in the estrangement of literature from science. His own philosophical world is therefore founded on a double gesture by which literature and the past together take part in a pluralistic concept of reason.[14] A pluralism of rationalities becomes, in turn, the very condition of clarity about the crisis of our times, a crisis marked by the untrammelled power of the physical sciences in a world that needs physics together with ethics, the sciences with philosophy and literature. Much rides, then, on showing that Lucretius is right, too.

Lucretian Time

Serres's Lucretius is defined by his unexpected proximity to us. But what is the common ground on which the ancient past and the cutting edge of the present meet? In the simplest terms, it is a shared understanding of physical reality, one independently arrived at via twentieth-century physics. Serres resists the idea that ancient atomism is only a vague intuition of the structure of nature, holding such a view responsible for the isolation of Lucretius in poetry and philology. In order to restore reason to the *DRN*, Serres aims to show that the poem participates in a rigorously mathematical physics. His strategy is twofold.

First, Serres seeks to dismantle the claim that a mathematical physics appears only in the Renaissance, before which time mathematics and physics were seen as essentially separate disciplines. While he concedes that in classical antiquity, mathematics is separate from what the Greeks called "physics" (*ta physika*)—that is, philosophies of nature—he, nevertheless, argues that the two branches of knowledge could be seen even in antiquity as interdependent and that this is exactly what we find in atomist physics. There are faint traces of such interdependence in the fragmentary remains and testimonia concerning Democritus (a lost work on irrational lines and solids, for example, and traces of a calculus of the infinitesimal).[15] But the physical model of atomism was most rigorously mathematized, Serres argues, by the third-century BCE Greek mathematician Archimedes, whose significance for Epicurean physics has been obscured by the formal separation of mathematics and physics in antiquity. Serres seeks to demonstrate this significance by reestablishing the common ground between atomist physics and Archimedes's mathematics.

The affinities between Archimedes and atomism are many, on Serres's analysis, but foremost among them is the centrality of hydraulics. The mathematics of fluids is crucial not least of all because it rescues what has long been seen as one of the most whimsical and unscientific elements of Epicurean atomism, namely, the swerve or *clinamen*, described by Lucretius as the sudden deviation in the movement of an atom without external cause "at an unassignable time and in unassignable places" (*incerto tempore . . . incertisque locis*).[16] Serres, acknowledging the swerve's checkered reputation, rehabilitates it by assimilating it to the appearance of turbulence within laminar flow, that is, a type of flow in a liquid or gas in which neighboring layers do not mix and flow at different velocities. In the beginning, the atoms in their original state flow in perfect parallel: no twisting, no knots, no collisions. And yet, a little wildness necessarily emerges at some indefinable point as the property of such a system in the form of vortices. The *clinamen* is the minimal angle of deviation that gives rise to these vortices. Far from being the error that renders Epicureanism irrational and thus exiles it from science "proper," the *clinamen* is now a foundational event within a physics addressed to flow and turbulence, "present and possible, from the beginning, in the geometry of the first atomist."[17]

The vortices formed by the *clinamen*, in turn, give rise to the world of compound objects, formed by ephemeral entanglements of atoms. Serres repeatedly stresses the way in which the appearance of disorder within laminar flow is coextensive with the emergence of the order of the created world: once the equilibrium of the flow is disturbed, we see the rise of order in the form of the stabilities, albeit temporary, of compound objects. "Fall assures difference, as creation," he writes. "Once again, the fall gives order, as well as drift, decline, disorder. Always the double operator: the fall, here, is productive."[18] The vortex at the juncture of instability and stability is observed in the spinning top, which confounds the Platonic categories of rest and movement, or the current of a river.[19] Yet the vortex is not only an observed phenomenon, speculatively analogized by the Epicureans to the subphenomenal terrain of the atom. It is also a phenomenon demanded by the mathematics of angles, curves, and tangents in Archimedes. Not least of all, the vortex is also a philosophical phenomenon, the impetus toward imagining an ethics developed under the aegis of Venus, as we will see below.

The historical conflict between two different mathematical systems supports the second prong of Serres's strategy to redeem the rationality of ancient atomism. What has kept us from seeing the mathematical elegance of the theory of the swerve, he argues, is the dominance of classical physics within the history of science. The fixation on solids rather than fluids within that tradition has blinded us to the reality to which Epicurean physics provides, in Bruno Latour's memorable phrasing, "the soundtrack."[20] It is as the children of the geometers of solids, Plato and the Stoics, Serres claims, that contemporary readers judge Epicurus and Lucretius as irrelevant to the history of science.[21]

What transforms the dominant perspective is not that we moderns have learned, on our own, to become better readers of Lucretius. The impetus comes, rather, from physics itself, as it discovers the science of flows. As we awaken to the idea of order within and through constant fluctuation, the limits of classical physics are exposed and the claims of the *DRN* can appear in a new light. If Lucretius had once appeared prehistoric, Serres writes, the moderns now appear prehistoric to us, with our interest in open systems and chaos. "And," he goes on, "the *De rerum natura* is there ahead of us. Outside in the storm and the rain. On the banks of the Nile."[22] With the displacement of ancient atomism from the dusty annals of history to the new horizon of physics, our notion of time, too, is upended: we can no longer assume a linear march forward. For Serres, who associates the progressivist model with an "infantile" history of science in which sons murder fathers and assume "great ignorance and obscurities in the early reaches the better to mark progress in the later," the turn away from linear time is a salutary development.[23] It requires the rejection of a model according to which the present is always in possession of the best possible reason.[24] Once we imagine time as topological rather than strictly linear, Lucretius becomes our transhistorical intimate and unexpected contemporary, reasonable anew.

For as classical physics recedes and gives way to a physics of fluid and turbulence, Lucretius appears not just prescient but also, as I emphasized earlier, right. "Each important discovery suddenly reveals an intelligent past behind a recent obstruction."[25] Serres is lavish with a mathematician's compliments in talking about the *DRN*. The poem offers a model of time with "unassailable precision" (*une exactitude imprenable*) and theorems of "extraordinary precision" (*une extraordinare précision*); the logic of its mathematics has an "unassailable rigor" (*une rigueur imprenable*).[26] Lucretius describes a form of flux that "remains exact" (*demeure exacte*).[27] Twentieth-century physics comes to function like a Rosetta stone that allows us to finally read the *DRN* and, in so doing, to realize that everything we know is already there, that we are carrying through a revolution in understanding that has already been essentially accomplished in ancient atomism.

These claims of completeness and sufficiency demonstrate Serres's tendency at times to cast Lucretius's poem as long-lost but perfectly conserved, arriving on the threshold of the present uncompromised by the vagaries of transmission. Unlike the simulacrum whose edges are worn down by long-distance travel in the Epicurean theory of perception, the poem's truth, such a model suggests, is in no way distorted by the centuries that intervene between us and it. It is no doubt to this rhetoric of undisturbed integrity that Latour is responding when he compares the poem in Serres's reading to Sleeping Beauty, put to bed in the prescientific era: "A kiss; and here it is; yawning, stretching, breathing again, as young as when it was written."[28] The poem, that is, is like a body that was once cryogenically frozen. Serres suggests as much when he tells Latour a story about a Swiss mountain guide who, after disappearing half a century earlier, is rediscovered, perfectly conserved, inside a glacier and buried by his now-old sons.[29] And he repeatedly emphasizes the DRN's total sufficiency at its origin: "Everything is there, nothing is lacking, with no error or excess. The inventory is exhaustive . . . Everything is there, nothing is lacking, the inventory is complete."[30] The poem thus seems to exist outside the dynamics of history, enclosing a world to which nothing is added, nothing is lost.

Such a reading exercises an undeniable attraction. It is as if at such moments Lucretius begins to function as images of the gods do in Epicureanism, as a message from a space outside our world that arrives, as it were, in a bottle. The past emerges as a kind of intermundium, the space between worlds that is inhabited by the perpetually happy, blissfully indifferent deities of Epicurean theology. What makes the gods so pivotal in Epicureanism, despite their utter lack of concern for human life, is the crucial role they play in helping us recognize our proper ethical telos— namely, ataraxia—by emitting simulacra that give us a glimpse of a life undisturbed by the vagaries of matter or the tumult of our own fears and desires. Perhaps Lucretius can fulfill this role as well precisely because he is an interloper among us.

The slide from physics to ethics is not an accidental deviation: the intertwining of the two domains defines Epicureanism as well as being at the core of Serres's reading of Lucretius. Before exploring it further, however, I would like to complicate the idea of Lucretius as Sleeping Beauty or Epicurean god by looking at another model of history at work in *The Birth of Physics*.

On the model of the crumpled handkerchief, topological time, as we saw above, brings two apparently distant points into proximity. The very conjunction of these two points both confirms and is confirmed by the principles of Epicurean physics. That is, the arrival of Epicurean physics in our own time is enabled by a time that obeys the principles of flow and turbulence that govern the atom and thereby delivers Lucretius as if on a wave or within a pocket of water that is suddenly accelerated into our own

time: "Time flows," Serres says, "in an extraordinarily complex, unexpected, complicated way...[it] is paradoxical; it folds or twists."[31] There
are countercurrents and turbulences that disrupt our ordering of geometrical time; at times, there is local reversibility within global irrevers-
ibility, with the result that "Ophelia's boat goes upstream, here and there,
Moses had a good chance of not dying at sea, the poetic waters of dreams
know little of river transport and hydrodynamics. Everything does not go
uniformly to death."[32] If time behaves exactly as matter does in Epicurean
physics, it is because time and matter are entirely isomorphic: like matter,
history is "chance, aleatory, and stochastic"; it is cloud and noise.[33] From
these conditions Serres draws the house-of-mirrors conclusion that the
very arrival of Lucretius in the present vindicates his physics of flow over
and above its validation within physics itself: How could Lucretius sit next
to Ilya Prigogine unless time is turbulent?

But the isomorphism of time and matter yields another way of
thinking about atomism in history, one based on what Serres calls the
"quasi-invariant." On this model, ancient atomism is a truth that recurs
throughout history in a serial manner, periodically emergent. Serres
reads the so-called scientific revolution, for example, in just these terms.
"Scientific modernity does not enter history by a fault or a break, but by
the revival of a philosophy of nature that has been spreading ever since
Antiquity."[34] The Renaissance, too, conforms to the model: "Everything
indeed takes place as if the institution of applied modern sciences was
not, as has long been thought, a break...No, physics and mechanics were
not born in an instant, from the void or contemporary pressure alone, at
the moment of the Renaissance, they are reborn, that's all."[35] The basic
principle here is that ostensibly new knowledge is always ancient wisdom.
The Renaissance or the early stirrings of "modern" science or Carnot's
breakthroughs in thermodynamics thus function as eruptions of atomist
wisdom analogous to the revelation of Lucretius's poem as entirely reasonable in our own period of history.

The serial model may appear at first glance to return us to a notion of
linear time, albeit one punctuated by moments of insight. Yet like the
model of the crumpled handkerchief, it, too, is shaped by a concept of history as turbulent and fluid. Here it may be useful to think back to Serres's
emphasis on the emergence of compound bodies from chaos as islands of
stability within the prevailing instability of an atomic cosmos. The most
central of these islands is the ataraxia of the soul, but in history, too, there
are islands of order that are organized out of noise: history, Serres writes,
is "the formation of *syrrhèses*, of systems, of orders, originating from this
endless cloud."[36] These *syrrhèses*—literally, "flowings together"—are the
mechanism by which the truth of atomism appears and disappears as a
quasi-invariant, creating a cycle not unlike the circular evolutionary time
that structures Book 5 of the *DRN*.

Under these conditions, Lucretius is neither a fossilized artifact nor
Sleeping Beauty. Rather he enacts a truth that obeys the (Epicurean) law

of the eternal return. Such a law takes seriously the prefix quasi- in the idea of the quasi-invariant in understanding that truth is always reconstituted with an element of difference or singularity: the series is repetition and difference. Serres suggests this when, for example, he tells Latour that contemporary physics allows us to reread Lucretius "in an oblique manner," where "oblique" means that you cannot translate atom by atom but instead have to look more globally at systems of turbulence. In other words, the principle of recurrence is not equal to a law of the same— indeed, emphatically not, for a law of the same belongs to a history of science that recognizes only one kind of right, one kind of reason, its own.[37] Serres offers a different perspective on the micro-variability in the model when he compares ancient atomism to a tectonic plate, moving at a glacial pace: up above, the surface layer may change dramatically, while the tectonic substratum is nearly stable, albeit still subject to displacement.[38]

Serres gives us, then, at least two ways of thinking about Lucretius's poem: on one hand, the fossil or the frozen body that lies outside turbulence and time; on the other hand, as something—a system, or an idea— that emerges out of turbulence as the recurrent pattern, a *quasi*-invariant in an evolutionary dynamics; and the pattern as subterranean stability. Both models rely on the concept of "liquid" or nonlinear history, while also diverging in their points of emphasis.

It is possible to reconcile the two models by imagining, for example, that the poem of Lucretius is a perfectly preserved artifact while the truth that it enacts is the quasi-invariant. But we might then ask what the value of the poem is if the truth of Epicurean physics is periodically emergent, as chaos theory demonstrates. Indeed, in some sense, the validity of the contemporary scientific theory sometimes seems to be what vindicates Lucretius in Serres's eyes, rather than Lucretius validating chaos theory. Lucretius is right, but he is superfluous. If we reject this idea, as Serres does, what value *do* we accord the rightness of ancient atomism? Is it simply a question of getting the history of science right, of giving credit where credit is due? These questions have been made more urgent by recent attention within the growing field of reception studies to the nature and consequences of classical receptions. At the same time, the majority of work in reception has been carried out in relationship to literary works and works of art, rather than to ancient physics. I turn now to consider some of the implications of Serres's concept of history and his claims on behalf of Lucretian truth for thinking about the temporality of reception studies as well as the very practice of the history of science in the present.

Lucretian Receptions and Lucretian Reason

For readers accustomed to dealing with literary receptions, Serres's approach can feel strange, if not simply dead wrong.[39] The idea that a text is

the carrier of a timeless truth, while implicit in more traditional constructions of the classical canon, is hardly uncontested in reception studies as it
has taken shape as a field over the past few decades. Indeed, the theoretical
orientation of the field has historically been toward privileging the reader,
best summed up in the mantra that meaning is always realized at the point
of reception.[40] Whether that tag is taken to imply a privileging of the aesthetic experience of the reader or the sociocultural context of his or her
encounter with the text, it is designed to destabilize a belief in the text as
the hermetically sealed bearer of meaning simply delivered to the reader.
Moreover, the reception encounter can be seen as complicated further by
the text's (linear) trajectory through time. Many scholars of antiquity and
later periods alike would agree with Julia Haig Gaisser's description of
classical texts as "pliable and sticky artifacts gripped, molded, and stamped
with new meanings by every generation of readers," texts that "come to
us irreversibly altered by their experience."[41]

Even if one did believe that the text represents a kind of timeless truth, it
would not make much sense to see it as separable from the text itself—for
example, that the truth conveyed by Homer's *Iliad* or Sophocles's *Antigone*
could be conveyed by other means equally well. It is possible to say that
tragedy as a genre, for example, recurs at particular historical moments
without canceling out the unique value of earlier expressions of the genre.
There are many meditations on the human condition after Homer but
they do not replace Homer.

Serres does not believe that chaos theory renders Lucretius obsolete
either. And yet the emphasis on the mathematical exactitude of his break-
through makes it difficult to see why not. The situation is made particularly difficult by the uncertain question of influence, that is, the question
of whether appearances of a fluid-state physics after Lucretius owe a debt
to him, or any other ancient atomist at all, the way that Euclidean geometry owes something to Euclid. Serres himself does not explicitly make
the claim in *The Birth of Physics* that eruptions of atomism are themselves
catalyzed by readings of Lucretius, as Stephen Greenblatt has, emphasizing instead that it is because we now know how to construct open systems
that the discourse of nature penned by Lucretius is newly legible—or, as
Serres says, audible—to us.[42] The "we" here who receives Lucretius does
so from the perspective of a scientific insight that has already been realized. For Lucretius to be more than a historical curiosity, then, we need
to know why subsequent iterations within the series of atomist physics do
not exhaust Lucretian reason.

One way to conceptualize such excess is through the domain most
emphatically isomorphic with physics on Serres's reading of the Epicurean
system—namely, history. The revolutions within physics over the course
of the twentieth century have left virtually untouched dominant concepts
of historical time, no doubt because of the vast divide that separates physics and history in our era.[43] A core part of Serres's project is thus to rejoin
physics and history as themselves variants on the same logic of fluids—a

discovery he credits to Lucretius—and, in so doing, to transform the very terms under which Lucretius and other historical figures exist in our time. On the topological model, as we have seen, ancient atomism erupts at particular moments, including the late twentieth and early twenty-first century, with a vitality foreclosed by linear models of history. Serres's claims about nonlinear time are thus a valuable provocation for reception studies, insofar as they demand that we think more explicitly about the models of temporality that we assume when we move between the past and the present. If, at times, it is necessary or desirable or strategic to affirm that texts are sticky objects that come to us with the accretions of every generation between us and antiquity, a claim that takes the notion of linear history very seriously, at other times, it is preferable to confront the sudden, live emergence of an ancient text at a space and time far removed from its point of origin. The second model, of course, describes the rediscovery of the *DRN* itself in the fifteenth century. Yet there may be conditions other than strictly material ones that invest a text with untimely power.[44]

The potentially destabilizing effects of such temporal displacements remain an untapped resource for reception studies, where there is a tendency to anchor the interpretation of the text in the local context of the encounter. On this model, the reading of the ancient text becomes a product of its immediate milieu—social, intellectual, cultural—and so is approached primarily with the historian's tools rather than as a genuinely transhistorical event.[45] There is always the risk, of course, that downplaying context will enable the return of a retrograde notion of the timelessness of Homer and Sophocles, with whom we commune in some idyllic, ahistorical space guaranteed by an unreconstructed humanism. But that is not the only alternative. Until now, reception studies as practiced by classicists have not engaged, for example, the various forms of anachronism and anachrony being developed by postclassical stewards of the Western past in medieval, Renaissance, and early modern studies.[46] Nor has the field embraced the intellectual resources of comparatism and the leaps and folds it requires.[47] Serres, in fact, is a comparatist at heart, as his long-standing fascination with Hermes suggests. "Comparatism," he tells Latour, "proceeds by short circuits and, as we see in electricity, this produces dazzling sparks."[48] The metaphor points to what is unsettling about working comparatively, which always carries with it the threat of abandoning method. Yet are we willing to give up the idea that our ancient texts are still live wires?

Serres's transhistorical reading of Lucretius poses particular challenges, however, insofar as it seems to understand the *DRN* not as a work of art but as a discourse on physics.[49] From one perspective, as we have seen, there should be no problem at all, if we accept that what is transhistorical about the poem is a grasp of scientific truth. Yet the question then becomes: If we accept the claim, even in a weak sense, that Lucretius is right, what is the particular difference of the poem that makes it valuable? One possible answer I have outlined is that atomist physics is singular in the model of liquid history that it yields according to Serres's reading and that part of what imbues this model with value is that it forces us to reconsider our assumptions about linear time.

It is our very willingness to allow our concepts of time to be disrupted by Serres's Lucretius that points to the broader implications of Serres's reading. For that disruption is a sign that physics cannot be kept in isolation from history, nor from literature, nor from philosophy. What Serres is advocating is not the application of physics to history, the subordination of history to scientific reason (analogous, say, to the subordination of literary studies to neuroscience)—far from it. Instead, the seemingly straightforward claim "*Lucrèce a raison*" grows increasingly complicated over the course of Serres's reading of Lucretius as the apparently singular idea of reason or rightness proper to historical epistemology, which judges whether past thinkers discovered scientific truths (that are absorbed into the present) or fell into error, is steadily decimated by the articulation of a uniquely Lucretian reason.[50]

In the interviews with Latour, Serres describes the move by which he puts Lucretius together with the most current hypotheses in physics—a move that I would argue is summed up in the double meaning of the phrase "*Lucrèce a raison*"—as something of a strategy or ruse to answer another question. He defines this question in terms of loss:

> Everything has its price. As science advances, we rarely evaluate the substantial cultural losses that correspond to the gains. Literature becomes evanescent through a loss of substance, while, on the other hand, there is a considerable gain in scientific intelligence—in both content and institutions. This is behind my temptation to write a defense and an illustration of the humanities—in the face of, in opposition to, and for the benefit of the scientists themselves. To say to them: "Lucretius thinks more profoundly and even more rationally than many of today's scientists..." I want to show a certain reason in its emerging state (*une raison à l'état naissant*) and illustrate it for the benefit of academic reason.[51]

Serres's claim that atomist physics is rigorously mathematical, I would argue, is not a ruse in the sense he is not actually committed to his conjunction of Lucretius with Archimedes on the common ground of liquid matter. It is a ruse, rather, in the sense of gaining the attention of physicists and philosophers of science and then slowly breaking down the singular idea of scientific reason by constructing another reason, Lucretian reason, that is both intelligible and strange, of our time and not of our time. Here, independent of what Lucretian reason looks like, its very validity undermines, in one gesture, the privileging of the sciences over the humanities and the present over the past.

The redefinition of reason against the model of singular reason that Serres dates to the Enlightenment comes to the fore in the final pages of

The Birth of Physics under the heading of "Morality." And it is no accident that Serres's study of Lucretius ends with morality, for it is the poem's very imbrication of physics with ethics and morality that is a hallmark of its reason, in marked contrast with the rigorous separation of "is" and "ought," at least in theory, in our own physics. Like the entwining of history and physics, the very thinking together of ethics and physics is a rejoinder to Enlightenment reason as the master discourse and an enactment of another practice of thinking, a practice at once comparatist and committed to local difference.[52]

The co-thinking of physics and ethics also has crucial consequences for ethics: "Nature is controlled by laws, the wise man in accordance with nature controls himself by these same laws. If he understands physics, he conducts himself morally."[53] What is it that has to be understood about physics? Namely, "how nature is born in local singularities in which atoms are inflected by declination."[54] What could this possibly have to do with happiness? Serres here returns, with good reason, to a literal reading of the Epicurean ethical ideal, ataraxia, as non- or minimal disturbance. The happy life arises from a meditation on limits that mark that life as an ephemeral, local singularity, where finitude is the condition of happiness. We are here in a physics—and an ethics—"of the plurality of worlds, and of their temporary existence."[55] The Garden, for Serres, is a place that respects limits.[56]

One of the ways that Serres understands these limits is as the very limits of one form of reason. The importance of limits is what accounts for the at-first-glance paradoxical intolerance that Serres demonstrates toward the reason of the moderns: to accept the terms of that rationality is to be imprisoned within its limits under the illusion of always being right. The illusion has consequences not just for how we live our single and unique lives but also for how we, as a collective and as different collectivities, relate to one another, as well as to the physical world.[57] For Serres sees in the totalizing and universalizing aspirations of the moderns' reason a propensity toward violence: Mars not Venus. And not just the moderns' reason, for Epicureanism itself, on his account, is a self-conscious choice of Venus over Mars. It is a choice taken in full knowledge, Serres suggests, of the risks of totalizing reason, made not in the name of irrationality but of another science and another reason altogether organized around peace, an ethics of the local, the logic of the *clinamen*. Though Serres mocks the recuperation of the swerve as subjective free will, this is not to say that we do not ourselves participate in its fluxion, its inclination: ethics resurfaces, rather, within physics. These choices concern not just how we treat each other but also how we relate to what we call nature, as adversaries or contractual partners.

At the foundation of objective knowledge, as in its historical beginning, there lies a series of decisions or preliminary choices that often pass unnoticed. Here is one of them: either the contractual pact, or military strategy...What about this so-called nature? Is it enemy or slave, an adversary or our partner in a contract that Lucretius calls Aphroditean...Life or death, this, finally, is the question.[58]

The choice that Serres describes here ends up driving a wedge between the two figures he was at pains to join together on the common ground of the nature of fluids at the beginning of the book. The path of military strategy, which stands under the sign of Ares, is taken by Archimedes with his war-machines and complicity with state-sponsored violence. Lucretius takes the other route, following Epicurus in a self-conscious turn away from a martial physics toward the law of Venus. Although the Archimedean choice is by far the more common one in Western science, with its historical commitment to war, Lucretius demonstrates that the same physics can operate under the sign of Venus: "From the same piece of iron we can make a sword or a plough."[59] Lucretius thus paves the way not for a war against nature or mastery of the irrational by means of reason but for a contract, a *foedus*, with nature, the subject of another of Serres's books.[60]

The very ambiguity within the provocative claim "*Lucrèce a raison*" thus enacts the double-sidedness of Lucretius's contemporaneity in Serres's reading. Serres plays with the idiomatic meaning of the phrase to suggest the *DRN* as a cryogenically frozen body, rediscovered by a physics of fluids as nonlinear history. But as the reading develops, the second, more literal meaning of the phrase comes to unwork the very universality implied by "being right." By developing this line of meaning, Serres fleshes out a specifically Lucretian reason, one organized not only by a physics of fluids but also by the imbrication of physics in ethics and politics and committed to ataraxia in all its forms, from an ethics of minimal deviations to an ecological politics. Here it is precisely the strangeness of Lucretius's Aphroditean vision that endows it with its vitality and its power. Such power is put in the service not of confirming scientific results—of providing them with publicity, as Serres says scathingly of historical epistemology—but of disrupting their universal applicability, a presumption that is, for Serres, already complicit with a physics of Mars.[61] Lucretius thus arrives in the present not via a law of the same but in a series of quasi-invariants where even minimal difference pluralizes the singularity of modern scientific reason. By splintering Reason, Serres brings antiquity and literature alike, brought together in Lucretius, into the domain of rationality, thereby setting them in play in the present as a precondition of nothing less than a future under the sign of Venus, not Mars.[62]

Notes

1. Michel Serres, *The Birth of Physics*, trans. Jack Hawkes, ed. David Webb (Manchester: Clinamen Press, 2000), 3 (= Michel Serres, *La naissance de la physique dans le texte de Lucrèce: Fleuves et turbulences* [Paris: Éditions de Minuit, 1977], 9). Quotations from Serres are from the Hawkes translation.

2. Serres, *Birth of Physics*, 4 (= Serres, *Naissance de la physique*, 10).

3. See W. R. Johnson, *Lucretius and the Modern World* (London: Duckworth, 2000), esp. 127–33 (though Johnson believes Lucretius can help us "in our efforts to reconstruct the idea of science and of the world it has, in recent centuries, for worse or for better, remade" [136]); Stuart Gillespie and Donald Mackenzie, "Lucretius and the Moderns," in *The Cambridge Companion to Lucretius*, ed. Stuart Gillespie and Philip Hardie (Cambridge: Cambridge University Press, 2007), 306–24.

4. As in, for example, David Sedley, *Creationism and Its Critics in Antiquity* (Berkeley: University of California Press, 2007).

5. Serres, *Birth of Physics*, 77 (= Serres, *Naissance de la physique*, 98).

6. Ibid., 25 (= Serres, *Naissance de la physique*, 35–36).

7. Michel Serres with Bruno Latour, *Conversations on Science, Culture, and Time*, trans. Roxanne Lapidus (Ann Arbor: University of Michigan Press, 1995), 51 (= Michel Serres, *Éclaircissements; cinq entretiens avec Bruno Latour* [Paris: Éditions François Bourin, 1992], 80).

8. Ibid., 53 (= Serres, *Éclaircissements*, 83).

9. On Serres's notion on nonlinear history, see Maria Assad, "Ulyssean Trajectories: A (New) Look at Michel Serres' Topology of Time," in *Time and History in Deleuze and Serres*, ed. Bernd Herzogenrath (London: Continuum, 2012), 85–102; Jane Bennett and William Connolly, "The Crumpled Handkerchief," in Herzogenrath, *Time and History*, 153–71; Kevin Clayton, "Time Folded and Crumpled: Time, History, Self-Organization, and the Methodology of Michel Serres," in Herzogenrath, *Time and History*, 31–49; Stephen Clucas, "Liquid History: Serres and Lucretius," in *Mapping Michel Serres*, ed. Niran Abbas (Ann Arbor: University of Michigan Press, 2005), 71–83; Ming-Quian Ma, "The Past Is No Longer Out-of-Date," *Configurations* 8 (2000): 235–44.

10. Serres, *Conversations*, 60 (= Serres, *Éclaircissements*, 80).

11. Ibid., 47 (= Serres, *Éclaircissements*, 74).

12. Ibid., 66 (= Serres, *Éclaircissements*, 101).

13. Serres, *Birth of Physics*, 189 (= Serres, *Naissance de la physique*, 233).

14. See esp. Serres, *Conversations*, 50–52 (= Serres, *Éclaircissements*, 79–81).

15. Serres, *Birth of Physics*, 10 (= Serres, *Naissance de la physique*, 18).

16. Lucretius, *De Rerum Natura*, 3 vols., Books 1–6, commentary by Cyril Bailey (Oxford: Oxford University Press, 1947), 2.218–19. All translations are my own.

17. Serres, *Birth of Physics*, 11 (= Serres, *Naissance de la physique*, 19).

18. Ibid., 28 (= Serres, *Naissance de la physique*, 38).

19. Ibid., 28–30 (= Serres, *Naissance de la physique*, 38–41). On the spinning top, see Plato, *Republic*, ed. and trans. Chris Emlyn-Jones and William Preddy, 2 vols., Loeb Classical Library (Cambridge, MA: Harvard University Press, 2013), 436d (1:407).

20. Bruno Latour, "The Enlightenment without the Critique: A Word on Michel Serres' Philosophy," in *Contemporary French Philosophy*, ed. Allen Phillips Griffiths (Cambridge: Cambridge University Press, 1987), 83–97, at 97.

21. Serres, *Birth of Physics*, 112 (= Serres, *Naissance de la physique*, 141).

22. Ibid., 68 (= Serres, *Naissance de la physique*, 86).

23. Ibid., 59 (= Serres, *Naissance de la physique*, 75).

24. Serres, *Conversations*, 49 (= Serres, *Éclaircissements*, 77 ["*la meilleure des raisons possibles*"]). See also ibid., 50 (79).

25. Ibid., 56 (= Serres, *Éclaircissements*, 87).

26. Serres, *Birth of Physics*, 35, 57, 44 (= Serres, *Naissance de la physique*, 47, 73, 57).

27. Ibid., 56 (= Serres, *Naissance de la physique*, 72).

28. Latour, "Enlightenment without the Critique," 88.

29. Serres, *Conversations*, 61 (= Serres, *Éclaircissements*, 94). Latour here refers to the story as "cette bizarrerie biographique et philosophique" ("this biographical and philosophical bizarreness").

30. Serres, *Birth of Physics*, 24 (= Serres, *Naissance de la physique*, 35).

31. Serres, *Conversations*, 58 (= Serres, *Éclaircissements*, 89).

32. Serres, *Birth of Physics*, 152 (= Serres, *Naissance de la physique*, 188).

33. Ibid., 164 (= Serres, *Naissance de la physique*, 202). On the isomorphism of physics and other domains such as history, see David Webb, "Michel Serres on Lucretius: Atomism, Science, and Ethics," *Angelaki: Journal of the Theoretical Humanities* 11 (2006): 130–31, rightly arguing against a reading that would see isomorphism in terms of a reduction of all domains to physical laws.

34. Serres, *Birth of Physics*, 41 (= Serres, *Naissance de la physique*, 55).

35. Ibid., 25 (= Serres, *Naissance de la physique*, 36).

36. Ibid., 164 (= Serres, *Naissance de la physique*, 202). See also ibid., 189 (= Serres, *Naissance de la physique*, 234) where history obeys the law of the *clinamen*.

37. Ibid., 191 (= Serres, *Naissance de la physique*, 237 ["*la répétition d'une loi homogène*"]).

38. See Serres, *Conversations*, 139 (= Serres, *Éclaircissements*, 203), with David Webb, "Michel Serres on Lucretius," 131–32, 135 ("If the general model itself flows, the atomist currency of flow, clinamen, equilibrium, disequilibrium, conjunction, difference, limit, and path have themselves to be translated into the language of our own science, literature, reason, philosophy, and general practice") and Bennett and Connolly, "Crumpled Handkerchief," esp. 160–62.

39. See Duncan F. Kennedy, *Rethinking Reality: Lucretius and the Textualization of Nature* (Ann Arbor: University of Michigan Press, 2002), 4.

40. See Charles Martindale, *Redeeming the Text: Latin Poetry and the Hermeneutics of Reception* (Cambridge: Cambridge University Press, 1993) and Charles Martindale, "Thinking through Reception," in *Classics and the Uses of Reception*, ed. Charles Martindale and Richard Thomas (Malden, MA: Blackwell, 2006), 1–13.

41. Julia H. Gaisser, "The Reception of Classical Texts in the Renaissance," in *The Italian Renaissance in the Twentieth Century*, ed. Allen J. Grieco, Michael Rocke, and Fiorella Gioffredi Superbi (Florence: L. S. Olschki, 2002), 187, cited by Martindale, "Thinking through Reception," 4.

42. Serres, *Birth of Physics*, 70 (= Serres, *Naissance de la physique*, 89); Stephen Greenblatt, *The Swerve: How the World Became Modern* (New York: W. W. Norton, 2011).

43. At other points in the reception of Epicureanism, however, the isomorphism of physics and history has been taken up more readily: see esp. Gerard Passannante, "Homer Atomized: Francis Bacon and the Matter of Tradition," *English Literary History* 76 (2009): 1015–47, on Bacon's atomist understanding of the classical tradition.

44. See, for example, Konstan in this volume.

45. The comments of Christopher Wood, "Reception and the Classics," in *Reception and the Classics: An Interdisciplinary Approach to the Classical Tradition*, ed. William Brockliss et al. (Cambridge: Cambridge University Press, 2011), on the papers presented by the classicists at a Yale conference on reception studies target precisely this contextualist approach, closely associated with cultural studies (see esp. 166–67). He, in turn, advocates a notion of the (Greek and Roman) classics as true, but, by contrast with Serres, this truth belongs to an aesthetic order, not a scientific or ethical one.

46. See, for example, Alexander Nagel and Christopher S. Wood, *Anachronic Renaissance* (New York: Zone Books, 2010).

47. On comparatism and reception studies, see further Brooke Holmes, "Cosmopoiesis in the Field of 'the Classical,'" in *Deep Classics: Rethinking Classical Reception*, ed. Shane Butler (London: Bloomsbury, 2016).

48. Serres, *Conversations*, 69 (= Serres, *Éclaircissements*, 106).
49. Wood and Nagel, for example, privilege the artwork as an anachronic object: "No device more effectively generates the effect of a doubling or bending of time than the work of art, a strange kind of event whose relation to time is plural" (*Anachronic Renaissance*, 9).
50. For Serres's rejection of the tradition of historical epistemology in France, see esp. Serres, *Conversations*, 52–53 (= Serres, *Éclaircissements*, 82–84).
51. Serres, *Conversations*, 54–55 (= Serres, *Éclaircissements*, 85–86). See also Serres, *Birth of Physics*, 189 (= Serres, *Naissance de la physique*, 234): "Another reason is in the process of being born, one delineated by Lucretius."
52. The practice of comparatism represents a third way between an ethics of the local and the tyranny of the global (on which see below), enabling movement beyond the limits of one local site into those of another.
53. Serres, *Birth of Physics*, 184–85 (= Serres, *Naissance de la physique*, 229).
54. Ibid., 185 (= Serres, *Naissance de la physique*, 229).
55. Ibid.
56. Ibid. (= Serres, *Naissance de la physique*, 230). Compare Deleuze's reading of Lucretius's rejection of "the false infinite" in his appendix, "Lucretius and the Simulacrum," to his *Logic of Sense* (New York: Columbia University Press, 1990) (= *Logique du sens* [Paris: Éditions du Minuit, 1969]) with Brooke Holmes, "Deleuze, Lucretius, and the Simulacrum of Naturalism," in *Dynamic Reading: Studies in the Reception of Epicureanism*, ed. Brooke Holmes and W. H. Shearin (New York: Oxford University Press, 2012), 316–42.
57. That "we" is alert to economic disparities such that, although Serres anticipates with remarkable prescience the concept of the Anthropocene in his interviews with Latour, he does not fall into the error often associated with that term of eliding global inequities with the universal term "man" (*anthrōpos*): see Serres, *Conversations*, 167–204 (= Serres, *Éclaircissements*, 243–94).
58. Ibid., 114 (= Serres, *Naissance de la physique*, 142–43).
59. Ibid., 116 (= Serres, *Naissance de la physique*, 144).
60. Michel Serres, *The Natural Contract*, trans. Elizabeth MacArthur and William Paulson (Ann Arbor: University of Michigan Press, 1995) (= Michel Serres, *Le contrat naturel* [Paris: F. Mourin, 1990]).
61. On historical epistemology as publicity, see Serres, *Conversations*, 128 (= Serres, *Éclaircissements*, 187).
62. I am grateful to the audiences at the "Lucretius and Modernity" conference, the Mahindra Humanities Center workshop at Harvard, the "Postcontextualisms" workshop at the Max Planck Institute for the History of Science in Berlin, the "Classics and Critical Theory" panel at the 2013 CAAS Meeting in Philadelphia, the "Bodies of Ideas: Science and Classical Reception" conference at the Warburg Institute, and the Department of Classics and Ancient History at Bristol for their comments and questions. I would also like to thank the editors, Liza Blake and Jacques Lezra, for their feedback and encouragement, and Emilio Capettini for editorial assistance.

CHAPTER TWO

Lucretius and the Symptomatology of Modernism

JOSEPH FARRELL

Lucretius between Ancient and Modern

Considerations of Lucretius and modernism generally take it for granted that Lucretius's modernity, proto-modernity, or impact on modernity is exceptional. The usual story is that Lucretius, in some way, anticipated and perhaps made possible certain intellectual developments that one commonly associates with the modern. He was "ahead of his time," and, in this way, we may see Lucretius as somewhat like ourselves, in contrast to more representative denizens of classical antiquity. This perspective is presumably meant to do honor to Lucretius, but it is not without its share of self-regard.

That it is possible to define a fundamental distinction between the categories of "ancient" and "modern" is a cornerstone of intellectual history and, especially, of modernist self-fashioning.[1] Personally, I suspect that these categories are misleading when they are used as anything other than value-neutral chronological markers. That is, of course, one of the uses of the words "ancient" and "modern," but it is often difficult to be certain when merely chronological distinctions come to stand for different modes of consciousness. This is not the place to explore the entire question of "ancient v. modern," however, so for the sake of the argument I am willing to accept what appear to be two widely shared premises: (1) that a broad distinction between antiquity and modernity does exist and is meaningful not only in chronological terms but also with reference to intellectual history; and (2) that these chronological and intellectual markers do not always line up, in that there were at least some figures who lived in the chronological period that we call antiquity, but who exhibit a modern or at least proto-modern consciousness that transcends the intellectual horizons of their contemporaries—if not of all, then of the vast majority.[2]

The title of this chapter refers to the study of symptoms, suggesting that modernity as a state of mind can be identified by certain characteristic signs, and that any culture that presents these symptoms can be considered modern.[3] This is an idea that I find appealing.[4] Again, though, the question is not whether it is globally true; for the sake of the argument, I accept that it is. The question, rather, is a more focused one: does Lucretius himself exhibit the symptoms of modernity, either uniquely or to an unusual and significant degree, in comparison with other ancient intellectuals? Is he therefore modern, and is modernism in some way peculiarly Lucretian? Most of the chapters in this book make a case that the answer to one and perhaps both of these questions is "yes." I would like to argue the other side of the case.

If the point were, what specific elements of the modern worldview are owed to Lucretius, or what specific elements of modernity did Lucretius anticipate, then it would be a relatively straightforward problem to investigate those ideas that would not exist if Lucretius's poem had been lost, or those ideas that found readier acceptance because they had precedents in Lucretius. Atomism, of course, is the most obvious aspect. Closely related to this is a radical materialism that recognizes no place for the immaterial, however conceived. Gods so marginalized as to play no role in anything that happens in the universe make Lucretius look like an ancient ancestor of modern atheism, and in the randomly ordered universe that he describes the role played by natural selection is another very important point. These are among the topics that are brilliantly illuminated elsewhere in this book.

But if the point is more general—if we are speaking not of specific individual anticipations and contributions but of *symptomatic* ones—then the problem is much greater. Did Lucretius contribute to the formation of a modern perspective on the world? Did he even share such a perspective? Was Lucretius in fact "modern," and is "modernism" in some sense Lucretian?[5] I would like to address these questions by considering, or reconsidering, Lucretius as a scientist—not, however, in the light of his supposed anticipations of modern scientific discoveries, but in that of comparison against the achievements and influence of ancient science in general.

Lucretius in the Context of Ancient Science

Let us begin with this question: is Lucretius, of all the scientific thinkers of classical antiquity that we can name, the one who best represents whatever it is that we mean by "modern"? Is he, for instance, a more or less "modern" figure than the geographer and astronomer Claudius Ptolemaeus, better known simply as Ptolemy?

The question probably seems absurd. Lucretius, as the story goes, anticipated atomic physics and Darwinian biology by thousands of years, while Ptolemy's geocentric universe is today regarded as an emblem of all that modern science had to overcome before it could begin to make real progress in understanding the nature of things. But this uninformed perspective, while popular, is hardly tenable. Ptolemy was the last and the most advanced astronomer of antiquity and the one who was able most accurately to take account of observed phenomena in mathematical terms.[6] Any responsible scientist or historian of science would admit that Ptolemy's mathematically based account of the geocentric universe is remarkably consistent with the phenomena that one can observe from earth without the aid of instruments. Indeed, one could say similar things about a long series of ancient astronomers who were Ptolemy's predecessors, including Eudoxus, Autolycus, Aristarchus, Apollonius, Hipparchus, and many others.[7] What all of these scientists had in common, apart from an agreement that a geocentric model of the universe fit the observational data to a much greater degree than any other model, was that such data—and this is the important point—*expressed in mathematical form* offered a much more effective way than any other, not only of accurately *describing* the universe, but also of gradually *refining* that description, as more accurate observational data and more sophisticated mathematical techniques became available.

Lucretius also enjoys an exalted and richly deserved reputation as a keen observer, but the difference between *qualitative* Lucretian observation and *quantitative* scientific observation is categorical and absolute. Because Lucretius is, for all intents and purposes, innumerate.[8] The only numbers that he knows are "one," "many," and "infinite." Calculation does not enter into his thinking. In this sense, even the much-maligned astronomical and astrological poet Manilius has more in common with scientific method than does Lucretius, and certainly men like Ptolemy behaved like modern scientists in a way that Lucretius simply does not.[9]

For such reasons, it might be interesting to consider whether Aristarchus of Samos, the first ancient scientist to argue in favor of a heliocentric universe, was even more modern than Ptolemy and all the other proponents of the standard geocentric model.[10] Like Lucretius's atomic physics, Aristarchus's astronomical model did anticipate the modern conception of the solar system by many centuries. Also like Lucretius, Aristarchus favored a model that could not be proved or disproved by the means available to him. But—and this is an important point—Aristarchus's model resembles our own conception of the solar system much more closely than Lucretius's atomic model resembles modern physics. That is to say, Lucretius's atoms have almost nothing in common with modern atoms.[11] But Aristarchus's heliocentric universe is, for all intents and purposes, identical with our solar system. Unlike Lucretius, then, Aristarchus proposed a model that not only is the same as ours, but could also be, and eventually was, proved to be correct.[12] So Aristarchus probably deserves more credit than he gets, but his work was so far from the mainstream of ancient science that almost nothing he wrote survives. We know about his heliocentric theory only because Archimedes, who did not subscribe to it himself, makes provisional use of it as affording him the most effective way of demonstrating a new technique that he (Archimedes) had developed to facilitate calculations involving very large numbers.[13]

Both Aristarchus, then, and Archimedes, in my view at least, deserve consideration as the most modern of the ancients. But in historical terms and direct scientific influence, Ptolemy eclipsed all earlier classical astronomers, and it is for this reason that Nicolaus Copernicus, when he published his treatise *On the Revolutions of the Heavenly Spheres* (1543), actually positioned himself explicitly as a successor to Ptolemy by presenting his calculations as refinements upon those contained in Ptolemy's definitive premodern account of celestial mathematics, the *Almagest*. Like an Augustus among astronomers, Copernicus disguised a revolution by presenting it as the incremental refinement of an earlier system. But there was no disguise, no effort to deceive: in Copernicus's view, the new system really was basically a refinement of the older one. As James Evans has put it:

> Copernicus' work, great as it is, turns out to be less radical than one might suppose. The revolutionary part—the Sun-centered cosmology—is introduced in the first book and constitutes only about 5% of the text. The rest of *On the Revolutions* is a sort of rewrite of Ptolemy's *Almagest*. Theorem by theorem, chapter by chapter, table by table, these two works run parallel. Although Copernicus disagrees with Ptolemy about the arrangement of the universe, he makes use of Ptolemy's observations and methods. In the technical details, Copernicus follows Ptolemy more often than not. Copernicus may be regarded as one of the last, and one of the most accomplished, astronomers in the Ptolemaic tradition.[14]

In this sense, it is clear that modern astronomy is a direct descendant of its ancient ancestor in a way that is certainly not true of atomic physics; or to put it differently, it is clear that Aristarchus, Ptolemy, and Copernicus were all engaged in essentially the same scientific pursuit, whereas Lucretius and Dalton, Rutherford, or Bohr certainly were not.

What I have been saying about astronomy is obviously true as well with regard to the closely allied science of mathematics. In this respect, one could discuss the ways in which geometers like Eratosthenes anticipated Descartes in devising an abstract system of numerical coordinates to describe a set of spatial relations.[15] For reasons such as this, it seems to me that one could much more confidently consider any number of ancient astronomers or mathematicians as "modern," or at least as forerunners of the modern, than one could Lucretius.

This conclusion is only strengthened if one considers Lucretius's own opinions about astronomical matters. All of the astronomers whom I have named, except Ptolemy, lived before Lucretius. Their theories were well known and can be said to have defined in Lucretius's day the standard scientific view concerning the structure of the universe. One almost universal tenet of this view was that the sun, like all the other heavenly bodies, revolved around the earth. Lucretius, however, was not sure about this. Not that he agreed with Aristarchus about the heliocentric model; practically no one did. But Lucretius was willing to entertain a much odder theory. In a notorious passage from Book 5, he allows that the usual explanation of observed phenomena might be right—that is, that the sun might revolve around the earth—before turning to an elaborate explanation of an alternative possibility, namely, that a new sun was born each morning behind Mt. Ida in northwest Asia Minor.[16] Lucretius then goes on to discuss why the lengths of the day and the night vary throughout the year, giving a quite adequate account of the sun's journey along the ecliptic between the tropics, then advancing the possibility that the thickening of the air in certain seasons retards the sun's movement through the sky, and then returning to the possibility of solar palingenesis.[17] I find it extraordinarily difficult to say why Lucretius does this. In such a situation we can exclude no possible explanations, even if they raise new problems of their own; and in that spirit I offer the following suggestion.

Elsewhere Lucretius famously and programmatically declares that "clarity" is an important element of his poetic credo.[18] In general terms, indeed, the forceful clarity of his expression is one of his most impressive and effective traits. That said, there are also passages in which Lucretius is extremely subtle, and subtlety is not exactly the same thing as clarity.[19] In other passages he can only be considered downright misleading—provisionally misleading, perhaps, but misleading nonetheless. Most notable among such passages is the almost ecstatic "Hymn to Venus" with which Lucretius saw fit to begin a poem dedicated to proving by logical argument that the gods have no concern for us.[20] Critics once thought that such inconsistent behavior was proof of St. Jerome's infamous notice that Lucretius was insane.[21] Most have now come to see this and other instances of misleading argumentation as strategically motivated. The "Hymn to Venus," for instance, is convincingly interpreted in light of a famous programmatic simile as "honey on the rim of the cup," something to draw the reader in so that eventually he will find himself drinking the bitter medicine of unvarnished truth about the nature of material reality.[22] Thus the attractive Venus of Book 1 is eventually reduced in Book 4 to the status of a metonymic label: the sex urge in its most unromanticized form.[23] In much the same way, the poem's astonishing finale—a rhetorically and imagistically extravagant description of a plague that struck Athens during the Peloponnesian War—seems to be at odds with an earlier pronouncement that death is no concern of ours.[24] But this conclusion has come to be seen as a peculiarly apt test of whether the reader has learned from the previous books of the poem to look upon such things with dispassion.[25]

In view of these solutions, then, it may be that Lucretius's purpose in citing a frankly bizarre theory of solar palingenesis as if it were equal in authority to the obviously superior one of solar revolution along the ecliptic may simply not yet be apparent. It may even be that his occasional way of making a point by saying something quite the opposite of what he must mean has affinities with a postmodern rather than the modern sensibility. But in terms of the present argument, this particular theory of new suns born each morning was anything but current scientific or even educated opinion at the time when Lucretius wrote. And in this connection, it seems necessary to observe that Lucretius may not have accepted the scientific consensus of his time that the earth is spherical. Not only ancient geographers but also most people in Hellenistic and Roman times who had the benefit of a general education knew that the Earth is a sphere and even had a good idea of how big it was. Lucretius—and this is important—is no exception. He had certainly been exposed to the standard, and correct, view of these matters, but he never endorses it and in some passages seems to imply that he thought the Earth to be flat.[26] There is some question as to whether he fully grasped what was at stake, because real uncertainty about basic facts is the best explanation as to why he does not accept that the length of the sun's seasonal movement between the tropics along the ecliptic is the reason why the length of daylight hours varies with the seasons, and this entails a further belief in the permanence of the sun. But, after all, the most convincing explanation for Lucretius's drastically outmoded opinions about all of this is that, to judge from what indications we have, he appears to believe exactly what Epicurus had believed.[27]

Lucretius in the Context of Evangelical Fundamentalism

At this point I shift from considering Lucretius as a scientist to considering him as a religious devotee. To do this is at odds with a widespread tendency to regard Lucretius as an ancient representative of free thinking of a kind that would not become common in Western civilization until the Enlightenment. But one of Lucretius's most outstanding characteristics is, in fact, his devotion to the ideas of a philosopher who lived three centuries before his own time. What does this extraordinary devotion mean, both per se and in terms of Lucretius's putative modernity?

To consider first the former question: To understand Lucretius's place in the history of Epicureanism has always been complicated by the fact that he is our most complete surviving source for Epicurean philosophy. But over time that situation has changed with the recovery of more material particularly from the library buried at Herculaneum and especially with the dramatic improvements, both technical and philological, in our ability to interpret its contents.[28] Much of what has been recovered so far belongs to the writings of Epicurus himself and those of Lucretius's contemporary, the Epicurean philosopher Philodemus of Gadara.[29] And one of the most remarkable aspects of Philodemus's writings is the difference that one finds in them between his own concerns and those of Epicurus on one hand and those of Lucretius on the other.

Philodemus deals with all sorts of questions that Epicurus treated with neglect, lack of interest, or downright hostility. The most remarkable among these is poetry: we know from fragments of Epicurus's own writings that he took a dim view of poetry, and he seems neither to have written any himself nor to have written about it from a philosophical perspective.[30] Philodemus, on the other hand, was a well-regarded poet who wrote extensively on poetry as a philosopher.[31] Both aspects of Philodemus's interest in poetry have some bearing on our assessment of his contemporary Lucretius. This is mainly the case because Philodemus's own involvement with poetry helps to explain how Lucretius ever could have conceived of the apparently un-Epicurean idea of expounding Epicurus's system in poetic form. Why he did so has long been a puzzle of Lucretian scholarship, and even if it is not quite solved by the recovery of Philodemus's works, at least Philodemus's poetic interests make Lucretius look a bit less isolated and anomalous within the Epicurean tradition.

But the poetic form of the *De Rerum Natura* (*DRN*) is the most un-Epicurean thing about it, or at least, it is the aspect of Lucretius's work that seems most at odds with the attitudes of Epicurus himself. On the other hand, in virtually all other respects, comparison between Philodemus and Lucretius actually reinforces the perception that the *DRN* has much more in common with the writings and thought of Epicurus than with the advances made by later philosophers working within the Epicurean tradition. We can say this because one of the great values of Philodemus's work is its extensively doxographic quality; and even if Philodemus is an exceptionally hostile witness in regard to the vast majority of Hellenistic philosophers, he at least allows us to form some idea of the questions that interested himself and them. Many of these are quite interesting responses to problems implicitly raised by Epicurus's exclusively materialist conception of all phenomena—including poetry, even if Epicurus did not concern himself with poetry at all. Thus we now know that Hellenistic philosophers staked out a range of opinions regarding the basis on which poetic excellence might be judged.[32] Some evidently adhered to a conception similar to that of Plato, which is that poetry is to be judged primarily on the basis of its content.[33] Aristotle with his formalist concerns represents a move in the direction that we might call aesthetics in the proper sense, as it would eventually be defined by thinkers like Kant; and Hellenistic philosophy, as we now know, moved much farther down this road. One group of Hellenistic philosophers in particular, whom Philodemus labels "the critics" but modern interpreters usually call "euphonists," held that sound is the only proper criterion by which to judge the excellence of a poem *qua* poem; content and meaning having nothing to do with poetics as such.[34] Philodemus himself seems to believe that sound and sense must somehow work together; just how they do so and just how he would account for this interaction in terms of the materialist physics that is the basis of his own and of all Epicurean philosophy, we do not know.

What we do know is that Lucretius shows no interest in this or in any related topics that he did not find in the writings of Epicurus himself. David Sedley has argued convincingly that Lucretius fashioned his poem not as a summa of contemporary Epicurean philosophy in the mid-first century BC, but as a versified redaction of Epicurus's own mammoth treatise on the nature of things, his 37 books *Peri physeos* ("On Nature," which would serve as a reasonable translation of Lucretius's title, *De Rerum Natura*, as well), which was written about three hundred years earlier.[35] Similarly, in a very prominent passage of Book 1 in which he goes to the trouble of refuting the basic assumptions of non-Epicurean thinkers, Lucretius confines himself to the views of three pre-Socratic philosophers, Heraclitus, Empedocles, and Anaximander.[36] That means he does not mention Plato, with whom Epicurus himself had taken issue, or either Aristotle or Zeno—the founders of the three major philosophical schools, the Academics, the Peripatetics, and the Stoics, which were the chief rivals to Epicureanism in Lucretius's own time.[37] His poem, then, is not designed to take account of later challenges to or refinements of Epicurus's original system. Rather, it is a poetic embellishment of that system as Epicurus originally presented it to the world. This helps to explain, among other things, why Lucretius is able to regard the antiquated theory of daily solar palingenesis as a possible explanation for the alternation of day and night, including the varying length of each throughout the year: he accepts it because Epicurus had done so before him.[38]

Epicurus also regarded the sun and the other heavenly bodies as being not very distant from the earth and declared that the heavenly bodies must be exactly the size that they appear to us to be.[39] Both of these positions are not merely wrong, but bafflingly so. Astronomers who lived and worked shortly after Epicurus's time proved that the sun and all other heavenly bodies must be enormously far away (because, despite changes in their apparent position in the sky, their light always strikes the earth directly and with no detectable change in angle of incidence). On the basis of what they could deduce from observing solar and lunar eclipses, they produced some very reasonable estimates of the relative size of the sun, moon, and earth.[40] None of this had any impact on Lucretius, who reports Epicurus's bizarre opinions as if the intervening three hundred years of scientific inquiry and discovery had not occurred.

This brings me to my third and final point. Lucretius, as has often been observed, represents Epicurus's philosophy almost as a form of revealed wisdom—revealed, that is, not to Epicurus by some god, but discovered by Epicurus and revealed by him to humanity, with the result that Lucretius considers him a god.[41] This is an aspect that admirers of Lucretius's rationalism never fully acknowledge. Lucretius does stress, of course, the fact that Epicurus's system is rational, that all of it is accessible to reason, that it is informed by and is accurately described as *ratio*. His insistence on this point, his enthusiasm for logical and analogical forms of argument, for evidence-based proof, and, above all, perhaps his open hostility to conventional religiosity, all have contributed to making him seem to many the most convincing candidate that the ancient world has to offer as the classical prototype for the modern, enlightened mentality. I, on the other hand, have been pointing out some characteristics that do not comport so well with this idea. And I am hardly the first to point them out; where my assessment differs from others is that I regard these inconcinnities as being not exceptional but typical. And the reason I do so is because, in my view, Lucretius's lapses of reasoning or information are not mere anomalies, but are of a piece with and, I would say, are due to his willful ignorance of the scientific advances that the ancient world had made since Epicurus's time. And this willful ignorance is due, in turn, to the fact that Lucretius, by his own confession, regards Epicurus not just as a thinker who discovered a method of thought that could immediately relieve many of the cares of human life and that could be continually improved so as to become a better way of understanding the world, but also as the promulgator of a wholly and permanently adequate perspective on the human condition that is complete in every way and is neither in need of nor capable of improvement. In this respect, Lucretius appears not so much as a proto-Enlightenment thinker as he does a proto-fundamentalist religious fanatic.

I expect that this statement may be controversial, so let me linger on it. Lucretius, obviously, differs from most religious fundamentalists because he believes that the divinity has no concern whatever with human affairs for good or ill, and that the human soul is both material and mortal and that, consequently, no reward or punishment awaits the individual after his or her death. This is the aspect in which he claims to differ from most pagans and also in which he is taken to resemble a modern atheist; and it is this aspect of his message that tends to receive the most emphasis. But on the other hand, Lucretius expresses the religious sensibility of one who finds a salvific message in the teachings of a great man. Those teachings, once enshrined in authoritative texts, became the focal point of a sect committed both to living in accordance with the teachings of the founder and to taking his message to those who had not heard it in a conscious effort to spread his word.[42] There is nothing tendentious in this description so far. The main point of contention that I can see would consist in my use of the word "salvific," since the nature of Epicurean salvation differs from (say) the Christian and Muslim varieties by being focused on this world rather than on any putative afterlife. But Lucretius himself gives us ample testimony that he regards Epicurus as a culture hero and as a liberator of humankind from religious oppression and the fear of death, and does so to such an extent that the title "savior" seems scarcely inappropriate.[43]

If we pursue this line of reasoning, I think it is clear that Lucretius regards Epicureanism as salvific not only with respect to eliminating superstition about the afterlife, but also with respect to a particular symptom of modern consciousness that he is generally taken to have embraced. Here I refer to the concept of alienation, which is recognized by some theorists as a more or less inevitable concomitant—and, in fact, a symptom—of modernization brought about by the loosening or dissolution of the traditional bonds of family, tribe, and so forth and their replacement by a concept of individualism that tends toward the radical isolation of the human subject.[44] Lucretius gives poetic form to this concept, eloquently, in Book 5 when he compares a newborn baby to a shipwrecked sailor, absolutely alone and lacking every necessity to sustain its life. In somewhat the same way, Lucretius's acceptance of death as annihilation might easily be confused with the acceptance of a life spent in isolation, but this is an un-Epicurean perspective. Epicureans, if anything, feared individual isolation in life more than or instead of death. Friendship is the basis of their ethical system, and the hope of friendship with Memmius is one of the things that makes Lucretius labor so lovingly over his poem.[45] It has often been said that the Epicurean ideal of friendship and community is one of the most attractive elements of the entire system. I would submit that, according to conventional conceptions of contemporary individual isolation, it is also one of the most unmodern.

But there is more. Just as in the case of Christianity and Islam, when a religious teaching comes to terms with the world, it usually evolves and makes accommodations of various sorts. For instance, among the Roman nobility there were many who regarded themselves as Epicureans. They were numerous enough that Cicero regarded the tendency as alarming.[46] And well he should: because Epicurean dogma in its original form is antithetical to the ethos of civic and military involvement on which the ideals of the Roman ruling class were based. Clearly the Roman nobility, no less than the most Christians and Muslims today, found ways to work around or overlook the incompatibility of their professed beliefs and the conventional behavior demanded of them by society. One such person was the senator L. Calpurnius Piso, father-in-law of Julius Caesar and patron of the aforementioned Epicurean philosopher Philodemus.[47] And Philodemus was a willing accomplice in Piso's double consciousness. The most eloquent testimony to this fact is the essay that Philodemus wrote, called "On the Good King According to Homer," a kind of instruction manual on how to be, simultaneously, a professing Epicurean and an active statesman in a strife-ridden polity like that of Rome as the republic entered its death throes.[48]

Accommodation, then, was Philodemus's approach, and in the history of most religions we can find many comparable figures. But in most religions we can also find some adherents who objected to any accommodations with society as distortions or even betrayals of the founder's message. And so with the Epicureans, as well. In fact, Lucretius himself, who expounds a version of Epicureanism much more closely and anachronistically tied to that of the founder than is the version professed at exactly the same time by Philodemus, has for this very reason, as I noted before, been labeled an "Epicurean fundamentalist."[49] And if we contrast what he says to Memmius, his patron or addressee in the *DRN*, with what

Philodemus says to Piso, the difference could hardly be more extreme. Philodemus eases Piso's conscience by teaching him how to be both a good Epicurean and a player in the power politics of his time. Lucretius lures Memmius into his poem not only with an appealing representation of Venus, but also with flattering words about how indispensable he is to his country at its hour of need.[50] But before long, he insinuates that any hope that Memmius may actually place in that entire way of life is a sham and a fraud.[51] And this is typical of him. An enormous part of Lucretius's appeal is that he does nothing by halves. He is a zealot. And if that commitment put him at odds with many fellow Epicureans, than it was evidently a price that he was willing to pay.

But what does it mean to consider Lucretius in such a light? Does his religious devotion to Epicurus's message make him modern? And does his fundamentalist's commitment to the original version of that message make him more or less so?

At this point, the structure of my investigation threatens to break down. The case for Lucretius as a modernist rests partly on the idea that he is a virtual atheist and a committed rationalist. And yet his commitment to a kind of gospel and his willingness to blind himself to the voice of reason if it contradicts that gospel are there for all to see. I have mentioned certain forms of ancient science that are, in my view, more continuous and homologous with their modern avatars than is Lucretian atomism; and I would suggest, accordingly, that the thinkers who gave us those sciences are entitled to some consideration as ancient moderns. But if we are speaking of continuities and homologies, I would have to admit that the great religions of the book stand alongside astronomy and mathematics as products of the ancient world that continue to shape the consciousness of many, and perhaps most, people who are alive today. Is this sort of religious belief, then, also modern? And is Lucretius more approximately modern in his devotion to Epicureanism as a means to salvation than he is in his mistaken adherence to its outmoded science? Or is Philodemus or any other of Lucretius's ancient coreligionists who adapted the master's teachings to the realities of their world, in fact, more modern than he?

I hope it is clear that my concern throughout this chapter is with Lucretius himself—that is, not with Epicurus or Democritus on one hand, and not with the reception of Lucretius on the other. I hope that the chapter also helps to explain why I believe that the intellectual character of Lucretius, and in different ways those of other ancient writers, as well, challenge the idea of modernism as it is most often defined. But even if we accept the definitions of ancient and modern that are the most current among literary, intellectual, and cultural historians, I hope to have made the case that Lucretius, far from being a modern or proto-modern, actually has less claim to be considered as such than many other ancient intellectuals. This is in no way to disparage Lucretius, for I use "modern" as a descriptive term, and not one of praise. My goal has been simply to give what I think is a more accurate assessment of Lucretius than some that have appeared of late.[52]

Notes

1. On the genealogy of this trope from Schiller to Hegel and Nietzsche, see Andrew Bowie, *Aesthetics and Subjectivity from Kant to Nietzsche* (Manchester: Manchester University Press, 1990). The tradition continues in the work of Lukács, Auerbach, and Bakhtin.
2. Presumably, the converse is also true, and there are among us in this chronologically modern period holdovers and recidivists of premodern consciousness. This point will become important below.
3. This is indeed the usual approach. Thus religious free-thinking, high literacy rates, the popularity of the novel, the industrial revolution, rapid transportation over land, densely concentrated urban population centers, and a variety of other symptoms have been identified, alone or in combination, as the defining features of modernism in one or another domain.
4. My own view is that many of the conventional symptoms of modernity, or close analogues of them, existed and were characteristic of urban society in the Hellenistic and Roman Imperial periods—and in some respects, even more characteristic of that society than of its early modern counterpart. But to argue that case would go well beyond the purposes of this chapter.
5. For the record, if I were asked to recommend a single meditation on the subject of Lucretius and modernism, my preference would be for Italo Calvino's marvelous *Six Memos for the Next Millennium,* trans. Patrick Creagh (Cambridge, MA: Harvard University Press, 1988), which were written as the Charles Eliot Norton Lectures on Poetry for 1985–86. Lucretius, with Ovid, frames the five lectures that Calvino lived to write. Regarding Lucretius's reception during the Renaissance and his impact on early modernism, I would cite Alison Brown, *The Return of Lucretius to Renaissance Florence* (Cambridge, MA: Harvard University Press, 2010), Gerard Passannante, *The Lucretian Renaissance: Philology and the Afterlife of Tradition* (Chicago: IL University of Chicago Press, 2011), and Ada Palmer, *Reading Lucretius in the Renaissance* (Cambridge, MA: Harvard University Press, 2014).
6. Ptolemy erected an inscription in 146 or 147 AD in which he records an earlier version of work that he would later present in the *Almagest*, which is accordingly dated to no earlier than about 150; and since he refers to the *Almagest* in several later works, he is assumed to have gone on working for some time. On this basis, he is estimated to have lived from about 100 to 175. For details, see G. J. Toomer, "Ptolemy," in *Dictionary of Scientific Biography,* ed. C. C. Gillespie, vol. 11 (New York: Charles Scribner, 1975), 186–206.
7. In fact, already by the mid-fourth century BC, when Aristotle wrote his treatise *De caelo*, the Earth had been proven to be a sphere, and its size had been estimated with reasonable accuracy. Subsequent advances in geometry and trigonometry permitted Eudoxus of Cnidos (c. 410–350 BC), Autolycus of Pitane (c. 360–290 BC), Aristarchus of Samos (c. 310–230 BC), Apollonius of Perga (c. 262–190 BC), and Hipparchus of Nicaea (c. 190–120 BC) to refine considerably their understanding of cosmic distances and of solar and lunar movements. For an overview, see James Evans, *The History and Practice of Ancient Astronomy* (New York: Oxford University Press, 1998), 20–23.
8. I have deliberately left this and the preceding sentence unaltered from the version of this paper that I read at the original conference, precisely to maintain the sharpest possible contrast with the more favorable, and brilliantly provocative, perspective

on Lucretius's mathematical intuition that my friend David Konstan presents in his chapter of this book.

9. Cf. the dismissive assessment of Manilius's greatest editor, A. E. Housman: "The inordinate length of Manilius' exposition is perhaps after all less due to a low estimate of his reader's knowledge than to the pleasure he takes in exercising that eminent aptitude for doing sums in verse which is the brightest facet of his genius" (*M. Manilii Astronomicon liber secundus*, 2nd ed. [Cambridge: Cambridge University Press, 1937], xiii). For a more sympathetic treatment of Manilius, see Katharina Volk, *Manilius and His Intellectual Background* (Oxford: Oxford University Press, 2009).

10. On Aristarchus, see Thomas Heath, *Aristarchus: The Ancient Copernicus* (Oxford: Oxford University Press, 1913); J. J. O'Connor and E. F. Robertson, "Aristarchus of Samos," *The MacTutor History of Mathematics Archive* (St Andrews: School of Mathematics and Statistics, 1999), accessed April 19, 2013, http://www-history .mcs.st-and.ac.uk/~history/Biographies/Aristarchus.html. Sextus Empiricus uses the phrase "followers of Aristarchus the mathematician" [οἱ περὶ Ἀρίσταρχον τὸν μαθηματικόν] in *Sextus Empiricus in four volumes*, trans. R. G. Bury, vol. 4, *Against the Professors* [*Adv. Math.*] (Cambridge, MA: Harvard University Press, 1944), 4.174, but the only such follower we can identify is Seleucus of Seleucia (190 BC?), whom Plutarch names along with Aristarchus as a proponent of heliocentrism; see Paul Murdin, "Seleucus of Seleucia," in *Encyclopedia of Astronomy and Astrophysics*, ed. Paul Murdin (New York and London: Nature and Institute of Physics, 2001), accessed April 19, 2013, http://eaa.iop.org.

11. For Lucretius's place in the history of atomism, see Duncan Kennedy, *Rethinking Reality: Lucretius and the Textualization of Nature* (Ann Arbor: University of Michigan Press, 2002), a balanced assessment of what is at stake in emphasizing either continuity or discontinuity in tracing the history of a concept such as "the atom," noting its "historical tenacity" but admitting that "we stress [the element of] continuity only by negotiating or suppressing some potentially discomfiting discontinuities" and asking in what sense the atom of Lucretius is really the same as that of Dalton, Rutherford, or Bohr (3). Monte Johnson and Catherine Wilson, "Lucretius and the History of Science," in *The Cambridge Companion to Lucretius,* ed. Stuart Gillespie and Philip Hardie (Cambridge: Cambridge University Press, 2007), 131–48, write that "the Lucretian conception of nature as 'accomplishing everything by herself spontaneously and independently and free from the jurisdiction of the gods' was a major driving force in the Scientific Revolution experienced in Western Europe beginning in the early seventeenth century." But they go on to note that "there are nevertheless profound differences between ancient and modern materialism" (147). More recent interventions, particularly Stephen Greenblatt's *The Swerve: How the World Became Modern* (New York: W. W. Norton, 2011), seem to me to have greatly exaggerated perceived continuities between Lucretius and modernism; consequently, my aim in this chapter is to redress the balance by emphasizing certain discontinuities. In general, however, I believe that accounts like Kennedy's and Johnson and Wilson's are correct.

12. The possibility that Aristarchus directly influenced Copernicus is raised by Owen Gingerich, "Did Copernicus Owe a Debt to Aristarchus?" *Journal for the History of Astronomy* 16 (1985): 37–42.

13. Archimedes wished to demonstrate his method by calculating the number of grains of sand it would take to fill up the universe. Aristarchus's heliocentric theory called for the universe to be much larger than did the geocentric model, and the amount of sand needed to fill it would be correspondingly larger, and therefore would show off Archimedes's technique much more impressively. The only work of Aristarchus

that survives, "On the Size and Distances of the Sun and Moon" (Greek text and English translation in Heath, *Aristarchus*; see note 10 above) does not mention his heliocentric theory.

14. Evans, *History and Practice of Ancient Astronomy,* 26; cf. 414–27.

15. Geodetic coordinates (i.e., latitude and longitude) translate readily into Cartesian form. Dicaearchus of Messana (c. 350–285 BC) invented the concept of 0° latitude from which other positions of latitude might be measured. Eratosthenes of Cyrene (c. 276–194 BC) followed up by proposing five bands of latitude corresponding to the equator, the tropics, and the polar circles. Hipparchus of Nicaea (c. 190–120 BC) refined Eratosthenes's plan by measuring latitude in terms of 360° and explicitly including those parts of the globe that were unexplored and thought to be inaccessible. His system is the one used by Ptolemy and, in effect, it remains in use today. Longitude was a much more difficult problem. Hipparchus understood the theoretical aspects, but had no practical means at his disposal to calculate accurate meridians, something that was not finally accomplished until the eighteenth century (Daniela Dueck and Kai Broderson, *Geography in Classical Antiquity* [Cambridge: Cambridge University Press, 2012]), 95–97, and Dava Sobel, *Longitude: The True Story of a Lone Genius Who Solved the Greatest Scientific Problem of His Time* [New York: Walker, 1995]). Nevertheless, ancient geographers came close to developing a geodetic system based on analytical geometry, the key figure in this area being Apollonius of Perga (c. 260–190 BC). According to Carl B. Boyer, *A History of Mathematics,* 2nd ed., rev. Uta C. Merzbach (Hoboken, NJ: John Wiley), 1991, 156: "The methods of Apollonius in the *Conics* in many respects are so similar to the modern approach that his work sometimes is judged to be an analytic geometry anticipating that of Descartes by 1800 years…However, Greek geometric algebra did not provide for negative magnitudes; moreover, the coordinate system was in every case superimposed *a posteriori* upon a given curve in order to study its properties. There appear to be no cases in ancient geometry in which a coordinate frame of reference was laid down *a priori* for purposes of graphical representation of an equation or relationship, whether symbolically or rhetorically expressed. Of Greek geometry we may say that equations are determined by curves, but not that curves are determined by equations.…That Apollonius, the greatest geometer of antiquity, failed to develop analytic geometry, was probably the result of a poverty of curves rather than of thought. General methods are not necessary when problems concern always one of a limited number of particular cases."

16. Lucretius, *De Rerum Natura* (hereafter *DRN*) 5.656–79. I cite the Latin text as printed in Bailey's *editio maior* (*Titi Lucreti Cari De Rerum Natura libri sex,* vol. 1, prolegomena, text and critical apparatus, translation, ed. Cyril Bailey [Oxford: Oxford University Press, 1947]); all translations are my own. Lucretius's explanations of astronomical phenomena are minutely and illuminatingly analyzed by F. A. Bakker, "Three Studies in Epicurean Cosmology" (PhD diss., University of Utrecht, 2010), 39–53, especially 48–50. Bakker argues persuasively against the view that Lucretius expresses any preference for the different explanations that he offers.

17. The first two explanations presuppose the permanent existence of the sun (movement along the ecliptic, *DRN* 5.682–95; varying atmospheric resistance, 696–99); the third, which involves daily palingenesis (700–4), does not actually explain why the length of the daylight hours varies throughout the year.

18. Note, in particular, the language of *claritas* and *obscuritas* at *DRN* 1.136–48, 921–34 (≈ 4.1–9) and, in contrast, the criticism of Heraclitus as being *clarus ob obscuram linguam,* "famous for his obscure manner of expression" (*DRN* 1.639).

19. For instance, Lucretius, for the most part, develops his ethical position not through explicit argument, but through suggestion, as in his treatment of distant views, ostensibly as a physical phenomenon, but by implication an ethical one, as well: see Phillip De Lacy, "Distant Views: The Imagery of Lucretius 2," *Classical Journal* 60 (1964): 49–55.

20. This is a famous and much discussed paradox; see Monica Gale, *Myth and Poetry in Lucretius* (Cambridge: Cambridge University Press, 1994), 208–23, with further references.

21. Jerome, *Chronica* s.a. Abr. 1923 = Ol. 171.3 (94 BC): *Titus Lucretius poeta nascitur. Qui postea amatorio poculo in furorem versus, cum aliquot libros per intervalla insaniae conscripsisset, quos postea Cicero emendavit, propria se manu interfecit anno aetatis XLIIII* ["The poet Titus Lucretius is born. Later, having become insane by drinking a love potion, after writing during periods of remission several books, which Cicero later edited, he committed suicide at the age of forty-four"], in *Eusebius Werke*, ed. R. Helm, vol. 7, Die Chronik des Hieronymus, 3rd ed., Die Griechischen Christlichen Schriftsteller der Ersten Jahrhunderte, 47 (Berlin: Akademie-Verlag, 1984), 233. Excellent reflections on the reception of Lucretius's "insanity" can be found in W. R. Johnson, *Lucretius and the Modern World* (London: Duckworth, 2000), 79–133.

22. *DRN* 1.921–50 ≈ 4.1–25 (cf. note 18 above); this is another much discussed passage. See Margaret Graver, "The Eye of the Beholder: Perceptual Relativity in Lucretius," *Apeiron* 23 (1990): 91–116; Gale, *Myth and Poetry*, 141–43.

23. Cf. *DRN* 4.1058, *haec Venus est nobis*, "this is Venus for us," that is, this is what Venus really is, not as a goddess, who in Epicurean terms is perfectly happy and so utterly unconcerned with mortal affairs, but as a metonym of human sexuality. This revelation is made as the culmination of a lengthy diatribe: see Robert Brown, *Lucretius on Love and Sex: A Commentary on* De Rerum Natura *4.1030–287, with Prolegomena, Text, and Translation*, Columbia Studies in the Classical Tradition 15 (Leiden: Brill, 1987).

24. "Plague of Athens," *DRN* 6.1138–236; see Gale, *Myth and Poetry*, 223–28; Peta Fowler, "Lucretian Conclusions," in *Classical Closure: Reading the End in Greek and Latin Literature*, ed. D. H. Roberts, F. M. Dunn, and D. P. Fowler (Princeton, NJ: Princeton University Press, 1997), 112–38. On the irrelevancy of death, the statement *nil igitur mors est ad nos neque pertinet hilum*, "Therefore, death is nothing to us, nor does it pertain to us at all" (*DRN* 3.830), is the conclusion that Lucretius draws from a series of proofs that the soul is mortal (*DRN* 3.417–829). The remainder of Book 3 (830–1094) is a diatribe against the fear of death: see Barbara Price Wallach, *Lucretius and the Diatribe against the Fear of Death: De Rerum Natura III, 830–1094* (Leiden: Brill, 1976).

25. Again, see Fowler, "Lucretian Conclusions."

26. This issue also is carefully examined by Bakker, "Epicurean Cosmology," 146–238.

27. Epicurus's views on the movements of the heavenly bodies are best preserved in *Epistle to Pythocles*, 91–93, which is probably a summary of *Peri physeos*, 11, both in *Epicuro: Opere*, ed. G. Arrighetti, 2nd ed. (Turin: Einaudi, 1973); see David Sedley, *Lucretius and the Transformation of Greek Wisdom* (Cambridge: Cambridge University Press, 1998), 119–21. For an overview of the place of cosmology in Epicureanism see Liba Taub, "Cosmology and Meteorology," in *The Cambridge Companion to Epicureanism*, ed. James Warren (Cambridge: Cambridge University Press, 2009), 105–24. It is worth noting that a fragment of the inscription in which Diogenes of Oenoanda lays down his own Epicurean beliefs, refers to someone as "dismissing the unanimous opinion of all men, both laymen and philosophers, that the heavenly bodies pursue

their courses round the earth both above and below" (Martin Ferguson Smith, ed. and trans., *Diogenes of Oenoanda: The Epicurean Inscription*, La scuola di Epicuro, 1 [Naples: Bibliopolis, 1993], fr. 66). This implies that in the second century AD, when Diogenes wrote, even professing Epicureans accepted the idea of a geocentric world.

28. See Richard Janko, *Philodemus, On Poems, Book One* (Oxford: Oxford University Press, 2000), 11–119.

29. On the remains of Epicurus's works, see Sedley, *Transformation*, 94–133, and his "Epicureanism in the Roman Republic," in *The Cambridge Companion to Epicureanism*, ed. James Warren (Cambridge: Cambridge University Press, 2009), 29–45. On Philodemus, see Marcello Gigante, *Philodemus in Italy: The Books from Herculaneum*, trans. Dirk Obbink (Ann Arbor: University of Michigan Press, 1995). For the possibility that the same library contained a copy of Lucretius's poem, see Dirk Obbink, "Lucretius and the Herculaneum Library," in *The Cambridge Companion to Lucretius*, ed. Stuart Gillespie and Philip Hardie (Cambridge: Cambridge University Press, 2007), 33–40.

30. On Epicurus's hostility to poetry, see Gale, *Myth and Poetry*, 14–16.

31. On these aspects, see Dirk Obbink, *Philodemus and Poetry* (Oxford: Oxford University Press, 1995).

32. The key text is his *De Poematis* in five books, of which Richard Janko has edited books 1 (*Philodemus, On Poems, Book One* [Oxford: Oxford University Press, 2000]) and 3–4 (*Philodemus, On Poems, Books 3–4, with the Fragments of Aristotle, On Poets* [Oxford: Oxford University Press, 2010]) and is working on book 2; see his Introduction to book 1 for a general discussion of the shape of the work and of its central themes; for the entire treatise, see his "Reconstructing Philodemus, *On Poems*," in *Philodemus and Poetry*, ed. Dirk Obbink (Oxford: Oxford University Press, 1995), 69–96. Book 5 of *De Poematis* is being edited by David Armstrong, Jeffrey Fish, and James Porter.

33. These Philodemus characterizes as "the philosophers": see Elizabeth Asmis, "Crates on Poetic Criticism," *Phoenix* 46 (1992): 128–69; Janko, *Philodemus, On Poems, Book 1*, 129–34.

34. Janko, *Philodemus, On Poems, Book 1*, 169–81; James Porter, "Content and Form in Philodemus: The History of an Evasion," in *Philodemus and Poetry*, ed. Dirk Obbink (Oxford: Oxford University Press, 1995), 97–146.

35. Sedley, *Transformation*, 134–65.

36. *DRN* 1.635–920.

37. On the debate over Lucretius's interest in philosophy after Epicurus, see James Warren, "Lucretius and Greek Philosophy," in *The Cambridge Companion to Lucretius*, ed. Stuart Gillespie and Philip Hardie (Cambridge: Cambridge University Press, 2007), 22–25, with further references.

38. *DRN* 5.650–55, like its source, Epicurus's *Epistle to Pythocles*, 92, offers both the theory of daily extinction and palingenisis and the theory that the earth blocks the light of the sun during the night as possible explanations of the phenomenon. Some scholars believe that Lucretius expresses a preference for the theory of palingenesis, but this idea has been refuted by Bakker, "Epicurean Cosmology," 35–53, who shows that the Epicurean principle of multiple explanation is incompatible with such a preference.

39. Epicurus, *Epistle to Pythocles*, 91; cf. Cicero, *On Ends* [*De Finibus*], trans. H. Rackham (Cambridge, MA: Harvard University Press, 1914), 1.6.20; Cicero, *Academica*, in *Cicero: De Natura Deorum, Academica*, trans. H. Rackham (Cambridge, MA: Harvard

University Press, 1933), 2.26.82; Aetius 2.21.5 (= [Plutarch], *Moralia*, ed. G. N. Bernardakis [Leipzig: B. G. Teubner, 1893], 11.61); *DRN* 5.564–84.

40. Evans, *Ancient Astronomy*, 68–74, 385–87.

41. *DRN* 5.8 with C. D. N. Costa, *Lucretius De Rerum Natura V* (Oxford: Oxford University Press, 1984), 50 ad loc.; cf. Bernard Frischer, *The Sculpted Word: Epicureanism and Philosophical Recruitment in Ancient Greece* (Berkeley: University of California Press, 1982; rev. ed. 2006), 412–36, accessed April 18, 2013, http://quod.lib.umich.edu /cgi/t/text/text-idx?c=acls;cc=acls;view=toc;idno=heb90022.0001.001

42. For a speculative but persuasive account of Epicurean recruitment strategies, see, in general, Frischer, *Sculpted Word*.

43. Culture hero, *DRN* 5.54; liberator from religious superstition and fear of death, *DRN* 1.62–145; cf. Frischer, *Sculpted Word*, 387–404.

44. The literature on this subject, which goes back to the foundational works of Marx, Weber, and Durkheim, is vast. In general, sociologists distinguish between "traditional" and "modern" societies by recognizing that various forms of material and technological advancement in the latter are purchased by the loss of many structures (religious, hierarchical, ceremonial, and so forth) that created social cohesion in the former. Although most social scientists consider either that the benefits of "modernization" are worth the cost, or else that the cost of maintaining cohesion in "traditional" societies is exorbitant, contemporary perspectives on alienation expand upon the classic sociological theory to consider alienation from many perspectives, questioning, for instance, whether the economic and social history of Western Europe is a suitable or adequate paradigm for evaluating the experience of "modernization" and "development" in other parts of the world, or from an ecological perspective whether alienation from the environment is too high a price to pay for the human race as a whole. For a spectrum of ideas on the subject, see Lauren Langman and Devorah Kalekin-Fishman, eds., *The Evolution of Alienation: Trauma, Promise, and the Millennium* (London: Rowman & Littlefield, 2006).

45. *DRN* 1.140–45.

46. Cicero, *Tusculan Disputations*, trans. J. E. King (Cambridge, MA: Harvard University Press, 1950), 4.6–7.

47. On Piso and Philodemus, see, briefly, R. G. M. Nisbet, *Cicero, In L. Calpurnium Pisonem oratio* (Oxford: Oxford University Press, 1961), 183–86, with further references.

48. See Oswyn Murray, "Philodemus On the Good King According to Homer," *Journal of Roman Studies* 55 (1965): 161–82 and Oswyn Murray, "Rileggendo *Il buon re secondo Omero*," *Cronache ercolanesi* 14 (1984): 157–60.

49. Sedley, *Transformation*, 62–93.

50. *DRN* 1.21–43.

51. *DRN* 2.37–54 and 323–32.

52. I would like to thank the editors and the other participants in the NYU conference and the organizers of and participants in a conference on "Lucretius in theory: literary-critical approaches to the *De Rerum Natura*" held at the University of Edinburgh on September 30 and October 1, 2013, at which I gave a revised version of the NYU paper. The published version has benefited greatly from the opportunity to present and discuss these ideas with two very different but very stimulating groups of colleagues.

CHAPTER THREE

Lucretius the Physicist and Modern Science

DAVID KONSTAN

In a 2011 issue of *The New Yorker*, there appeared a feature article by Stephen Greenblatt titled "The Answer Man," and bearing the subtitle, "An Ancient Poem was Rediscovered—and the World Swerved"[1]—a kind of advance notice for his book, *The Swerve: How the World Became Modern*, published in September of that same year.[2] The article records Greenblatt's encounter with Lucretius's poem when he was a student at Yale, and how it struck him for its astonishing modernity. Lucretius defended various ideas that have since been proved false, such as the notion that the sun circled the earth. "But, at its heart," Greenblatt writes, "'On the Nature of Things' persuasively laid out what seemed to be a strikingly modern understanding of the world."[3] Greenblatt was especially sensitive to the ethical message of Epicureanism, but this vision was founded on and inseparable from the atomic theory and its unflinching materialism. Years later, when Greenblatt held in his hands a Renaissance copy of the only manuscript by which Lucretius's text survived, he was still under its spell: "In the great Laurentian Library, surrounded by the achievements of Renaissance Florence, I felt the full force of what this ancient Roman poet had bequeathed to the world, a tortuous trail that led from the celebration of Venus, past broken columns, high-domed churches, and inquisitorial fires, toward Jefferson, Darwin, and Einstein."[4] Modern science was given a profound, perhaps indispensable boost by the rediscovery of Lucretius's poem.

But how modern was Epicurean physics—was it a science, indeed, in the modern sense of the word at all? In a book provocatively titled, *The Forgotten Revolution*, and subtitled *Greek Scientific Thought and Modern Science*, Lucio Russo argues that "modern science was born in the Hellenistic age" ("la scienza nacque con l'ellenismo").[5] Like Greenblatt, Russo, too, holds that the great discoveries and scientific vision that marked this epoch went underground with the decline of the Roman Empire, and only resurfaced in the Renaissance. Yet Russo all but neglects atomic physics in favor of ancient mathematics, optics, technology, and medicine. Epicurus earns a brief mention in three footnotes, and Lucretius fares only a little better, mentioned chiefly in connection with evolution rather than the atomic theory as such. It is as though ancient atomism, for all its resemblance to one of the crucial achievements of modern physics, never reached the level of true scientific method.

The reasons for the relative condescension toward Epicurean physics are various. Epicurus himself is, in part, responsible, inasmuch as he maintained that physics was wholly subordinate to the ethical or rather psychological goals of his philosophy; as he put it: "If we had never been troubled by celestial and atmospheric phenomena, nor by fears about death, nor by our ignorance of the limits of pains and desires, we should have had no need of natural science" (*Principal Doctrine* 11). Or take his remark in the *Letter to Menoeceus* (134): "It would be better to follow the mythology about gods than be a slave to the 'fate' of the natural philosophers";[6] Epicurus is not asking whether determinism is true or false, but whether, in depriving us of confidence in our free will, it threatens to undermine our possibility of achieving that serenity or ataraxy that is the goal of Epicurean teaching.[7] In addition, Epicurus's notorious insistence on allowing for all possible explanations of celestial phenomena such as eclipses, without seeking to discover the true cause, smacks not so much of justifiable skepticism in relation to remote and untestable phenomena as it does of intellectual idleness or, at all events, a lack of proper scientific curiosity (see especially Epicurus's *Letter to Pythocles*; Lucretius adopts the same approach: see *DRN* 5.416–770, 6.703–11). Then, too, the relative absence of experiment in Epicurus, who in this respect did not differ from the proponents of theories of nature generally in antiquity, leaves his system open to the charge of excessive speculation, far removed from the empirical foundations of modern science (Epicurus inferred the existence of atoms and void from observed phenomena such as the fact of motion and the susceptibility of objects to disintegration). Add to this the fact that Epicurus's conception of atoms is, in fact, very different from the modern view, and a healthy skepticism would seem to be in order in regard to ostensible analogies between ancient atomism and the modern version, even if the encounter with Epicureanism, in large part through the efforts of Pierre Gassendi, had a huge impact on thinkers from Hobbes to Newton and beyond.[8]

But perhaps the deepest reason for distancing Epicurean theory from modern scientific method is the apparent incoherence of ancient atomism itself, and most fundamentally its apparent indifference to mathematics, whether then or now. For in introducing the notion of minima—not the atoms themselves, but rather the irreducible constituents of atoms— Epicurus seems to have violated the elementary principles of geometry, according to which, for example, the diagonal of a square or cube is incommensurable with the side. If there are minimal entities in the sense that they have extension but nothing smaller can be imagined, won't these minima necessarily have internal dimensions? If one of them is shaped like a cube, its sides must be smaller than its diagonal—so which of these lengths is minimal? Puzzles like this, and others, have called into question the seriousness of Epicurus's enterprise, and exposed him to the charge that he neglected elementary logic. Thus, Anthony Long and David Sedley, in their valuable selection of Hellenistic philosophical texts, comment à propos Epicurean minima: "One further consequence should be the falsity of conventional geometry. If, for example, the perfect geometrical square could exist, its side and diagonal would be incommensurable—incompatibly with the theory of minima, in which, as we have seen, all magnitudes share a common submultiple. There is good historical evidence that Epicurus accepted this consequence..., but none that he worked out in detail an alternative geometry."[9]

Today, we are familiar with alternative geometries, such as those associated with the names of Riemann and Lobachevsky, not to mention modern quantum mechanics, where sophisticated notions of minima are employed. I quote from the abstract of an article by Luis J. Garay titled "Quantum Gravity and Minimum Length": "The key ingredients for the appearance of this minimum length are quantum mechanics, special relativity and general relativity. As a consequence, classical notions such as causality or distance between events cannot be expected to be applicable at this scale. They must be replaced by some other, yet unknown, structure."[10] But it is just here, where modern theories invoke highly complex mathematical theories, that we become conscious of what seems like an unbridgeable distance between ancient atomism and its modern descendant. Is it not foolhardy in the extreme to see in Epicurus's system even a remote anticipation of physical theories that are derived from entirely different premises?

Before addressing this question head on, by proposing an interpretation of Epicurus's theory that may bring it into relation, albeit distantly, with contemporary physics, I pause (begging the reader's patience) to make some observations about the nature of modernism more generally and its relation to the past. British writers in the eighteenth century developed a conception of the novel that had the result, perhaps not entirely by accident, of ascribing the invention of the novel to the British. This was achieved by a certain sleight of hand, according to which criteria were established by which to define novels in the strict sense, as opposed to mere romances. Earlier narratives that might seem to compete for precedence were simply demoted to the status of romances, among them the ancient Greek novels, as they are once again respectfully called nowadays.[11] Among the works that failed to meet the criteria for the realistic bourgeois novel is Cervantes's *Don Quixote*, and not just, I think, because it is a parody of the chivalrous tales that were the prime target of the new conception of the novel. Just to recall the curious history of *Don Quixote*, Cervantes had published in 1605 what is today the first part of the work, and evidently regarded it as finished. But the appearance of a sequel composed by another writer, whose identity is still obscure, provoked Cervantes to

issue his own continuation ten years later, in 1615, constituting what is
today the second part. In this latter part, Don Quixote hears of another
knight with the same name, who is pursuing his adventures at the same
time: there is a mirroring of two fictions here, in a way that would seem
to be highly modern—or, if we reserve the term "modern" for the high
period of the naturalistic novel, that is, the eighteenth, nineteenth, and
early twentieth centuries, then we might employ the term "postmodern"
for the kinds of experiments in contemporary fiction that *Don Quixote*
seems to anticipate. One might make a similar case for works such as
Diderot's *Jacques le fataliste*, in which a character in the novel argues with
the author over the question of whether he has free will—not to mention
an oddity like *Tristram Shandy*. My purpose in introducing these examples
is to suggest that the constraints placed on the early modern novel tight-
ened up the rules for the genre in such a way as to exclude both most of
the fiction that preceded it and much of what has been written since in a
modernist vein. We might regard the naturalistic novel as a kind of parenthetical moment in the trajectory of fiction generally, at the limits of
which what we may call non-Euclidean alternatives to the standard narrative form had been, or were again to become, admissible.

Something similar can be said about the reign of perspective in painting: there is a kind of convergence between pre-Renaissance art and modern techniques, which have the advantage of liberating the viewer from
the constraint of having to behold the image from a single vantage point,
or at the most a restricted viewing position. The abstract construction of
the image around a single vanishing point came into being along with the
modern rediscovery of the science of optics, but it is only from within
this theory that it can be seen as an unambiguous advance, as opposed to
one particular fashion in the history of art.[12] Literary criticism, too, has
made something of a return to ancient models, with the new emphasis
on rhetoric and persuasion as opposed to finding a single meaning or
authorial viewpoint in a text.[13] In the introduction to *The Protestant Ethic
and the Spirit of Capitalism*, Max Weber sought to define the Zeitgeist of
the modern world, and affirmed that only in Western Europe did there
develop, after the Renaissance, a commitment to or vision of rational
structure in the fields of science, history, architecture, and art, along with
music (the subordination of the entire orchestra to the leadership of the
conductor) and statecraft, in the form of a highly trained and disciplined
bureaucracy.[14] Capitalist industry, too, is built on this same rational foundation, and this is the secret of its success. Although the ancient Greek
enlightenment in some ways anticipated this revolution in perception and
social organization, the real take-off point came with the rise of capitalism concomitantly with the Protestant values that stimulated it. For
Weber, of course, this rationality represented progress in human history.
Postmodernism has called this teleological view into question, and it is
now possible to interpret the congruence of ostensibly rational organization across a wide variety of fields of life as a symptom of a particular

historical moment, which, in turn, has given way, in many areas, to new visions, some of which bear a resemblance to ways of thinking, viewing, listening, and so forth that prevailed in the premodern period or in societies outside the so-called West.

Now, I wish to unpack Weber's neatly boxed account of how rational structure came to prevail over the various arts, sciences, and practices in the modern world: this was not a uniform movement, nor will it be dismantled or superseded by some new configuration across the whole range of human activity. Euclidean mathematics persisted from antiquity to the nineteenth century as the paradigm of geometry; the codifications of the ancient grammarians are still dominant in the teaching of English grammar in the schools. The various fields of human endeavor do not march in lockstep, and they exhibit paradigm shifts at different times. What is more, even if something like a scientific worldview did emerge in classical antiquity, as Lucio Russo avers, it did not enjoy the overwhelming ideological privilege that it acquired after Newton. Plato and Aristotle, who were both highly respectful of mathematics, nevertheless entertained very different conceptions of science than anything we might recognize today, and their subsequent influence was pervasive. The absence of a dominant ideology or outlook such as emerged in post-Newtonian physics may have impeded the development of a scientific establishment, but it did not necessarily mean that alternative ways of interpreting reality were less systematic or well grounded. On the contrary, there may have been more room for working out unorthodox or indeed non-Euclidean theories, just as Cervantes, writing before the age of Richardson, Fielding, and Defoe, was free to experiment with narrative form, unimpeded by the constraints of the new naturalism. Thus, while it would be absurd to claim that Epicurus or Lucretius achieved anything like the rich theoretical vision of modern physics, they may have come closer, in some respects, than we would be inclined to allow if we measure ancient physics exclusively by the yardstick of Newtonian mechanics, and imagine that any alternatives were dead-end enterprises, like the sad-eyed hominids that are represented as occupying the lower branches of the evolutionary tree.

With this preamble, I return to the question of minima in Epicureanism, and to the possibility that the atomic hypothesis may have been more coherent than scholars have allowed, due in part, perhaps, to ingrained doubts about the plausibility of a mathematical minimalism as well as to the fragmentary state of the sources. What, then, is an Epicurean minimum? Lucretius explains:

> In addition,
> since there are always extreme particles
> [which in objects are the tiniest things
> we see, there should, in the same manner, be
> a smallest point] in those things which our sense　　　600
> cannot perceive—and that point, quite clearly,

has no parts and consists of the smallest
element in nature; it has never been
isolated on its own and cannot be
in future, since it is itself a part,
the single primary part, of something else. (1.599–606)[15]

The translation I have adopted assumes a lacuna after the first line quoted, which is filled in on the basis of a conjecture by the great Lucretius scholar, Hugh Andrew Johnstone Munro. I believe that some such supplement is required, but the point does not substantially affect my argument, though it does indicate by what a slender thread our understanding of Epicurean physics hangs, and nowhere more than in the subtlest details of the theory. The Epicureans maintained, as we have seen, that the universe consists of matter and void, and that matter comes in the form of microscopic particles that are never visible to the eye—I do not say "naked eye," since the notion that atoms might be perceptible through enhanced optical instruments seems not to have been raised. The closest Lucretius comes to indicating the size of these subliminal entities is in his image of dust motes floating in a sunbeam, where he suggests that their constant motion and sudden shifts of direction are caused by their interaction with still smaller, unperceived particles that are either themselves atomic or are ultimately buffeted about by atoms somewhere down the line (2.114–28). But if atoms are imperceptible, they are not unimaginable, and our thought picture of them reveals some of the properties they must possess, on the analogy of macroscopic objects. When we contemplate an observable thing, we can discern parts of it, but our ability to subdivide it fails at the corners; so, too, Lucretius argues (here with good support from Epicurus's own texts), the tips of atoms cannot be imagined as being further divisible (1.599–604). Now, this is not a very good argument: we could say that, just as the corner of a perceptible object is, in reality, composed of particles beneath the visible threshold, so, too, minima can be further reduced to ever smaller components. But, in fact, that analogy with macroscopic objects is not, I think, intended as a proof but is rather a way of illustrating what a minimum is like: among other things, it serves as a limit or edge to the atom, and this is something that atoms require, if they are to have any structure at all—that is, any way that they can retain their individuality in the event that two atoms brush up against one another. The real argument concerning minima follows (1.605–14):

Then other parts like it and still others
in a series fill, in a compact mass,
the substance of that corporeal stuff.
Because they cannot exist on their own,
these parts must adhere to certain places
where there is no way they can be detached.
Thus, primary basic stuff is purely solid—

a close-packed mass of smallest elements,   610
not combined in an aggregate of parts,
but rather with a unitary force
which is eternal. Nature does not let
any part be separated from them
or diminished, reserving them as seeds
for objects.

The minimal bits of which atoms are constituted are inseparable from the composite: there is no such thing as a freestanding minimum. Hence, atoms cannot be said to be made up of minima (*non ex illorum conventu conciliata*; 1. 612), in the sense that minima are somehow assembled to form atoms; they are always embedded in matter.

This is the place where someone familiar with modern physics is likely to think of quarks, which likewise never exist independently, but are, as it were, fractions of larger wholes. The analogy is not exact, for reasons that will become clear in a moment, but the way of thinking about matter is perhaps not altogether different. The real source of the Epicurean view lies, or so I have argued elsewhere, in Aristotle's discussion of the relationship between points and lines in the sixth book of his *Physics*.[16] Aristotle observes that if you put two points together (assuming for the sake of argument that a freestanding point could exist), they will simply overlap; the reason is that points by definition have no edges—they are partless, after all—and so cannot be placed edge to edge. It follows that no amount of points can be assembled so as to create a line, surface, or solid; they will always collapse into a single point. A line contains points—an infinite number of them, according to Aristotle, since they are dimensionless—but it cannot be constructed out of them. Epicurus, in turn, adapted Aristotle's purely mathematical reasoning concerning points and lines to his analysis of the physical constituents of nature. His minimal parts do have extension, since they are corporeal, not mere abstract, entities. Hence, enough of them will add up to a finite span, for example, the size of an atom (I will consider in a moment how much is "enough"). But since they are like points in that they lack internal differentiation of any sort, they, too, have no edges, and so they cannot be lined up to form larger substances but exist only as parts.[17] Atoms, of course, do have boundaries, which I take to consist of the outermost layer of minima. This perhaps accounts for why they do not fuse when they meet: they touch edge to edge, just like macroscopic objects. Since atoms are said to be separated by void (this claim is attributed to Democritus, at all events), some later thinkers, who were puzzled by what happens when atoms touch and so leave no void between them, concluded that atoms in fact do not meet: there is always some tiny amount of space between them. Thus, Philoponus, in his commentary on Aristotle's treatise, *De generatione et corruptione* (1.8, p. 158) affirms: "Democritus did not speak precisely of contact when he said that the atoms are in contact with one another...but rather what he called contact was the atoms being near one another and not standing very far apart."[18] Some modern scholars suggest that atoms do not fuse simply because they are by nature inalterable, others that atoms meet only at a minimum, which effectively does not count as a joined surface.[19] I mention these alternatives to show how Epicurus elicits quite sophisticated explanations of his theories from sympathetic critics today.

We come now, however, to the crux of the problem: Epicurus's minima are not points, but have extension; any extended substance, of the sort that when multiplied by a sufficiently large number yields a finite mass, must have internal dimensions, such as height and width. Suppose a minimum is one hundredth the size of an atom, or a thousandth, or a millionth. It will still have some shape, and whether or not that shape is symmetrical (as in a cube, perhaps, or a sphere), it will be subject to the objection that its side or circumference is incommensurable with its diagonal or diameter, and so it cannot represent a true minimum. Did Epicurus have a solution to this dilemma? I believe that he did.

The key is to be found, paradoxically, in Epicurus's discussion of large magnitudes. Like other thinkers, Epicurus distinguished between finite and infinite quantities. However, he also introduced what looks like an intermediate order of magnitude, in the form of what he called "not strictly [or simply: *haplôs*] infinite," which he also describes as "inconceivably" large (*oukh haplôs apeiroi alla monon aperilêptoi: Letter to Herodotus* 42). Certain features of the universe are measured by this peculiar quantity, for example, vast cosmic distances (these are mentioned in the discussion of the speed at which atoms travel: *Letter to Herodotus* 42, 46–47; cf. Lucretius 4.141–217) and, above all, the number of different shapes that atoms come in. The number of atoms in the universe is infinite, of course, and so, too, the number of atoms of any given shape. The variety of shapes, however, is not. And yet, neither is the number of shapes strictly finite. It is somewhere in between: not infinite, but nevertheless incalculably large.

As is well known, Georg Cantor distinguished between denumerable and non-denumerable infinities (the set of integers is an example of the former, the set of real numbers an example of the latter), but neither of these classes corresponds to Epicurus's category, since that quantity is explicitly said not to be infinite (or not simply so). For a long time, I simply took it for granted that, intriguing as it was, Epicurus's conception was mathematically incoherent. He could exploit it to solve problems raised by his atomic theory, but alas, modern science could have no use for such a hybrid quantity. The reader may imagine my surprise when I read only a few years ago that modern mathematicians have discovered, or perhaps the better term is "constructed" or "defined," just such a value—one that is not infinite but is, nevertheless, theoretically (and not just practically) incalculable. The number has been assigned the name "omega": "Omega is perfectly well defined and it is a specific number, but it is impossible to compute in its entirety."[20] I do not mean to suggest that Epicurus had a comparable definition in mind, but it now seems to me that his notion of an incalculably large quantity should not be dismissed as mere nonsense. The Stoics, too, seem to have admitted such an intermediate quantity. Plutarch (*De comm. not.* 1079B–C), at all events, reports the following: "'When we are asked,' says Chrysippus, 'whether we contain any parts and how many and of what parts *they* are composed and how many, we shall employ a distinction, on the one hand positing on a large scale that we are composed of head and torso and limbs, for this was all there was to the question and the paradox; but if they extend this questioning to ultimate parts,' he says, 'we must not answer any such thing, but rather we must say neither out of what things we consist nor, similarly, out of how many, whether of an infinite or a finite number.'" Plutarch condemns this reply as evasive: "For if, just as there is the indifferent between good and bad, there is some middle term between finite and infinite, he should have resolved the puzzle by saying what this is."[21] Perhaps he misunderstood the Stoic position. Epicurus, at all events, was unambiguous.

Why should Epicurus have insisted that the variety of atomic shapes must be larger than any specifiable finite number and yet not strictly infinite? The number had to be very large in order to account for the enormous diversity of items in the world: not just the many species of animals but differences within each species, such that a cow can recognize its own calves, for example, and not confuse them with others. An infinite variety, however, would have the consequence that any and every kind of creature could exist, and this plainly is not the case: maples all differ among themselves, but there is a clear division between maples and oaks; we do not find in nature every intermediate type, which would blur the boundary between the two. But Lucretius offers another reason as well to limit the number of atomic shapes. Any given number of minima, he says, can be arranged in only a finite number of ways, and he offers the following thought experiment: "Take particles made of two or three minima, or increase them by a few more" (2.485–86), and locate the parts top and bottom, left and right, in any which way; at a certain point, it will be impossible to vary them further, unless you add more minima. Thus, to generate infinitely many kinds of atoms, you will have to keep increasing the quantity of minima, and eventually the atom will become large enough to be visible. But there are no visible atoms; hence, the variety of atomic shapes is less than infinite.

Here we see an important link between two mathematically innovative concepts: quasi-infinite atomic shapes and quasi-infinitesimal minima. An infinite number of extended minima will produce a huge object, indeed, one of infinite size.[22] A finite number will remain well below the threshold of perception, but an atom composed of just two minima, say, will raise the same geometrical difficulties as a single minimum. But suppose that all atoms, whether small or large, though always of microscopic size, are composed of an incomprehensibly large but not strictly infinite number of minima. The incalculable variety of phenomena is thereby preserved—every grain of sand, Lucretius says, is distinct from every other—but no atom need reach visible proportions. The Epicurean minimum, I propose, is precisely the inverse of the incalculably large or not strictly infinite order of magnitude: it is, in other words, one over omega.

This definition of the minimum helps to resolve a number of conundrums to which Epicurean physics has given rise.[23] But it is perhaps no accident that a proper understanding of one of the foundational principles of Epicurean atomism had to await the rise of a new, post-Euclidean and post-Newtonian era in mathematics and physics. It is not that Epicurus was ahead of his time or that he anticipated the achievements of modern science. Rather, his thinking took shape at a time when the Euclidean consensus was emerging but still not all-encompassing, as it would later become.[24] A theory like that of Epicurus, or for that matter of the Stoics, could still compete with the conception of numbers and geometry that was to prevail for two thousand years, to the point that Epicurean minima seemed absurd and not worthy of serious consideration. Perhaps we can say, then, that Epicurean atomism is to modern physics as *Don Quixote* is to postmodern fiction: a flourish of creative freedom from a time before a single model came to dominate the field and that found an echo only when that model gave way to rival structures of thought.

Notes

1. Stephen Greenblatt, "The Answer Man: An Ancient Poem Was Rediscovered—And the World Swerved," *The New Yorker*, August 8, 2011, 28–33.
2. Stephen Greenblatt, *The Swerve: How the World Became Modern* (New York: W. W. Norton, 2011).
3. Greenblatt, "The Answer Man," 33.
4. Ibid.
5. Lucio Russo, *La rivoluzione dimenticata: Il pensiero scientifico greco e la scienza moderna*, 5th ed. (Milan: Feltrinelli, 1998 [first edition 1996]), 26.
6. Translations of Epicurus are taken from A. A. Long and David N. Sedley, *The Hellenistic Philosophers*, 2 vols. (Cambridge: Cambridge University Press, 1987), 102. The standard edition of the Greek texts of Epicurus is *Epicuro: Opere*, ed. Graziano Arrighetti (Turin: Einaudi, 1960), with commentary and Italian translation.
7. Joseph Farrell, in this volume, sees in Lucretius's adherence to Epicurus's views a kind of fundamentalist commitment that rendered him indifferent to the scientific advances of his time; as he puts it: "Lucretius appears not so much as a proto-Enlightenment thinker as he does a proto-fundamentalist religious fanatic." I am rather inclined to believe that the Epicureans were more coherent in their defense of their physical theories, without denying that they were driven by both the therapeutic ambitions of their philosophy and an excessive attachment to the ideas of the founder.
8. See David Konstan, "Ancient Atomism and Its Heritage: Minimal Parts," *Ancient Philosophy* 2 (1982): 60–75; more generally, Howard Jones, *The Epicurean Tradition* (London: Routledge, 1989); W. R. Johnson, *Lucretius and the Modern World* (London: Duckworth, 2000); Catherine Wilson, *Epicureanism at the Origins of Modernity* (Oxford: Oxford University Press, 2008).
9. Long and Sedley, *Hellenistic Philosophers*, 44.

10. Luis J. Garay, "Quantum Gravity and Minimum Length," *International Journal of Modern Physics* A10 (1995): 145. The article is also available at http://arxiv.org/PS _cache/gr-qc/pdf/9403/9403008v2.pdf, accessed September 9, 2011.

11. English is the only language that makes this terminological distinction between novels and romances; see Ioan Williams, ed., *Novel and Romance 1700–1800: A Documentary Record* (London: Routledge and Kegan Paul, 1970); David Konstan, *Sexual Symmetry: Love in the Ancient Novel and Related Genres* (Princeton, NJ: Princeton University Press, 1994), 4–5, 205–6; Cheryl Nixon, ed., *Novel Definitions: An Anthology of Commentary on the Novel, 1688–1815* (Toronto, ON: Broadview Press, 2009).

12. See Margaret Iversen, "The Discourse of Perspective in the Twentieth Century: Panofsky, Damisch, Lacan," *Oxford Art Journal* 28 (2005): 191–202; Kirsti Anderson, *The Geometry of an Art: The History of the Mathematical Theory of Perspective from Alberti to Monge* (New York: Springer, 2007).

13. See also Jane P. Tompkins, *Reader Response Criticism: From Formalism to Post-Structuralism* (Baltimore, MD: Johns Hopkins University Press, 1980); Joseph Chaney, "The Revolution of a Trope: The Rise of the New Science and the Divestment of Rhetoric in the Seventeenth Century," in *Signs of Change: Premodern →Modern →Postmodern*, ed. Stephen Barker (New York: State University of New York Press, 1996), 155–74.

14. Max Weber, *The Protestant Ethic and the Spirit of Capitalism*, trans. Talcott Parsons (New York: Charles Scribner's, 1958 [originally published in 1930]); see also Richard Swedberg, ed., *Max Weber: The Protestant Ethic and the Spirit of Capitalism* (New York: W. W. Norton, 2009).

15. Lucretius, *Lucretius on the Nature of Things*, trans. Ian Johnston, 2010; available online at http://records.viu.ca/~johnstoi/lucretius/lucretiusbookoneweb.htm#t21, accessed September 10, 2011. Unless otherwise noted, all English translations are taken from this translation. The Latin text is that of Cyril Bailey, ed., *Lucreti De rerum natura libri sex* (Oxford: Oxford University Press, 1963).

16. For a fuller discussion, see David Konstan, "Atomism," in *The Oxford Handbook of Epicureanism*, ed. Phillip Mitsis (Oxford: Oxford University Press, forthcoming). For Aristotle, see the translation of the *Physics*, trans. R. P. Hardie and R. K. Gaye, in *The Complete Works of Aristotle: The Revised Oxford Translation*, ed. Jonathan Barnes, 2 vols. (Princeton, NJ: Princeton University Press, 1984).

17. Lucretius offers a similar but not identical argument at 1.628–34:

And then if nature,
creative mother of things, were accustomed
to forcing all things to be broken down
into smallest particles, she could not
restore things now from those same particles,   630
because things not endowed with any parts
do not possess the properties required
for generative stuff—different bondings,
weights, collisions, combinations, motions,
through which all actions happen.

Point-like entities could not move independently, as Aristotle argued in the *Physics*, nor would they have, Lucretius adds, any of the other properties that are characteristic of atoms.

18. This view is adopted by S. Luria, "Die Infinitesimaltheorie der antiken Atomisten," *Quellen und Studien zur Geschichte der Mathematik* (B: Studien) 2 (1932–33): 154–56; C. C. W. Taylor, *The Atomists: Leucippus and Democritus: A Text and Translation with a Commentary* (Toronto, ON: University of Toronto Press, 1999), 187. The Greek

text of Philoponus's commentary is published in the series *Commentaria in Aristotelem Graeca*, vols. 16 and 17, ed. Girolamo Vitelli (Berlin: G. Raimer, 1887–88). The translations here are my own; for an English translation, see C. J. F. Williams, *Philoponus on Aristotle's On Coming-to-Be and Perishing 1.6–2.4* (Ithaca, NY: Cornell University Press, 1999).

19. For discussion, see also Istvan M. Bodnár, "Atomic Independence and Indivisibility," *Oxford Studies in Ancient Philosophy* 16 (1998): 35–61.

20. Gregory Chaitin, "The Limits of Reason," *Scientific American* 294:3 (2006): 79. The quantity is also referred to as a "Chaitin constant."

21. For Greek text and facing translation of Plutarch's essay, see *Against the Stoics: On Common Notions*, trans. Harold Cherniss, in *Plutarch's Moralia*, 621–873, vol. 13, part 2 of the Loeb Classical Library (Cambridge, MA: Harvard University Press, 1976).

22. Lucretius's formulation of this argument runs (1.615–27):

And furthermore, if there were
no smallest body, the minutest stuff
would be made up of infinite pieces,
since, as you see, the half of any part
will always have its own half, and nothing
will bring the process to an end. And thus,
between the total sum and the smallest things
what difference will there be? Nothing at all
will distinguish them, for though the universe,   620
the total sum of things, is infinite,
the smallest particles there are will still
equally consist of infinite parts.
But since true reasoning rejects this claim
and asserts the mind cannot believe it,
you must concede, admitting there are things,
the very smallest natural elements,
which have no pieces, and since these exist,
you must also grant that they are solid
and last forever.

23. For further examples, see Konstan, "Atomism."

24. See also Anna Angeli and Tiziano Dorandi, "Gli Epicurei e la geometria: Un progetto di geometria antieuclidea nel Giardino di Epicuro?," in *Lucrezio, la natura e la scienza*, ed. Marco Beretta and Francesco Citti (Florence: L. S. Olschki, 2008), 1–9, and Thomas Bénatouil, "Les critiques épicuriennes de la géométrie," in *Construction: Festschrift for Gerhard Heinzmann*, ed. Pierre-Edouard Bour, Manuel Rebuschi, and Laurent Rollet (London: College Publications, 2010), 151–62. Brooke Holmes, this book, observes that Michel Serres adopts a more radical view, according to which Lucretius's physics is, in fact, correct as against modern Newtonianism; according to Serres, she writes, Lucretius "is advancing a physics of flow and turbulence that is shored up by the mathematics of Archimedes and validated as science by twentieth-century physics in its turn away from solids to fluids and from classical mechanics to chaos theory. Against readings of Lucretius grounded in literary criticism and cultural history, Serres reintroduces a framework of evaluation that is unapologetic about truth in the sense of an alignment between theory and physical reality: Lucretius is right" (Holmes, p. 22; citing Michel Serres, *La naissance de la physique dans le texte de Lucrèce* [Paris: Minuit, 1977], translated as Michel Serres, *The Birth of Physics*, trans. Jack Hawkes [Manchester: Clinamen Press, 2000]). Like Holmes, I am deeply skeptical of Serres's reconstruction of Lucretian physics.

PART II

What Is Lucretian about Modernity?

CHAPTER FOUR

The Presence of Lucretius in Eighteenth-Century French and German Philosophy

CATHERINE WILSON

Lucretius! His principal teachings were that everything—matter, life, and mind—arises from the motion and entanglement of atoms; that the soul is material; that there is no superhuman designer, fabricator, supervisor, or judge of the world; that human intelligence was behind the invention of language, law, and government; and that religious piety is a threat to human happiness.

The case for a Lucretian stamp on the eighteenth century—and so a stamp on more recent modernity—seems, in some respect, to make itself. The great critics and firebrands of the period, La Mettrie, Maupertuis, Holbach, Hume, and Rousseau, adopt with avidity certain of the above-mentioned doctrines, and scientific poetry gets a new lease on life. Yet the notion that Lucretius is a key figure in the formation of Enlightenment philosophy has not informed the writings of most scholars who have concerned themselves with its subversive themes recently, as well as earlier in the previous century. C. A. Fusil, whose articles of 1928 and 1930 were written in a spirit of deep admiration for the ancient poet, concluded that French intellectual life of the second half of the eighteenth century was not up to a proper understanding of Lucretius. Fusil refers in this connection to "an elegant, witty society, frivolous and sceptical; it discovered novelties; its thought was ambitious, but lazy."[1] The eighteenth century, Fusil believed, accomplished nothing great in poetry or philosophy: despite its "torrent of tears...it remained closed off from the profound and mysterious emotion" of Lucretius.[2] Wolfgang Fleischmann, studying the English case, agreed: Despite admiration for Lucretius's descriptive power, he says: "It is not possible to find a single Enlightenment figure whose central philosophical guide was Lucretius." The principal philosophical and theological use of Lucretius, he maintains, "was anti-Lucretian in intention."[3]

Fleischmann is certainly right to comment on anti-Lucretian sentiment. With the proliferation of new editions and translations of the
poem (19 in England alone between 1700 and 1740; 9 or so in France in
the course of the century, and several in the Netherlands and Prussia),[4]
the finger of blame for introducing absurd opinions with socially
destructive or seriously depressing effects was pointed consistently at
Lucretius. The Cardinal Polignac's didactic poem, the *Anti-Lucrèce*,
was published posthumously in 1747, warning against the "poison of
the Greeks."[5] Christoph Martin Wieland wrote *Die Natur der Dinge* in
1752, to combat atomists, mechanists, materialists, pantheists, and athe-
ists, arguing that if Lucretius had had the optical equipment of Hooke,
he would have known better to praise the Creator. It was the great
century of physicotheology with insect-theology, fire-theology, snow-
theology, and theology of rocks, meant to advance piety in step with
natural history.[6] Friedrich Carl Casimir Freyherr von Creuz, Prussian
academy member, composed an antimaterialist *Versuch über die Seele* in
1754, followed by a poem cycle, the *Lukrezische Gedancken*. Hermann
Samuel Reimarus wrote his *Abhandlung von dem Vornehmsten Wahrheiten
der natürlichen Religion* (1755) to refute, according to the subtitle of his
English translator, "the absurd doctrines of Epicurus, recommended by
all the charms of Poetry by Lucretius, and lately retailed by several artful
and admired French writers," namely Buffon, Maupertuis, Rousseau,
and La Mettrie.[7]

The philosophical effort, erudition, and poetic ability devoted to the
refutation of Lucretius and to the exposure of contemporaries as too much
under the influence indicates that the poet was being read in France and
Germany, as well as in Britain, and was taken seriously. At the same time,
there are no Lucretians of the eighteenth century (even in the sense in
which there are Spinozists of the eighteenth century) for a number of
reasons.

First, the reign of the schools and sects was long over: philosophers
had become eclectic and independent, helping themselves, as Leibniz
recommended, to pieces of the tradition they found useful. Natural philosophy was now on an established footing, with its academies, its reports
and memoirs, and even a university presence, and no longer needed to
draw on the ancients as a source of mathematical and physical theory, as
had been the case in the previous century. With Aristotle banished as
an authority in natural philosophy, Epicurus was not needed in order to
batter him.

Second, the initial stimulus to the emergence of the mechanical philosophy in the rediscovery of Epicurean atomism had expended its force.
The scientific ontology of hard, massy atoms was no longer dominant,
knocked off the stage, not to reappear until Dalton around 1803. The
atom of Boyle and Locke was not really consistent with the evolving
understanding of elasticity, percussion, and the nature of light; it raised
problems for chemistry, since the elements had secondary qualities and

"powers," yet were not decomposable. Newtonian physicists and chemists now emphasized the unknowability of the basic elements of nature or experimented with the idea of the atom as a virtual entity or a center of force; hylozooists introduced organic molecules or monads. Epicurean soul atoms—the especially light and tenuous particles that drift away from the body after death—were not favored by eighteenth-century materialists, who referred mentality instead to "organization" and to unknown mechanisms in the brain. However, in cosmology, the sciences of life, and anthropology—the speculative sciences of origins—the Epicurean theses so forcefully and memorably expressed by Lucretius set the agenda.

By way of arriving at an appreciation of the fortunes of Epicureanism and of Lucretius in the eighteenth century, meanwhile, some alleged connections need to be severed or at least nuanced, others discovered or strengthened. The doctrine that self-interest is the principal or only motivation of human beings is to be found neither in the moral and social teachings of Epicurus nor in their recapitulation in Lucretius, at least not in the form in which Francis Hutcheson[8] and Thomas Creech supposed it to be.[9] The thesis of "mechanical" man in La Mettrie, and the claim that man is helplessly subject to the laws of nature in Holbach, have no Epicurean pedigree; Descartes, Spinoza, Leibniz, and Wolff are their direct progenitors. The spontaneous emergence of order from disorder in Hobbes and in Mandeville is, by contrast, genuinely Epicurean.[10] Meanwhile, certain real points of connection have been missed. The "critical idealism" of Kant, I shall argue below, was an anti-Lucretian philosophical undertaking that was highly consequential for later philosophy. Through Kant's rejection of materialism and his defense of "pure philosophy" and immaterialist metaphysics, contemporary moral and political philosophy have been affected in ways that represent losses as well as gains.

If atomism, mechanical man, and self-interest were not the focus of eighteenth-century Lucretius reception, what was? Readers' attention was captured principally by the Lucretian story of the emergence of living forms and the story of the prehistory of humanity. Book 5, the evolutionary book of *De Rerum Natura (DRN)*, has three important themes: The first is the coming to be and eventual dissipation of our world and everything in it, including plants, animals, and human beings. The second theme is the evolution of civil society as human beings invented language and government, taught by "experience and vicissitudes," as the old atomist Democritus had first put it,[11] and developed new psychological characteristics, including pathological religiosity, along with better traits as their living conditions changed. The third important theme is the ambivalence between what the Germans call *Ascendenzlehre* and *Kulturkritik*, the celebration of the fruits of civilization and the deploring of their consequences in the miseries of labor and warfare. Political theory from Hobbes to Rousseau and Marx drew heavily on the Lucretian narrative.

Buffon and the Speculative Sciences of Origins

Fusil was, in some respects, right: it was as tragic author, as the philosopher of finitude, futility, and pity, that Lucretius had his greatest impact—though not, he thinks, until much later—and Fusil was also right to see George Louis Leclerc, the Comte de Buffon, as the true inheritor of the Lucretian sensibility and style. It was in part through the popularity of Buffon that the Lucretian ethos stirred imaginations and stimulated resistance. The critical reviews of Buffon's *Histoire Naturelle* that appeared in the *Journal de Trévoux* and the *Journal des savants* immediately upon the publication of the first volumes of the work expressed their disapproval of "the apostles in the system of Epicurus" who "lead men who might have been happy without the deadly effects of such doctrine, head down, to a miserable eternity."[12]

The exception Fusil made for Buffon did not, up to now, really add to the case for a positive Lucretius reception, insofar as, until recently, Buffon was rather scorned and disregarded by intellectual historians. He has been portrayed as a pompous, superficial writer, a popularizer, an indecisive, inconsistent philosopher, and a hypocrite, enjoying his wealth and estates and the *privilege du roi* while the outspoken, impoverished Diderot languished in prison. While he shared many of their commitments, he did not enjoy friendly relations with the Encyclopedists. His name was so perilously close to "buffoon" (in French *bouffon*) that semantic associations were inevitable.

Recent scholarship has begun to re-evaluate not only Buffon's significance but also his merits.[13] His name was a household word in the second half of the eighteenth century, thanks to his multivolume *Histoire* whose first three volumes appeared in 1749, and he is increasingly recognized as a significant philosopher of science and philosopher of history. Unlike the *philosophes*, Buffon avoided confrontation with the authorities, enabling him to publish his books with privilege through the Imprimerie Royale. Because of the way in which he casually inserted his most daring speculations into the discussion of familiar and interesting animals—the dog, the ass, the apes—and frequently declared his own hypotheses impossible and absurd, he insinuated them into the minds of readers who could not have been instructed in any other way. With his intimates, he was clear about his commitments. "I have always mentioned the Creator," he told his friend Hérault de Séchelles, "but one need only remove this word, and mentally substitute in its place the power of Nature, which results from the two great laws, attraction and repulsion."[14] His rhetoric in the grand opening discourse to the first volume of the *Histoire* evokes the amplitude and randomness of creative nature in a manner that appears calculated to prick and antagonize the physicotheologian:

> Nature's mechanism, art, resources, even its confusion, fill us with admiration... It appears that all that might be, actually is. The hand

of the Creator does not appear to be opened in order to give existence to a certain limited number of species. Rather it appears as if it might have cast into existence all at once a world of being some of whom are related to each other, and some not; a world of infinite combinations, some harmonious and some opposed; a world of perpetual destruction and renewal.[15]

The two distinct and rather inconsistent Lucretian motifs—Nature as creative goddess, constantly renewing and animating her works, and Nature as a set of impersonal and mindless fundamental entities and forces—are fused in his essay *De la Nature: Première Vue* in Volume 12 of 1764. There, Nature is described as "an immense living power." Although she is subordinate to God, she is "a worker perpetually alive, an active and unceasing operator...her power...is perfectly inexhaustible: time, space, and matter are her means, the universe her object; and motion and life her end."[16] From the fundamental entities she can neither create nor annihilate: brute matter, organic molecules, heat, and force, she produces all that exists and all of its alterations. Generation for Buffon did not begin with a preformed organism as the ovists and spermaticists of the period—Haller, Spallanzani, and Bonnet—held, but with an initial chaos from which all forms emerge. Living creatures are formed through the action of the infamous "interior moulds"—by which Buffon meant mechanisms that can form three-dimensional structures, by distributing organic particles to where they are needed.[17]

Speculative cosmologies and theories of the origins of the earth flourished in the first half of the eighteenth century, and almost 30 years later the elderly Buffon followed up with the *Époques de la Nature* (1778), the fifth supplementary volume to the *Histoire* and his "most vilified work."[18] Whereas Volume 1 of the *Histoire Naturelle* presupposed a created earth, albeit one with a more dramatic and extended geological history than reported in Scripture, the *Époques* proposed that the earth and the planets had originated from flaming vitreous material thrown off from the sun that was undergoing a long process of cooling. Seven epochs followed, according to Buffon, taking up 65,000 years (privately he thought in the millions), with humans appearing only in the fifth epoch, about 6,000 years ago, and developing civilization only in the seventh. They are "subject to the same laws, the same alterations, the same changes" as all the other animals, though they possess superior capacities, referred to throughout the work as the effects of "the soul." A contemporary critic in *Le monde de verre reduit en poudre* of 1779 wondered how "one of the most brilliant minds of the Christian world" could have come to revive "the extravagant opinions of the pagan philosophers who had no idea of the true creator of heaven and earth."[19]

The spontaneous generation of humans and animals in mother earth theorized by Lucretius (5.821–23) is a thesis by no means unique to him. Plato reports Aspasia as presenting the view in his curious dialogue

Menexenus. Nor is the insight that some possible forms are more viable than others, which Aristotle ridiculed in Empedocles. But both doctrines are memorably presented in Lucretius's poem. Book 5 proposed that nature had "experimented" with creatures, some of which were lacking mouths, eyes, or moveable limbs, or were unable to grow or mature sexually, so that "many species of animals must have perished and failed to propagate and perpetuate their race" (5.855–56). Such striking selectionism—the "system of perishing" as one later writer termed it, is not to be found in Buffon. Although he has no doubts about the extinction of prehistoric animals, he takes a more plastic view of modification or "degeneration," supposing creatures to arise from a small number of forms—or even a single form[20]—which vary and are modified by climate. Degeneration does not necessarily imply deterioration, only a departure from the existing stock. The rapid changes induced by breeders—Buffon observed that the modern street vendor would scorn the flowers of a generation before— suggested that recombinations at the subvisible level are always at work producing new visible characters.

The Origin of Human Societies

There are many ambiguities and contradictions in Lucretius. One, as noted, is the alternating personification and depersonalization of nature. At one moment, she is alma Venus; at another moment, a collection of atoms randomly knocking around in the void.

Another point of tension[21] is the coexistence of the stability that is said to arise as a matter of course in a world of random interactions, and the inherent instability of every composite entity. The "pact of nature" of the Epicureans refers to the stable and self-sustaining patterns that emerge slowly out of an initial chaos from entanglements and perishings. Eventually turbulent nature settled down, the cosmos assumed its present shape, and fewer monsters were produced: Now "all preserve their distinguishing characteristics in conformity with an immutable law of nature" (5.920), and "all things are subject to the same restriction"—held within certain bounds and limits (2.718–19). These pacts are strictly temporary. Every entity except the atom falls apart sooner or later.

A third contradiction in Lucretius is the coexistence of the Golden Age motif that portrays the first humans as happy and peaceful beings in the "springtime of the world," and the supposition that early humanity experienced a meteorologically challenging existence of violent storms, volcanoes, and earthquakes and lived in constant terror of accidents and wild beasts. The narrative of Book 5 suggests that the climate was initially mild and human life untroubled. "The earth provided her children with food, the warmth served as clothing, and the grass formed a couch thickly spread with soft down" (5.816–17). There was neither excessive heat, nor excessive cold, nor violent wind. Religion had not yet "filled cities with altars and prompted the institution of solemn religious rites" (5.1162–64). Rather than being a response to the anxiety felt by primitive humanity in the face of wild weather alone, superstition, on this account, was fostered by cosmic stability. According to Lucretius, when the heavens settled into their current pattern, the sight of the ether studded with sparkling stars, and the regular motion of the planets produced a new fear, the fear of divine powers (5.1206–10).

The Epicurean account of the origins of law and morality had human beings losing their primitive toughness as they discovered the comforts of huts, skins, fires, and living in families. They grew soft through being accustomed to warmth, tired out by sex, and charmed by their children. Their proximity to others led them "to form mutual pacts of friendship" to prevent harming and being harmed: reciprocal morality, as opposed to law. But the discovery of metal brought on servitude—the plow; and warfare—the sword, and as civil organization grew more complex, anarchy and regicide, a kind of war of all against all, "with all seeking sovereignty and supremacy for themselves" broke out, and private justice produced violent retaliation and feuds. Weariness and exhaustion brought in the law, and now fear of detection and punishment by the magistrate makes life miserable for wrongdoers and would-be wrongdoers alike (5.1145–60).

Rousseau's virtual line-by-line adoption of the account of the origins of society in his widely reviled *Second Discourse* has been documented by Morel.[22] The borrowing was noted by Rousseau's critics (much as Creech accused Hobbes of warmed over Epicureanism in the preface to his English translation). Jean de Castillon described Rousseau as having "revived the delirium of the Epicureans on our origins…he reduced our first parents to the level of the most stupid beasts,"[23] quoting the relevant passages of Lucretius in his Appendix. Adam Smith and Immanuel Kant disliked the work for other reasons. Yet the civilizations-critique of Marx and Engels, no strangers to Epicureanism, is unthinkable without the mediation of Rousseau.

It was not only the absence of our two parents, and the omission of any surveillance of early humans by God or even the gods that attracted attention in the Lucretian account of the evolution of social life, but also the counter-narrative of the origins of religion. The most impressive adaptation was the engineer Nicolas Antoine Boulanger's posthumously published *L'antiquité devoilée par ses usages* composed in about 1766. Boulanger, who died at the age of 36, but whose posthumous work filled 8 volumes,[24] investigated the common element of ancient religions in tears, austerities, mutilations, and macerations.[25] He saw prehistoric humans as terrified by floods and droughts, and as concluding that they were hated by the gods. The geographical records of these disasters are the "sublime anecdotes of nature, engraved over the whole earth, in ineffaceable characters."[26] To understand the origins of religion and despotism that "has precipitated all the nations into idolatry and slavery" is the key to leading men "out of the labyrinth" of mortification, sacrifice, and torture that religion enjoins.[27]

There is something peculiar about the conventional description of the eighteenth century as a century of "reason." Observation, wild conjecture, sentiment, and outrage—these motivate the critique of religion and society. Except in Hume's cool *Dialogues*, the theological scepticism fueled by the availability of the Lucretian natural history of religion did not take the form of rational dismantling of arguments for the existence of God. It departed from the authentically Lucretian view that religion is a source of persecution of the innocent and helpless, exemplified in the account of the sacrifice of Iphigenia for superstitious reasons in Book 1 and the account of mental suffering on account of the fear of hell and ghosts that torments the living. Religion is understood there as a mental disposition that was explicable and perhaps necessary in the early history of terrified humanity; it is an atavism that in modern times is not compensated for by its consoling powers. "O hapless humanity to have attributed such happenings to the gods... What sorrows did they then prepare for themselves, what wounds for us, what tears for generations to come!" (5.1194–97).

Enlightenment Pessimism

Tears—so uncommon in contemporary moral and political philosophy— are frequently encountered in Lucretius and in his followers. A favorite passage of later commentators was Lucretius 5.222–27. After asking why the seasons bring diseases and why premature death prowls about, the poet asks the reader to "consider... how a baby, like a shipwrecked sailor tossed ashore by the savage waves, lies on the ground naked, speechless and utterly helpless, as soon as nature has cast it forth... how it fills the place with its woeful wailings—as well it may, seeing that life holds so much sorrow in store for it." Wordsworth, paraphrasing, calls the baby's cry the "omen of man's grievous doom."[28] The chief threats to human happiness are bad conscience, fear of ghosts and Hell, and romantic love, inseparable from jealousy and anguish, while the chief threats to human existence include navigation, warfare, and pestilence.

True, there is a kind of celebration of culture and human capability at the end of Book 5:

> Navigation, agriculture, city walls, laws, arms, roads, clothing and all other practical inventions, as well as every one of life's rewards and refinements, poem, pictures, and polished statues of exquisite workmanship,... [all were invented by humans themselves]. People saw one thing after another become clear in their minds until each art reached the peak of perfection. (5.1448–57)

Book 5 is followed, however, by the final book of the poem, either unfinished or jarringly abrupt in its ending, a meteorological account of the invisible miasma of pestilence. Sick humans, wandering in public squares and streets, "their languid limbs half-dead, caked with filth, covered with rags,... already almost buried in dirt and ghastly ulcers" (6.1267–71) are helpless against it, and prayers to the imaginary or uninterested gods are useless.

Human mass cruelty—slavery and slaughter—is, for the first time, extensively and persistently condemned in the eighteenth century. Pierre Bayle's view of history as "no other than a collection of the crimes and misfortunes of mankind"[29] is turned to his defense of the Manichaeans, but eighteenth-century pacifism may well be an important and largely overlooked element of the Lucretian legacy. War, for the Epicureans, is not part of a providential plan, God is not on anybody's side, and death in battle is not an entré to heaven. Early man might have been torn by wild beasts, and terrified by storms, but "never in those times did a single day consign to destruction many thousands of men marching beneath military standards; never did the boisterous billows of the ocean dash ships and sailors upon the rocks" (5.999–1001). Voltaire's outright condemnation of war as atavism is one of the more appealing elements of his satire, along with his mockery, in the *Dictionnaire philosophique* of 1764, of divine wrath and his incomprehension at the moralists who "prove... that the women who touch up their cheeks with a little rouge will be the eternal object of the eternal vengeance of the Eternal God" but who ignore "the universal rage that desolates the world, that tears us into a thousand pieces."[30]

Buffon's own cultural pessimism was given eloquent voice in his *Première Vue* in which he begins by praising the powers of human beings to cultivate and improve the world by agriculture, animal breeding, mining, and building and manufacture. He goes on to note, however, that all these achievements are transitory, that with neglect, nature resumes her powers, "destroys the operations of man, envelopes with moss and dust his most pompous monuments, and in the progress of time, entirely effaces them."[31] Further, human beings destroy their works and themselves in a way that is difficult for the naturalist to comprehend since other species do not war amongst themselves:

Incited by insatiable avarice or blind ambition, which is still more insatiable, [man] becomes callous to the feelings of humanity... his whole thoughts turn upon the destruction of his own species, which he soon accomplishes. The days of blood and carnage over,... he beholds with a melancholy eye, the earth desolated, the arts buried, nations dispersed, an enfeebled people, the ruins of his own happiness, and the loss of his real power.[32]

The essay ends with a prayer to end "the devouring flames of war" to restore peace and harmony to a world, to allow nature "sterile and abandoned" to resume her former fecundity.

To Buffon's awareness of human folly is joined the conviction that time may be about up for the human race, that it will vanish along with other extinct species. As Lucretius declares, in time, "The ramparts that surround the mighty world will be taken by storm and will collapse and crumble into ruins...all things gradually decay and head for the reef of destruction" (2.1148–74). Buffon reminds the reader that the universe offers perpetual scenes of creation and destruction: "Suns...appear and disappear as if they were alternately kindled and extinguished." They can expire and annihilate a world or a system of worlds.[33] The "torrent of time carries off and absorbs all individuals,"[34] and the earth itself will cool down to a block of ice that spells the end of living nature.

Lucretius in Germany

There is accordingly good reason to accept the claim of Fusil that Buffon is the principal inheritor and expositor of the Lucretian pathos. The theme of the futility of human existence—perhaps on account of Protestant habits of self-scrutiny—is more marked in German letters than it is in French. The first three volumes of the *Histoire* were translated into German in 1751 by Albrecht Haller, and, as Philip Sloan rightly remarks: "To his contemporaries and successors, particularly those in the German tradition, no feature of Buffon's thought was more in need of philosophical repair than his historical pessimism which seemed to be a consequence of his scientific cosmology."[35] Lucretian topics, themes, and moods appear not only in the didactic poetry, but also in the debates over optimism, pessimism, and human purpose of the second half of the eighteenth century.[36]

These debates set the metaphysics of Leibniz and Wolff—their doctrine that everything is already metaphysically perfect and is becoming culturally more perfect—against Bayle's Manichaean outlook and Buffon's advertisements of futility. For the poet and metaphysician Friedrich Carl Casimir von Creuz, the Lucretian account of the formation of the world and the spontaneous emergence of plants, animals, and humans was an acceptable doctrine in 1754. The living polyp is the "faint trace" of the origins of life in the ancient chaos. But the titles of his later poems—"Der Tod," "Die Gräber"—reveal his anxiety over mortalism. In the physical world, he realizes, everything has limits and is determined by mechanical laws. The materialist La Mettrie pretended to take a torch in hand to illuminate the world, but his intention was to set it on fire.[37] We are tormented by the conflict "that only eternity can decide," between our conviction that we are immortal and our awareness of the wonderful but perishable order of nature.[38] In his widely read *Die Bestimmung des Menschen* of 1748, J. J. Spalding wrote in a similarly forlorn abandoned tone, grasping at the Stoic belief in a "source of agency in me, distinct from my self-love, but deeply entrenched in my nature"[39] and conducive to righteousness, probity, gratitude, and courage. The conviction of an immortal soul and of a personal relationship to the Christian God confirm the author's intention to rescue and decisively affirm the supersensible element in nature, but he betrays his anxiety at the end that, as he puts it, all this is only "the enraptured [*schwärmerische*] flight of an overheated imagination or the heavy, sour insensitivity of a superstitious mind against the ordinary and cheerful joys of life."[40]

His phrasing anticipates Kant's. Even before the "critical turn," Kant was growing scornful of just such enthusiastic flights of the overheated imagination or *Schwärmerei*, attacking them in his *Träume eines Geistersehers* (1766). He was as distressed as Spalding, however, by the threat of moral futility in a purely material world without divine reward and punishment. The Christian revelation was part of a system Kant abandoned in his adulthood, and it left a gap. Critical metaphysics was a moral undertaking, to which the epistemology of the phenomenal and noumenal worlds, the undecideability of the antinomies, and the doctrine of the active mind and its necessary constructions were meant to contribute. It was Kant's answer to the threat of futility.[41]

Kant knew Lucretius well. Lucretius was apparently his favorite author in his school days before he became enchanted by Newton.[42] Although the emergence of the critical philosophy is typically discussed in terms of Kant's search for a third way between the rationalism of Leibniz and Wolff and the empiricism of Locke and Hume, this narrowly epistemological interpretation scarcely does justice to his virtual obsession with the moral problematic posed by Epicurean materialism and the pessimistic view of history as undirected by Providence. Kant turned away from the philosophical empiricism of Locke, with its "thinking matter" and its mechanical theory of experience, and from Scottish moral sentiment-based accounts of ethics. At the same time, in the face of existential anxieties about the objectivity of moral duties and the finality of death, the argument-based metaphysics of a just and omnipotent God and an immortal soul were no longer available for intimidation and reassurance. As Creuz in "Die Gräber" (1760) lamented, "Die Wahreheit finde ich nicht die ich gesucht / Und grosse Zweifel sind des Demonstriens Frucht" [I cannot find the truth I sought / And grievous doubts are demonstration's fruit].[43]

Kant's reference late in the first *Critique* to the "cold-blooded David Hume, the destroyer of our beneficial illusions,"[44] is accordingly not to be understood in narrow epistemological terms. It was Hume's anti-theology, utility-based moral theory, and rejection of the substantial "self" that unnerved him, not the analytic brain teaser whether there is more to causation than constant conjunction. Even Hume's skeptical doubts about causation, however, had wider ramifications. Noting that the Epicureans maintain that the chance encounters of atoms have formed heaven and earth, Bayle says that it is hard to see where they derive the principles of order they perceive in the Universe:

> This hypothesis necessarily implies confusion, disorder, and anarchy in every body. No one can be assured that the sun will rise tomorrow, or that it will disintegrate during the night, the partisans of this system do not at all deny that our world is constantly exposed to total ruin.[45]

Kant's earliest published work, the *Allgemeine Naturgeschichte*, written around 1755 and published in 1763, drew on Buffon's early chapters in the *Histoire Naturelle*, and evoked Lucretian cycles of destruction and renewal. Futility clings to every finite thing, and nature works for its destruction. "Worlds and world-orders fade away and are swallowed by the abyss of eternity."[46] However, Kant argues: "Creation is always at work in other regions of the heavens constructing new formations, replenishing what is lost with new gains."[47] The building forces of nature tend to the production of ever more perfect rational creatures elsewhere in the universe.[48] With the critical turn, Kant gave up speculative cosmology and abandoned his project of becoming a popular philosopher and indeed turned around to attack popular philosophy, adopting the sober, technical tone, and the rebarbative constructions that fascinate or repel his students. Like Haller, on whom he drew, he accepted the need for hypotheses in the natural sciences, while rejecting metaphysical hypotheses.[49] The critical philosophy is partly auto-critique, a repudiation of the enthusiastic cosmology and belle lettristic anthropology of Kant's first forays into philosophical writing and that he later attacked in Buffon as "frivolity" and "recklessness" in speculation.[50]

Kant conceded to the materialist a modified physics—Newtonian physics—and even an anthropology in which humans are driven by the prospect of pleasure. But science, he says, deals not with "things in themselves," but with things as products of perception and cognition. Materialism is a metaphysical thesis and is accordingly unprovable. What we call "matter" is "only a species of representations (intuition), which are called external... because they relate perceptions to the space in which all things are external to one another, while yet the space itself is in us."[51] The Epicurean had therefore, according to the system of transcendental idealism, no philosophical license for his theses of the corporeality of the soul or his hedonistic morality, or even for mortalism. On the contrary, Kant claims: "If I remove the thinking subject the whole corporeal world must at once vanish: it is nothing save an appearance in the sensibility of our subject and a mode of its representations."[52] My immortality cannot be inferred, but, Kant says, "it is nevertheless possible that I may find cause, on other than purely speculative grounds, to hope for an independent and continuing existence of my thinking nature, throughout all possible change of my state."[53]

In his essays of the mid-1780s on politics and history and in certain sections of the *Critique of Judgment* of 1790, Kant turned to the theme of historical pessimism. His aim here was to defend his view of humanity as cosmologically distinguished and to defang the threat of futility without having to accept any claim about the creation of a purpose instilled into human life by a benevolent Creator and fair-minded judge. He evokes for the reader the cruelty and indifference of nature and maintains that the inner fortitude of a "Spinozist" is an inadequate response to it:

> Deceit, violence, and envy will always be rife around him … Moreover, as concerns the other people he meets: no matter how worthy of happiness they may be, nature, which pays no attention to that, will still subject them to the evils of deprivation, disease and untimely death, just like all the other animals on earth. And they will stay subjected to these evils always, until one vast tomb engulfs them one and all … and hurls them, who managed to believe that they were the final purpose of creation, back into the abyss of the purposeless chaos of matter from which they were taken.[54]

Insofar as the tone here is Lucretian via Buffon, such observations arising nowhere in Spinoza (although he, too, maintains that the Individual is no match for the destructive forces of Nature), there is evidence here of an Epicurus-Spinoza amalgamation. One might say that Kant thinks that Spinozist ethics are not adequate to the Epicurean world.

We are compelled, Kant argued, to consider living things as purposive in their structure, though they may well simply be products of mother earth, and to consider human beings as having a purpose in the universe and human history as having a positive direction. We cannot know that the earth did not come to be by chance or that it is not doomed to a fiery or icy death, and we cannot be certain that events such as the French revolution are really prognostic of the end of luxurious tyrannies. But we must not lapse into the fatalism suggested by natural history, anticipating that the species will be wiped out by a geological or cosmological catastrophe or destroy itself in warfare. We must not adopt the view that personal moral effort is pointless in view of our animal mortality and that political effort is pointless in view of the possibly quite short time remaining before the end of the world or the collapse of civilization in another revolution of the sort that (recently for the eighteenth-century paleontologist) buried the mastodon.

Kant had no patience with what he calls "the empty yearning" for a golden age[55] as depicted by Horace, Lucretius, and Rousseau. Nature's purpose must be the advance of culture, by which Kant means the increasing sophistication of taste, and the refinement of manners, as well as the growth of scientific knowledge. His position is summed up in the closing paragraph of section seven of the *Streit der Fakultäten*. Cultural progress is assured: this is not just a "practical" assumption, but a proposition "valid for the most rigorous theory, in spite of all skeptics."[56] Warfare, finally, is another manifestation of nature's achieving her own plan for us, which is not our plan for ourselves. Where Voltaire, the French materialists, and Herder deplored it, and Adam Smith considered it high human folly, Kant saw "oppressive domination, barbaric wars, etc.,"[57] as instruments of nature, realizing this higher purpose of advancing culture. "Though war is an unintentional human endeavor (incited by our unbridled passions), yet it is also a deeply hidden and perhaps intentional endeavor of the supreme wisdom," insofar as it prepares the way for "a unified system of [states] with a moral basis."[58] War is "one more incentive for us to develop to the utmost all the talents that serve culture."[59] "So long as human culture remains at its present stage, war is...an indispensable means of advancing it further," he argued against Herder, "and only when culture has reached its full development—and only God knows when that will be—will perpetual peace become possible and of benefit to us."[60]

Summary and Conclusions

The case for a distinctively Lucretian stamp on eighteenth-century moral and political philosophy is as robust as the case for a distinctively Epicurean stamp on seventeenth-century natural philosophy.[61] It is supported not only by European publication data for the *DRN*, but also by the signifi-cant religion-critique of the mid-eighteenth century, the anguish over the foundations of morals, and the reintroduction by the Comte de Buffon of the long-anathematized and essentially Lucretian "speculative science of origins." The theme of the spontaneous emergence of order from disorder figured in new accounts of the formation of the cosmos, life on earth, civil society, language, and the economy. The themes of finitude, futil-ity, and human political, as opposed to individual, perversity—Lucretian pessimism—exercised poets and philosophers.

At the end of the eighteenth century, there was a fork in the road. Some philosophers went down the path of Kantian idealism, with high hopes for the moralization and eventual pacification of the world, but with unfor-tunate results, as the ideals of duty, purity, the exercise of the will, and the civilizing mission turned destructive of people and their happiness in the nineteenth and twentieth centuries. The French socialists, and Engels and Marx, went down the path of materialism, with its anti-theology, egalitarianism, and emphasis on human welfare. This route, too, became vicious in unexpected ways. Neither side was paying attention to the underlying Lucretian ethical admonitions: limit your ambitions, preserve the weak and pity the troubled, and cultivate the arts and sciences—the source of all of life's refinements and rewards. Take your moral comfort not from the idea of heaven or even from some utopian vision of the way everything ought to be on earth. Take it from the observation that, so far, spring has always come round, after winter, and that in the endless combinatorial possibilities of the atoms there is always renewal and the creation of new life.

Notes

1. C. A. Fusil, "Lucrèce et les litterateurs, poètes et artistes du XVIIIe siècle," *Revue d 'histoire litteraire de la France* 37 (1930): 175–76; see also C. A. Fusil, "Lucrèce et les philosophes du XVIIIe siècle," *Revue d 'histoire litteraire de la France* 35 (1928): 194–210.
2. Fusil, "Lucrèce et les litterateurs," 176.
3. Wolfgang Fleischmann, "The Debt of the Enlightenment to Lucretius," *Studies on Voltaire and the Eighteenth Century* 15 (1963): 643.
4. From a bibliographic perspective, the highlights include Thomas Creech's admired Latin edition, used as the basis for many subsequent translations, and his English translations, which went through six editions. The French translation of Marolles (1650) was followed by Coutures (1692, 1708), Coustelier (1713), LaGrange (1768), and Le Blanc de Guillet (1788). A German translation of 1795 is listed. But, for the most part, we can suppose that people were reading Lucretius in Latin. A bibliography is given by Cosmo Alexander Gordon, *A Bibliography of Lucretius* (Winchester: St. Paul's Bibliographies, 1985).
5. Melchior de Polignac, *Anti-Lucrèce, sive de Deo et Natura libri novem posthumum* (Paris: Guerin, 1747), 5.
6. Wolfgang Philipp, *Das Werden der Aufklärung in theologiegeschichtlicher Sicht* (Goettingen: Vanderhoeck and Ruprecht, 1957).
7. Hermann Samuel Reimarus, *The Principal Truths of Natural Religion Defended and Illustrated, in Nine Dissertations; wherein the Objections of Lucretius, Buffon, Maupertuis, Rousseau, La Mettrie, and Other Ancient and Modern Followers of Epicurus Are Considered, and Their Doctrines Refuted*, trans. Richard Wynne (London: B. Law, 1766).
8. Francis Hutcheson, *An Essay on the Nature and Conduct of the Passions and Affections* (1742; repr., Hildesheim: Olms, 1990).
9. Catherine Wilson, "Political Philosophy in a Lucretian Mode," in *Lucretius and the Early Modern*, ed. David Norbrook, Stephen Harrison, and Philip Hardie (Oxford: Oxford University Press, 2015), 259–282.
10. Richard Tuck, "The Civil Religion of Thomas Hobbes," in *Political Discourse in Early Modern Britain*, ed. Nicholas Phillipson and Quentin Skinner (Cambridge: Cambridge University Press, 1993), 120–39; E. J. Hundert, *The Enlightenment's Fable: Bernard Mandeville and the Discovery of Society* (Cambridge: Cambridge University Press, 2005).
11. As reported by Galen, "On Medical Experience," in *Three Treatises on the Nature of Science*, trans. and ed. Richard Walzer and Michael Frede (Indianapolis, IN: Hackett, 1985), 47–108, 62.
12. John Lyon and Philip R. Sloan, *From Natural History to the History of Nature* (Notre Dame and London: University of Notre Dame Press, 1981), 278.
13. In addition to Lyon and Sloan, *From Natural History*, see Jacques Roger, *Buffon: A Life in Natural History*, trans. Sarah Lucille Bonnefoi (Ithaca, NY: Cornell University Press, 1997), and J.-C. Beaune et al., eds., *Buffon 88: Actes du Colloque international pour le bicentenaire de la mort de Buffon* (Paris: J. Vrin, 1992).
14. Hérault de Séchelles, *Voyage a Montbar* (1801; repr. Paris: Aulard, 1890), 367.
15. George Louis Leclerc, Comte de Buffon, "Discours preliminaire," in *Histoire Naturelle générale et particulière, avec la description du Cabinet du Roy*, 15 vols. (Paris: Imprimerie du Roi, 1749–57), vol. 1: 1–64; trans. Lyon and Sloan, *From Natural History*, 101.

16. Buffon, "De la Nature: Première Vue," *Histoire Naturelle* XII:iij, trans. James Smith Barr, in *Buffon's Natural History Containing a Theory of the Earth, a General History of Man, of the Brute Creation, and of Vegetables, Minerals, &c.*, 10 vols. (London: J. S. Barr, 1792), vol. 10: 325–26. See Lyon and Sloan, *From Natural History*, 270: "No more primordial germs, no more unfolding. Nature herself enjoys the right of forming herself, of organizing herself, and of passing freely from the inanimate state to that of a plant or an animal."

17. As when, for Lucretius in Book 2, "the assimilable elements in the food are absorbed into the system, united, and perform the appropriate motions," *Lucretius: On the Nature of Things*, trans. Martin Ferguson Smith (Indianapolis, IN: Hackett, 1969), 2.711–14. Further citations of Lucretius are to this translation. The parallel is noted by Roger, *Buffon*, 668, n. 114. On Buffon's version of epigenesis, see François Duchesneau, "Haller and the Theories of Buffon and C. F. Wolff on Epigenesis," *History and Philosophy of the Life Sciences* 1 (1979): 65–100.

18. M. S. J. Hodge, "Two Cosmogonies ('Theory of the Earth' and 'Theory of Generation') and the Unity of Buffon's Thought," in Beaune et al., eds., *Buffon 88*, 243.

19. Thomas-Maurice Royou, *Le monde de verre réduit en poudre: Ou Analyse et réfutation des Époques de la nature de M. Le Comte de Buffon* (Paris: Mérigot, 1780), 60.

20. Buffon, *Histoire Naturelle,* vol. 4: 381.

21. This should not be considered a contradiction in the scheme. We assume today that "emergence" does not violate the law of entropy.

22. Jean Morel, "Recherches sur les Sources du *Discours sur l'Origine de l'Inégalité*," *Annales de la Société Jean-Jacques Rousseau* 5 (1909): 119–98.

23. Jean de Castillon, *Discours sur l'origine de l'inegalité* (1756; repr., Amsterdam: J. F. Jolly 2006), vi.

24. Not including the *Anecdotes de la nature*, thought to have been semi-plagiarized by Buffon. *L'antiquité devoilée* is ascribed, in turn, by some scholars to Holbach.

25. Nicolas Antoine Boulanger, *Oeuvres de Boullanger*, 8 vols. (Paris, Jean Servieres, Jean-Francois Bastien, 1792), vol. 1: 241.

26. Ibid., vol. 4: 30.

27. Ibid., vol. 3: 280.

28. William Wordsworth, "To ___ Upon the Birth of her First-Born Child, March 1833," in *William Wordsworth: Last Poems 1821–1850,* ed. Jared Curtis (Ithaca, NY: Cornell University Press, 1999), 252, l. 12.

29. Pierre Bayle, *General Dictionary, Historical and Critical,* 10 vols., trans. John Peter Bernard, Thomas Birch, John Lockman, and other hands (London: Roberts, 1734–41), footnote (D), Art. "Manichaeans," vol. 7: 400.

30. François-Marie Arouet (Voltaire), Art. "War," in *Philosophical Dictionary* (1764), 3 vols., by Voltaire, trans. J. G. Gurton (London: Hunt, 1824), vol. 3: 344. Voltaire's antimilitarism is characteristic of the Encyclopedists, and of Rousseau and Diderot. "Every practice," says Diderot, "tending to stir up the people, to arm nations and soak the soil with blood is impious" (Denis Diderot, *Political Writings,* trans. and ed. John Hope Mason and Robert Wokler [Cambridge: Cambridge University Press, 1992], 29). The article "Guerre" in the *Encylopédie* (1751–72) of Denis Diderot and Jean le Rond D'Alembert, ascribed to Louis de Jaucourt, is similar in tone. See *Encyclopédie, our Dictionnaire raisonné des sciences, des arts, et des métiers,* 2 vols., ed. A Pons (Paris: Flammarion, 1993), vol. 2: 157.

31. Buffon, *Natural History*, vol. 10: 340.

32. Ibid., 341.

33. Ibid., 329.

34. Ibid., 347.

35. Lyon and Sloan, *From Natural History*, 132.

36. See Henry Vyverberg, *Historical Pessimism in the French Enlightenment* (Cambridge, MA: Harvard University Press, 1958).

37. Friedrich Karl Casimir Freyherr von Creuz, *Versuch über die Seele* (Frankfurt and Leipzig: Knoch und Esslinger, 1754), 186.

38. Ibid., 12.

39. Johann Joachim Spalding, *Die Bestimmung des Menschen*, 2nd ed. (Leipzig: Weidmann: 1768), 31. For none of the respected eighteenth-century philosophers, says Brandt, "was the theory of La Mettrie unknown, for in every school the materialistic didactic poem of Lucretius *De rerum natura* was read, so that everyone as well, recognized Spalding's message as counter work to materialism or indeed to nihilism. It was a recapitulation of the Stoics vs. Epicurean debates known to every schoolboy through Cicero and Seneca" (Rheinhard Brandt, *Die Bestimmung des Menschen bei Kant* [Hamburg: Meiner, 2007], 143).

40. Spalding, *Bestimmung*, 135.

41. Thus Kant, arguing in his own defense: "When the blind mechanics of the forces of nature can by themselves bring perfection out of chaos so marvellously," then, the ignorant suppose, "Epicurus lives again in the middle of Christendom and an unholy philosophy treads faith under its feet" (Immanuel Kant, *Gesammelte Werke* [Berlin: De Gruyter, 1900–], vol. 1: 222).

42. H. B. Nisbet, "Lucretius in Eighteenth Century Germany," *Modern Language Review* 81 (1986): 97–115, citing Hermann Hettner, *Gesch. der deutschen Literatur im Achtzehnten Jahrhundert*, ed. George Witowski, 4 vols. (Leipzig: P. List, 1928), vol. 2: 160.

43. Friedrich Karl Casimir Freyherr von Creuz, *Die Gräber: Ein Philosophisches Gedicht in Sechs Gesaengen* (Frankfurt: Maynz, 1760), vol. 2: 144. As Sloan remarks, Kant "departs most markedly from Buffon [despite taking over his cosmogenesis] in asserting an inherent teleology behind the self-organisation of the universe, his differential reply to an Epicurean cosmology," Lyon and Sloan, *From Natural History*, 131.

44. Immanuel Kant, *Critique of Pure Reason*, trans. Norman Kemp Smith (New York: Macmillan, 1965), A 745/B 773.

45. Pierre Bayle, *Continuation des pensées diverses*, 2 vols. (Amsterdam: Herman Uytwerf, 1722), vol. 2: 338.

46. Kant, *Gesammelte Werke*, vol. 1: 317.

47. Ibid.

48. Ibid., 331.

49. Thus Haller: "We should not ask after God's intentions, the state of the soul before birth and after death, what was the first origin of thought, how the revolution of first eternity was made subject to the beginning of time. These are hypotheses of which the knowledge is forbidden to me and which no creature should presume to search. Philosophy has its limits." Virtue is the object of the philosopher's desire and leads to God. Albrecht Haller, *Briefe über die wichtigsten Wahrheiten der Öffenbarung* (Bern: Neue Buchhandlung, 1772), trans. as *Letters from Baron Haller to his Daughter: On the Truths of the Christian Religion, Translated from the German* (London: John Murray, 1780), 47–49.

50. Kant, *Gesammelte Werke*, vol. 15: 389.

51. Kant, *Critique of Pure Reason*, A 370.

52. Ibid., A 383.

53. Ibid.
54. Kant, *Gesammelte Werke*, vol. 5: 452; English translation from Kant, *Critique of Judgment*, trans. Werner S. Pluhar (Indianapolis, IN: Hackett, 1987), 342.
55. Kant, "Conjectures on the Beginning of Human History," in *Political Writings*, ed. Hans Reiss, trans. H. B. Nisbet, 221–34 (Cambridge: Cambridge University Press, 1991), 233; *Gesammelte Werke*, vol. 8: 122.
56. Kant, *Conflict of the Faculties*, trans. Mary J. Gregor (New York: Abaris, 1979), 159; *Gesammelte Werke,* vol. 7: 88.
57. Kant, *Critique of Judgment*, 318; *Gesammelte Werke,* vol. 5: 430.
58. Kant, *Critique of Judgment*, 320; *Gesammelte Werke,* vol. 5: 433.
59. Ibid.
60. Kant, "Conjectures," 232; *Gesammelte Werke*, vol. 8: 121.
61. Catherine Wilson, *Epicureanism at the Origins of Modernity* (Oxford: Clarendon, 2008).

CHAPTER FIVE

Epicureanism across the French Revolution

THOMAS M. KAVANAGH

Understanding how the Epicureanism so central to the French Enlightenment fared during and after the difficult days of the Revolution leads to one of the most intriguing chapters within the complex history of *De Rerum Natura* and its readers. Jean-Charles Darmon has shown how, by the early seventeenth century, "Epicurean" had become a preferred term for designating where one placed oneself and one's enemies in the defining cultural conflicts of the early modern period.[1] "Epicurean"—whether used to denigrate or to celebrate—became the powerful and protean banner of a philosophical ferment in relation to which everyone felt they must know well where they stood. At the same time, this intense concern with the "Epicurean" left, as it were, little place for what might more legitimately be called the "Lucretian"—a term that comes only reluctantly to modern lips.

There is, in other words, a considerable cultural injustice in our culture's nominal elision of its immense debt to Lucretius. If the term "Epicurean" achieved the currency it did, it was because *The Nature of Things*—both in the original and in its many translations—held a power and fascination for its early modern readers nowhere matched in the dry representations of Epicureanism offered by Diogenes Laertius or Cicero. *The Nature of Things* is, in the fullest sense, a literary work—a work whose vibrant poetic diction grounds its abiding power to move and inspire its readers.[2] It is this literary dimension that sets Lucretius's poem apart from the other surviving classical commentaries that, as W. R. Johnson has put it, offer only something "truncated, reduced to footnotes, and transformed into evidence and authority."[3]

If the Epicurean subsumed the Lucretian, it was also because that first term had long been paired with a Stoicism understood as its opposing and enemy twin. Throughout the early modern period, and especially with the rise of the eighteenth-century *philosophes*, this pairing of the Epicurean and the Stoic became a short hand for the two major variants of a new secular humanism. While the Epicurean evoked the ethos of an individualism centered on the liberating experience of pleasure, the Stoic stood for the ethos of a new sense of sociability anchored in the demanding practice of virtue. Denis Diderot, even as he rejected the church's long-standing vilification of Epicureanism as little more than bestial self-indulgence, made it clear in his *Encyclopédie* entry on Epicureanism that its value lay finally in preparing the way to the higher ideal of Stoicism: "We are born Epicureans, but we become Stoics."[4] Hardly three decades after Diderot's entry, however, the coming of the Revolution would banish the Epicurean care of the self and its cultivation of pleasures in the name of a newly muscular Stoicism of civic virtue as punitive as it was prescriptive. The Stoicism of Republican Virtue denounced Enlightenment Epicureanism as co-substantial with abuses so nefarious that they could be designated only as the realm of what must no longer be—as *l'ancien regime*.

Eighteenth-century Epicureanism was a unifying theme for so many of the period's major figures—novelists and artists, *philosophes* as well as *libertins*—who set out to describe, analyze, and multiply the resolutely subjective experience of pleasure.[5] Pleasure in eighteenth-century France was an elixir to be found not only in a glass, but also in an intimate encounter, a novel, an opera, or a painting. During the three-quarters of a century between 1715 and the early 1790s the cultivation of pleasure became a driving obsession within French literature and culture. Their many meditations on pleasure foregrounded the dynamic tension between pleasure as idiolect and pleasure as lingua franca. To speak of pleasure was to speak of sensation in the key of the individual, of experience as something always personal. Yet representing that pleasure, making it real for others, involved not so much an objectification of those sensations, but their pan-subjectification—an enticing seduction of all who make up one's audience. The sometimes naïve optimism of the French Enlightenment sought to parlay the always individual pleasure of the one into the exuberance of the many. Enlightenment Epicureanism placed its faith in pleasure as a universal currency whose endless exchange could bind together self and society in a new concord of felicity.

The moment marking the end of pleasure's reign might well be situated in the bold claim made by Louis Antoine de Saint-Just in his March 3, 1794 address to the Convention that "Happiness is a new idea for Europe."[6] That statement was part of Saint-Just's appeal to the Convention that it speed the implementation of the recently adopted Ventôse decrees—legislation that extended the confiscations leveled against the church and the *émigrés* to the larger and far more amorphous category of all who might conspire against or even entertain doubts about the Revolution. In practical terms this meant that every commune in France would be expected to draw up two carefully prepared lists: one naming those whose skepticism toward the Revolution rendered them unworthy of their property and another of those true patriots afflicted with an unjust poverty. Simply put, Saint-Just's "happiness" as a "new idea" for Europe had less to do with any universal well-being than it did with punishing all who might doubt the new order of things.

Saint-Just's frightening premise makes clear the opposition between what had been the Epicurean's pleasure and what would be the Revolution's civic happiness. Pleasure was private and personal; happiness would be public and collective. Pleasure was grounded in the senses; happiness would flow from the congruence of all with the common good as dictated by the General Will. The quarter century from 1790 to 1815 saw a dizzying succession of efforts made in the name of this new "happiness" to refashion the personal in terms of the shifting ideological premises of Revolution, Terror, Empire, and Restoration. What, in the wake of such dizzying changes, might be the fate of that earlier Enlightenment Epicureanism proposing an economy of pleasures exchanged and multiplied? Following the bewildering imperatives of an ideological "happiness" in constant mutation, could the Epicureans' appeal to a deontology of the sentient body ever again find any real cultural purchase?

The beginnings of an answer to that question can be found in the meditations on the new science of gastronomy published at his own expense by Anthelme Brillat-Savarin in 1825. Born in 1755 in the small town of Belley, approximately 50 miles east of Lyon, Brillat-Savarin first discovered the larger stage of Paris when he was elected in 1789 to the Estates General as a representative of the Third Estate. During his two years as a member of the National Assembly, he grew close to and all but idolized the philosopher Constantin François de Volney and became an ardent advocate for reform. Allied for a time with the Jacobins, he was, nonetheless, obliged—even after having returned to his remote Belley—to flee the Terror, first to Lausanne and finally to the newborn United States where, for the three years from September 1793 to September 1796, he lived in New York, Connecticut, Boston, and Philadelphia, supporting himself as an itinerant violinist. Returning to France when the Directory removed his name from the list of *émigrés*, he was appointed a magistrate first in Bourg-en-Bresse and, a few years later, as a member of the *Cour de cassation* in Paris. His quiet life as a judge was interrupted only by his intemperate rallying to the Emperor upon Bonaparte's return from Elba during the 100 Days of 1815—an enthusiasm that once again brought him dangerously close to becoming a victim of Terror, this time white rather than red.

Brillat-Savarin, the placid appeals court judge, is best known as the unlikely author of *The Physiology of Taste*—a project he worked on for nearly ten years but published only two months before his death in February 1826. His choice of the term "physiology," borrowed from the medical vocabulary of the period, signaled a distinctly Lucretian intention to orient the analysis of his subject less toward the clinical than toward the more philosophical question of taste and its place within the dynamics

of human pleasure.[7] Brillat's intention to establish the pleasured body as
the foundation of his philosophical claims is nowhere more apparent than
in the signature term he used to designate the new science he would
celebrate: gastronomy. Fusing the corporeality of the digesting stomach—
gastro—with a philosophical enumeration of general principles, Brillat
defines gastronomy as "the reasoned knowledge (*la connaissance raisonnée*)
of all that relates to man and his nourishment."[8] Brillat's materialist, even
Democritian, approach to taste begins with his describing that faculty as
a breaking down of what enters the mouth to its constituent parts so that,
in their atomic simplicity, they become part of a recombinant experience producing taste: a chemical operation in which the moisture of saliva
releases "sapid molecules" (49) then absorbed by the sensitive projections,
buds, and suckers of the tongue and mouth. Brillat begins his treatise,
however, not with a discursive analysis of taste, but with a series of staccato
single-sentence aphorisms that stand as disjointed claims foreshadowing
the arguments that follow. These opening aphorisms move rapidly from
the embrace of a Lucretian totality of Nature—"The universe exists only
as life, and all that lives, eats"—to the posing of a hierarchy—"Animals
feed; men eat; only the wise man (*l'homme d'esprit*) knows how to eat" (19).
He ends his list with a grandiose claim as to the stakes riding on nature's
universal feast: "The destiny of nations depends on how they nourish
themselves" (19).

Staging gastronomy as a key to the understanding of history, Brillat
envisions his new science as animating and integrating all other sciences
within this new understanding of pleasure. Natural history is enjoined
with ordering and classifying alimentary substances, physics with examin-
ing the composition and quality of substances, chemistry with multiplying
the variations of its analyses and catalyses, cooking with adapting dishes
and making them maximally pleasing to the taste, business with securing
foodstuffs as inexpensively as possible while selling advantageously what
is produced, and finally political economy with attending to the revenues
generated by the exchange between nations of resources and products
orchestrated by the motor of gastronomy.

If this new science is central to so broad a spectrum of human enterprise, it is because taste, more than any other of the bodily senses, stands as
the primary avenue of the Epicurean's paramount value of pleasure:

> Taste as nature has endowed us with it is the sense which gives us
> the greatest pleasure: because the pleasure of eating is the only one
> which, indulged in moderately, is not followed by regret; because it is
> common to all periods of history, all ages of man, and all social con-
> ditions; because it recurs of necessity at least once every day, and can
> be repeated without inconvenience two or three times in that space
> of hours; because it can be joined with all other pleasures, and even
> console us for their absence; and because its sensations are at once
> more lasting than others and more subject to our will. (55)

What is distinctive about Brillat's style is his startling combination of such grandiose claims with a minute and almost clinical attention to the organs of taste and their functioning: to the tongue and what he calls its "powerful muscular force" (47) as it moistens, mashes, and churns one's food as well as to the insides of the cheeks, the roof of the mouth, and, above all, the nasal channel as they work together in perfect concord. This close examination of the physiological apparatus of taste must, however, be complemented by an appreciation of that sense's complex temporality. Far from occurring as a simple or immediate experience, taste must be understood as a symphony of sensation in three movements. What Brillat calls "direct sensation" (52) is the first to be experienced. It occurs as what is to be consumed makes contact with the mouth, the lips, and the fore part of the tongue. Next comes the "complete sensation" occurring only when the food passes to the back of the mouth and informs our entire gustatory organ with its taste and aroma. Finally, the "reflective sensation" takes place as an encapsulation of all the sensory dimensions of the first two movements of taste within a mental act of appreciation and judgment.

Brillat's close attention to the physiological mechanics of taste represents what might be described as the rematerializing of an important cultural tradition. Within the Enlightenment's many debates on the subject, taste, le goût, acquired the more abstract sense of a faculty designating an informed cultural appreciation of all that the senses experienced.[9] "Taste" became a synecdoche affirming the individual's ability to make culturally correct judgments of value. Those judgments might be based on data provided by the senses, but they served, above all, to demonstrate a capacity for evaluation and appreciation that confirmed the sensitivity, finesse, and merit of the sentient subject. Brillat, systematically reining in the Enlightenment's figurative expansion of what is meant by taste, puts the physiological reality of the papillated tongue and the gustatory apparatus at the center of his new science of gastronomy. Returning to the Enlightenment's materialist and Epicurean tradition, Brillat grounds his claims for the primacy of taste in the organic specificity of our contact with what is sapid.

This tightening of focus did not, however, prevent Brillat from speculating on the tasting mouth as the proper subject of its own "moral history" (histoire morale)—a history that becomes a mini-anthropology of the eating experience. In so doing, he follows the lead of Book 5 of The Nature of Things where Lucretius highlights that point in the history of primitive man when "the human race began to mellow" and "then neighbors who wanted neither to harm each other / Nor to be harmed, began to join in friendship... Signaling with their hands and stammering speech / That the weak must be pitied, as was just."[10] Firmly situating this "mellowing" within the act of eating, Brillat combines this Lucretian trope with a poetic expansion of Rousseau's anti-Hobbesian claim in his Second Discourse that pity, rather than fear or violence, must be seen as the hallmark of natural man. If primitive men were prompt to commiserate with their fellows, this was because of our species' singular capacity for suffering. We are destined to pain, Brillat argues, by everything from the sensitivity of our skin and the shape of our feet to an appalling genius for developing ever more devastating forms of warfare and destruction. This redefinition of *homo sapiens* as *homo dolens* allows us, in turn, to understand why, as suffering's antidote, the intensification of pleasure has served as the motor of cultural development. Looking to what he calls "the days of paganism" (169), Brillat points to how the most obvious experiences of pleasure gave birth to Bacchus, Venus, and Comus as quasi-divine figures.

The shared meal (*le repas*)—much like that "hearty meal" described by Lucretius in Book 5.1385–86 as preparing the discoveries of song and dance—provides an experience of pleasure that coaxes mankind to a new stage of social organization. No longer solitary self-sufficient savages, primitive humans became interdependent members of families. It was as humankind moved beyond the nutritional independence of a diet of simple fruits that there began what Brillat calls "the second age of mankind" (170). The careful preparation and allocation of cooked foods served to cement the institution of the family as the fathers' dividing of the results of the hunt among children and elders provided a lesson to be passed from generation to generation. For Brillat, this consolidation of the family unit around the shared meal, in turn, prepared the way for later transformations producing larger alliances extending to neighbors and friends.

It is as he who eats with others achieves the status of "guest" that the specifically human dimension of *les plaisirs de la table* emerges as the defining premium of Brillat's vision. To the extent careful attention is paid to how and where the meal is served as well as to a thoughtful choice of guests to be brought together, *le repas* (the meal) becomes infused with a conviviality of heightened exchange and communication. These pleasures of the table have far less to do with the satisfaction of hunger than they do with generating the kind of conversation and exchange capable of producing around the shared table nothing less than what Brillat describes as "a new order of things" (171). The tenor of this "new order" depends less on any conscious decision to interact with and charm others than it does on being swept up in the gustatory delight of savoring and appreciating the shared feast. What Brillat calls *gourmandise*—a term he marks positively and places at the antipodes of voracity and gluttony—

> combines Athenian elegance, Roman abundance, and French *délicatesse*. It expresses itself in the ability to choose wisely, to prepare carefully, to savor energetically, and to judge with profundity. (141)

Most importantly, this food-based conviviality bridges divisions and creates alliances. *Gourmandise* is defined as an attracting force that spreads in all directions its power to bring people together and to soften what he calls "the sharp corners of conventional inequalities" (147).

Gastronomy and *gourmandise*, the science and the appreciation of taste, come together in a dynamic whose effects extend far beyond the ritual of a shared meal. Recognizing that "a happily digesting person is not the same as a fasting person" (65) and that postprandial contentment disposes us favorably toward the ideas and solicitations of our fellow diners, Brillat speaks even of a "political gastronomy" so potent that "meals have become a means of governing, and the fate of nations can be decided at a banquet" (65). It is to this "political gastronomy" that Brillat points as a social force allowing his reader to understand what have been the most astounding surprises of the last quarter century. By the end of 1815 France found herself not only occupied, but also, under the terms of the treaty ending the Napoleonic wars, saddled with public and private reparations amounting to fifteen hundred million francs. Given that situation, it seemed certain that the value of French currency would plummet and that, starved for credit financing, the entire economy would grind to a halt. To everyone's astonishment, however, the opposite occurred. The required payments were made, credit became easily available, and people were willing to invest. The greatest surprise came when the exchange rate, "that infallible measure of the circulation of money" (144), moved in favor of the franc, providing what Brillat sees as "the arithmetical proof that more money came in to France than left it" (144). How could this happen? What could have caused such a miracle? Paris may have been inundated by the most exotic variety of foreign occupiers—Britons, Germans, Huns, Cimmerians, and Scythians—but all of them, aristocratic generals as well as common soldiers, brought with them "a rare voracity and stomachs of uncommon capacity" (144). Quickly abandoning their military messes, and anxious to discover the pleasures of Parisian delicacies, they flooded all the capital's restaurants, *traiteurs*, cabarets, and taverns. Superficial observers, Brillat cautions, may not have known what to make of this endless feasting (*cette mangerie sans fin et sans terme*), but the true Frenchman, chuckling and rubbing his hands together, knew exactly what it meant: "Now they are under our spell, and they will lay out far more gold tonight than the treasury handed over to them this morning" (145).

Extending well beyond any particular moment in France's history, this unanticipated and resolutely international feast would establish Paris as the capital of a realm of gastronomy far more enduring than Bonaparte's empire. Writing in 1825, ten years after France's debacle, Brillat takes an obvious pleasure in describing what proved to be defeat's paradoxical effects. Waterloo may have brought foreign victors from every part of Europe flooding into France and its capital. The pleasures they discovered there, however, generated memories that could hardly be expected to disappear as they returned to their homes. For the French, defeat and occupation had created a new international clientele fascinated by and clamoring to taste again the pleasures associated with what Brillat calls "a country where gourmands are made happy (*un peuple chez qui les gourmands sont heureux*)" (145). In a footnote to this observation, Brillat cites the example of Moët, Epernay's premier champagne producer. The troops streaming toward Paris in the summer of 1815 may have plundered over 600,000 bottles, but, less than a year later, Moët found itself more than amply compensated when those now departed pillagers became nostalgic customers spurring a growth in foreign sales that went on to multiply year after year.

While Brillat speaks, at times, almost as a statistician, his most moving evocations of gastronomy rely less on dry quantitative analyses than on a distinctly poetic and gustatory "pleasure of the text." Much as Lucretius uses a metaphor drawn from the delights of taste to explain his choice of poetry's honey-rimmed cup as the vehicle of his Epicurean philosophy, Brillat relies again and again on a personal and even performative dimension of poetic evocations resurrecting particular moments of taste's delights. Even as he expounds on the principles of his new science, he revels in digressions that foreground language's power to evoke and recreate remembered places where an anchoring experience of taste worked its magic of intensifying conviviality.

At one point in his argument that France should adopt the large-scale raising of American turkeys, he interrupts his enumeration of that measure's economic advantages to recreate for himself and his readers a moment from thirty years in the past: the two autumn days he spent in 1794 while traveling on horseback from New York to Boston at the Connecticut farm of a certain Mr. Bulow. Bulow and his four charming daughters not only graciously welcomed the weary traveler, but also introduced him to the pleasure of hunting in the virgin forests outside Hartford and of tasting for the first time the succulent flesh of the three American turkeys they had been lucky enough to bag. As Brillat evokes that happy interlude, the Bulow household is transformed into the recreation of a Golden Age: that of independent and self-sufficient farmers who draw from their fields and the forests around them a life of simple but ever-renewed pleasures.

In a less exotic setting, it is the question of how best to prepare a tuna omelet that triggers for Brillat the memory of a strangely vicarious dining experience that served to resolve what has long been seen as a vitiating antimony at the core of Epicurean philosophy. During a dinner party where he was a guest, his hostess and niece, Juliette Récamier, shared with those at her table the story of her visit earlier that afternoon to her *aumonier*, the priest who oversaw her charitable gifts to the poor. As she had forgotten that ecclesiastics dine early, her five o'clock arrival happened to interrupt the priest's meal. As she describes that scene for her guests, the high point of the priest's frugal Lenten repast comes in the form of a tuna omelet. It was, as she put it,

> round and bulging and cooked to the exact point of perfection. At the first touch of the spoon, its paunch let flow from the cut a thick juice which delighted both the eyes and the nose. The platter seemed afloat with it, and she admitted that it made her mouth water. (308)

What fascinates Brillat about his niece's anecdote is how her words—themselves a verbal representation of the Lucretian *simulacra* that first emanated from the priest's omelet toward Récamier's eyes and nose—trigger for all her guests, Brillat included, the synesthetic experience of listening to words capable of provoking for her guests a *phantasia* that carries with it all the sensory delights of taste and texture:

> She took great care in praising the dish in the exact terms of its height, its fullness, and its shape. And from what she told us about it, we agreed unanimously that it had been truly excellent. *Her words provided a sensuous equation whose delights all of us were able to taste in our own fashion"* [italics mine]. (309)

The dynamics of this anecdote—its multiplication of an omelet enjoyed not only by the solitary priest but now also by all the guests around Récamier's table—points to gastronomy's performative power to provoke a conviviality that has the unexpected effect of resolving the frequent objection to Epicurean philosophy, which Pierre-Marie Morel has aptly described as "the supposed antinomy between an egotistic seeking of pleasure as the sovereign good and the altruism at the core of friendship."[11] Initiating a sensory experience that is individual yet shared by all, the tuna omelet and its poetic evocation acquire a power to transform what was first tasted *only by one* into a synesthetic recreation of pleasure *enjoyed by all*.

In the entry on Brillat-Savarin that he wrote for Michaud's 1843 *Biographie universelle*, Honoré de Balzac describes *The Physiology of Taste* as a work that, as he puts it, "brings back to life, across the ice of time and the experience of the Revolution, the very spirit of the eighteenth century."[12] Epicurean, sensationist, and utopian, Brillat can certainly be read as an avatar of the Enlightenment's militant materialism. His mock-heroic enlisting of all sciences as acolytes to gastronomy in its physical, political, and economic dimensions rises even to the challenge of recasting France's most tumultuous quarter century as, despite defeat and occupation, an unexpected apogee of French influence and supremacy. For someone who lived his *fin de siècle* and *fin de régime* in the fray and up close—as *constituant* and as Jacobin, as *émigré* and as judge—Brillat manifests a surprisingly irenic attitude toward the conflicting ideologies he so carefully navigated. All the stark oppositions that punctuated those upheavals of the past—between reformer and conservative; between Jacobin and girondin; between republican, Bonapartist, and monarchist—dissolve into an economic boom none would ever have expected. The alternatively glorious and bloody chapters of the Revolution linger on—but only as topics of conversations one might imagine as animating the delightful meals presided over by the new science of gastronomy. Much as the Enlightenment's materialist Epicureans sought to defuse the bellicose intolerance born of religion's internecine conflicts, Brillat proposes his compendium of gastronomy as the basis of a new social contract promoting the serenity and prosperity of pleasures that are natural, sensual, and shared.

Focusing on gastronomy and conviviality, Brillat has nothing to say of Saint-Just's "new idea of happiness" for Europe. His choice of pleasure over happiness is grounded in the Lucretian conviction that life's defining texture lies not within ideological convictions but in the intimate subjectivity of our senses and the pleasures they provide. As someone who knew all too well the consequences of ideology's ambitions, Brillat refrained from all imperatives that would legislate any nebulous equality of happiness. In turning from ideas to the senses, he borrowed but at the same time redirected what was the preferred strategy of Enlightenment materialism. The libertine tradition—from the abbé T of d'Argens's *Thérèse philosophe* to the A and B of Diderot's *Supplement to Bougainville's Voyage*, to the Merteuil of Laclos's *Dangerous Liaisons*—proposed for a circumscribed elite a practice in private of sexual pleasures possible only so long as they refrained from any public challenge to the Church and its repressive social norms. Brillat places at the center of his anthropology not the dynamics of sexual desire—which he nonetheless promotes to the status of a full-fledged sixth sense that he calls "the genesique"—but the shared pleasures of taste and table. In opting for the gustatory over the sexual, he reworks the sensual materialism of the militant Epicureans while extending their enlightenment beyond a closed circle of initiates who enjoy in private their pleasures as secret sexual pioneers. All his readers, whatever their social status and means, are addressed as potential participants in an appreciation and cultivation of taste accessible to all who would come to the table. Gastronomy's pleasures of taste initiate a ritual to be practiced not in the privacy of the hidden, but as the communion of an ever broader conviviality so potent in its seductions that it has already provided the motor of what Brillat sees as an entirely new form of France's cultural preeminence.

I referred earlier to how the eighteenth century's many learned treatises on *goût* drew that term away from the specificity of what is tasted to a more diffuse cultural connoisseurship that served to mark out a true elite. It was the refinement of this new metaphoric "taste" and its acute sensitivity to comparisons that made it one of the principal targets of Rousseau's attack on society's ever-growing panoply of moral inequalities in his mid-century *Discourse on the Origin of Inequality*. In that text Rousseau echoes and offers his own extended elaboration on Lucretius's claim toward the end of Book 5 that the passage from pelts that protect from the cold to fine garments marking out one's social status brought with it a new and dangerous dynamic. Lucretius says of this new refinement:

> So people struggle blindly and in vain,
> Wasting their lives on foolishness; no wonder,
> For they can grasp no limits to their having,
> No limit to the growth of true delight.

That, little by little, sets their lives adrift
In the deep sea and the seething tides of war. (5.1425–30)

For Rousseau, *le bon goût* and its endless multiplication of distinctions served only to establish society as a locus of always metastasizing inequalities. Brillat, by tightening his focus on taste to the gustatory experience, recasts that faculty not as Rousseau's multiplier of inequalities, but as a motor of openness, exchange, and innovation. As Brillat redefined them, taste and its pleasures must be imagined as prompting us to expand and perfect the delights of the table by incorporating within them exotic foodstuffs and ways of cooking drawn from every quadrant of the known world. Brillat's celebration of taste serves less to mark out an established hierarchy than to foster a universal propensity to intensify, diversify, and perfect the pleasures of the senses. As recast by Brillat's gastronomy, these new pleasures of taste are always a work in progress opening onto yet unseen vistas of delight: "The limits of human pleasure have not yet been either understood or set, and we have not yet grasped to what degree our bodies might attain beatitude" (208).

What finally does Brillat tell us about how Epicureanism crossed the Revolution? Writing in the 1830s, Jean-Baptiste Sanson de Pongerville, an eminent classicist, a member of the French Academy, and a translator of Lucretius, pointed out how the post-Napoleonic restoration banished from the school curricula all study of Lucretius's *The Nature of Things*, a work that during the two preceding centuries had been a mainstay for the study of Latin. As Pongerville put it: "Lucretius was censored as an ally of the eighteenth-century *philosophes* and banished in a blanket proscription that included the authors of the *Encyclopédie* and of the *Dictionnaire philosophique*."[13] Brillat, born in 1755 and trained as a lawyer, had undoubtedly studied Lucretius closely. As a man of his generation and of his politics, he quite probably shared Pongerville's dismay that a voice so important to his troubled times should be so summarily silenced. We saw how Brillat's treatise on taste is not only Epicurean but also seeks to temper Rousseau's radicalizing of the Lucretian warning as to the dangers of fashion. There is, however, another strand within Brillat's dialogue with Rousseau that speaks directly to how Epicureanism crossed the Revolution. Rousseau's *Social Contract* of 1762 may have been the least popular of his major works during his lifetime, but it was in it that he elaborated a concept that would find a virulent second life in the context of the Revolution. The General Will, as Rousseau described it in the *Social Contract*, became the shibboleth of a near mystical refashioning of individual wills within a nebulous unanimity imagined as both emanating from and imposing itself on all members of a community. This unanimity of the General Will was so crucial to Rousseau's utopian community that to refuse it left only two options: exile or execution. Brillat, writing 60 years after Rousseau, knew only too well the consequences of that concept's deployment in the ideologically supercharged context of the Terror. Brillat also knew how the Terror would bring with it a reinterpretation and intensification of the traditional opposition between Stoic and Epicurean. By mid-1793 the new Stoicism of civic virtue had become first and foremost an iron-willed determination to stop at nothing in the elimination of the Republic's enemies. Those enemies, seen as guilty of preferring private pleasures over republican virtue, became the new and noxious avatars of the Epicurean.

Written as a response to the Revolution's systematic denegration of the Epicurean tradition, Brillat's *Physiology of Taste* sets out to rehabilitate and redirect the premises of Lucretian materialism and its focus on the subjectivity of the pleasured self. His gastronomy and its bold enlisting of all sciences in its multiplication of gustatory delights looks far more to an Aristippian maximizing of pleasure than to a minimizing of suffering within *ataraxia*. In this sense, Brillat might be seen as part of what Eric Baker has described as the nineteenth century's movement away from "Lucretian quietism" toward a more activist program aimed at "a maximizing of comfort and pleasure" through science and technology.[14] Despite that optimism, however, Brillat remains acutely aware that, in a Lucretian universe bereft of providential order and finality, the real danger is, as the classicist Pongerville put it in his own defense of Lucretius, "the suffering and evil which we would inflict upon our fellow men" (54). Reimagined within gastronomy, taste becomes for Brillat a faculty that finds in the shared pleasures of the table a new and positive conviviality outside any General Will promising collective happiness as an enforced cultural Gleichschaltung. In this sense, Brillat's epic of gustatory delight might best be seen as poised between the lost utopias of eighteenth-century Enlightenment and a more tempered optimism acutely aware of the recalcitrant realities of history.

Notes

1. Jean-Charles Darmon, *Philosophie épicurienne et littérature au XVIIe siècle* (Paris: Presses Universitaires de France, 1998).

2. On Lucretius's choice of poetic form for his exposition of Epicurean philosophy, see Leo Strauss, "Notes on Lucretius," in *Liberalism Ancient and Modern* (New York: Basic Books, 1968), 85–87; James H. Nichols, *Epicurean Political Philosophy* (Ithaca, NY: Cornell University Press, 1976), 24–45; P. H. Schrijvers, *Horror ac divina voluptas: Études sur la poétique et la poésie de Lucrèce* (Amsterdam: A. M. Hakkert, 1970), 27–49; Natania Meeker, *Voluptuous Philosophy: Literary Materialism in the French Enlightenment* (New York: Fordham University Press, 2006), 17–58.

3. W. R. Johnson, *Lucretius and the Modern World* (London: Duckworth, 2000), 81.

4. Denis Diderot and Jean d'Alembert, *Encyclopédie, ou Dictionnaire raisonné des sciences, des arts et des métiers* (1751–57; repr. [17 vols., plus plates and supplement in 5 vols.], New York: Readex Microprint, 1969), vol. 1: 1196.

5. On this subject, see Thomas M. Kavanagh, *Enlightened Pleasures: Eighteenth-Century France and the New Epicureanism* (New Haven and London: Yale University Press, 2010).

6. Louis Antoine de Saint-Just, "Rapport au nom du Comité de salut public sur le mode du décret contre les ennemis de la Révolution présentée à la Convention Nationale le 13 Ventôse an II (3 mars 1794)," in *Oeuvres Complètes*, ed. Anne Kupiec and Miguel Abensour (Paris: Gallimard, 2004), 673.

7. The *Littré* defines physiology as "the study of life phenomena in a philosophical and abstract way." On the complex semantics of this term and Brillat's use of it in relation to Anthelme Richerand's *Nouveaux élémens de physiologie* (Paris: Crapart, 1802), see Giles MacDonogh, *Brillat-Savarin: The Judge and His Stomach* (London: John Murray, 1992), 209.

8. Jean-Anthelme Brillat-Savarin, *La Physiologie du goût* [1825], ed. Jean-François Revel (Paris: Flammarion, 1982), 62. All subsequent quotations from this work will be followed by parentheses enclosing the page number from this edition. The translations are my own.

9. On the broad connotations of and heated debates surrounding the term "taste," see Elena Russo, *Styles of Enlightenment: Taste, Politics and Authorship in Eighteenth-Century France* (Baltimore, MD: Johns Hopkins University Press, 2007).

10. My quotations from Lucretius follow the Esolen verse translation: Lucretius, *On the Nature of Things*, trans. Anthony M. Esolen (Baltimore, MD: Johns Hopkins University Press, 1995), Book 5.1011 and 1016–17, p. 187. All subsequent quotations from Lucretius will be followed by parentheses enclosing the book, verse, and page references according to this edition.

11. Pierre-Marie Morel, "Les Communautés humaines," in *Lire Épicure et les épicuriens*, ed. Alain Gigandet and Pierre-Marie Morel (Paris: Presses Universitaires de France, 2007), 167–86, 184.

12. Joseph and Louis Michaud, *Biographie universelle ancienne et modern*, 85 vols. (Paris: Michaud Frères, 1811–62), vol. 5: 250.

13. Jean-Baptiste Sanson de Pongerville, "Lucretius," in *Dictionnaire de la conversation et de la lecture* (Paris: Belin-Mandar, 1832–39), vol. 36: 53. Subsequent quotations from this article will be followed by parentheses enclosing the page reference.

14. Eric Baker, "Lucretius and the European Enlightenment," in *The Cambridge Companion to Lucretius*, ed. Stuart Gillespie and Philip Hardie (Cambridge: Cambridge University Press, 2007), 274–88, 282.

PART III

Lucretian Figures of Modernity:
Freedom, Cause, Truth

CHAPTER SIX

How Modern Is Freedom of the Will?

PHILLIP MITSIS

How modern is freedom of the will? For many, such a question might recall Jacques Derrida's famous corresponding question about the age of psychoanalysis[1] and suggest that I am going to attempt to find my way through the theoretical brambles of origins, pre-origins, copies, and their multifarious relations. Unfortunately or fortunately, depending on one's views about these questions, I make no attempt to directly address such large theoretical issues here. For me, when looking at the fitfully paratactic history of Epicureanism, it seems difficult enough to try to point to the process by which some stray bit of Lucretius's poetry or argument comes to be noticed and then, for sometimes baffling reasons, gets put back into circulation—though, just as frequently as not, decked out in ways that would hardly have provoked *divina voluptas* in Lucretius himself. To make a corresponding attempt to do so for Lucretius's text as a whole strikes me as an improbable task, since at no time has the *De Rerum Natura (DRN)*, at least in any meaningful sense, popped back from the dead as a vital whole. At different times and in different guises, various parts of the poem have gone in and out of historical consciousness,[2] some making multiple appearances, while others, in good Epicurean fashion, have lived utterly hidden. Accordingly, any holistic view of the text's historical path may wrongly suggest some lively and coherent relations between parts and wholes in Lucretius's poem that have never been fully operative, perhaps even from the very outset.

I therefore will focus on just a few connected Lucretian texts and try to understand how they happened to strike a chord at a particular historical moment, in this case, in the late seventeenth century and in the thought of John Locke. Since one of my passages, however, is the very one in which Lucretius's doctrine of the swerve makes its sole appearance, such a narrow focus might seem in need of justification, especially in the wake of Stephen Greenblatt's recent brilliantly public splash into Lucretian scholarship with his book, *The Swerve: How the World Became Modern*.[3]

Greenblatt is playing, no doubt, with the paradoxical notion of the world becoming modern at a precise moment by means of a chance rediscovery of an ancient idea that itself claims we are human only because of events that happen by chance. I must confess, however, that I remain deeply skeptical about any such grand claims about the swerve and its role in the creation of modernity, however clever or arch. By my lights, the swerve, as one of Greenblatt's "dangerous ideas," seems, in his account, in danger of taking on a timelessly synecdochic role itself that is deeply misleading, especially since it is unclear to me that anyone, at any fixed time or place, has ever been able to say exactly how the swerve is supposed to do its work or how it precisely fits into Lucretius's larger concerns.[4]

Moreover, when one reflects on the fact that such great and influential early modern Epicureans as Gassendi rejected the swerve as nonsensical, it would be hard to be confident, even in Greenblatt's own recounting, that the swerve, rather than, say, atomistic materialism generally—already well known from many sources before Bracciolini's discovery of the manuscript of *DRN* in January 1417—played a critical role in the world "becoming modern." Accordingly, although I examine a set of issues touching on the swerve that similarly suggest a significant point of contact between Lucretius and modernity, I argue that, rather than creating modernity— whatever that means—these passages in Lucretius and their reception arguably raise serious questions about how we begin to go about drawing lines between antiquity and modernity in the first place, and about what it means for us to characterize a concept or argument as being "modern." My argument is therefore rather more in the spirit, though not of the letter, of Bruno Latour's *Nous n'avons jamais été modernes*.

So to return to my initial question, how modern is the will, or if you like, how old is the will? One might initially suppose that a conception of the will would be among the least promising places to try to isolate the kinds of meaningful connections that are meant to arise in a volume on Lucretius and modernity, especially since a near consensus has emerged among people as diverse as MacIntyre, Darwall, Foucault, Habermas, and Schneewind about a radical discontinuity between ancient and modern conceptions of the will. MacIntyre, for instance, claims that there is "no conceptual space"[5] in any ancient pre-Christian author for the notion of will. Even philosophers less prone to grand Hegelian pronouncements still write a lot of "invention" and "discovery" books about the early modern period—Schneewind's *The Invention of Autonomy*, Taylor's *Sources of the Self*, and so on—that make similar assumptions and, in so doing, reinforce the general notion that there is a critical conceptual divide between the way that ancients and moderns conceive of themselves as acting in the world as free human agents.

In my own subdiscipline of ancient philosophy, for instance, a view that seems to be winning the day is one formulated by Susan Sauvé Meyer[6] and then elaborated in relentless detail by Susanne Bobzien,[7] who claims that no Greek philosopher before Alexander of Aphrodisias—some three centuries after Lucretius—ever thought of free human agency as involving a choice between two alternative courses of action. Of course, when we begin talking about notions like free will across historical periods, it is all too easy to run into a variety of linguistic and conceptual minefields.[8] It is hard not to notice, for instance, that already two of the conceptual divides that I have just mentioned, those postulated by MacIntyre and Meyer, are really quite different in their claims and assumptions. In the hope of avoiding confusion, therefore, I am going to limit myself to the more specific argument that at least one recognizably modern and hugely influential account of free will—that of John Locke—corresponds in its goals and details to Lucretius's account in sufficiently relevant ways about our ability to freely choose between alternatives that it calls into question the notion of an unbridgeable conceptual divide between antiquity and modernity on the question of the will and human freedom.

At first glance, of course, it might seem rather foolhardy to try to link Locke and the Epicureans in order to make this argument because, like most of his contemporaries, Locke is regularly taken to be a determinist.[9] So it is certainly reasonable to wonder how my argument is ever going to gain any traction, given the shrillness of the anti-determinist arguments found among the Epicureans. A barely adequate answer here would require some lengthy detours into general questions about philosophical naturalism, I think, but one thing that is going to emerge from the comparison is how collaborative and cozy indeterminists and determinists can sometimes appear when their discussions are limited to purely phenomenal analyses of free human agency. Where the disputes get testier, especially among the materialists, is in deciding what view of matter and its atomic causal movements can best theoretically ground and explain the macro-level accounts of human freedom that both endorse.

Now, one further preliminary: suppose it turns out that there are, indeed, some important relevant similarities between Locke and the ancient Epicureans? Should we view these merely as an interesting conceptual coincidence or are there reasons for concluding that actual traceable lines of historical influence exist between their two accounts? Claims of philosophical influence are notoriously difficult to establish, of course, but there are many tantalizing suggestions, I would argue, that not only was Locke aware of the Epicurean account, both directly and through Gassendi,[10] but he also actually came to adopt key features of it in ways that suggest that we should think of him not so much as inventing or discovering a particular view of free will, but rather as reviving an Epicurean one and fitting it out anew. Having said that, however, let me issue a quick disclaimer. I certainly do not mean to claim that Locke's theory of free will does not, at the same time, also respond to a very different set of intellectual problems generated, for instance, by his adherence to Christian doctrine, the new science, emerging capitalist economies, and so on. Locke is obviously writing in a different social, political, and scientific framework from that of ancient Epicureans and it would be silly to discount these differences. Accordingly, what follows is not meant to be an exercise in some retrograde idealist form of the philosophical history of ideas. Nonetheless, I think that we have some reason to believe, at least on Locke's own view of his philosophical influences, that the arguments of ancient Hellenistic and Roman philosophers loom large in his thinking. To the extent that Locke's account of free human action was important in helping to articulate the variegated intellectual sources around him, in that very articulation, I would argue, we are able to hear, as did Locke, a distinctive and significant Epicurean voice. And it is this voice that has been regularly muted in recent autochthonous accounts of philosophical conceptions of autonomy in the early modern period.

In making this claim, I perhaps need to mention a few larger considerations about the practice of the history of philosophy in general, especially since the historical relations between ancient and early modern philosophers, for the most part, have lately been both neglected and woefully under-theorized.[11] Even though it is no longer common practice to dismiss philosophers of the Hellenistic and Roman periods in the way that Hegel did as a kind of regrettable downturn after Plato and Aristotle, there still has been a tendency to view the history of philosophy in the following cartoonish manner. Having first made a sudden and unprecedented appearance among the Greeks, philosophical thinking in the West quickly reached an initial zenith with Plato and Aristotle. Then followed a long period of decline from the death of Alexander the Great to the end of Rome, especially in the theoretical and political ambitions of philosophical thought. Next came (almost exclusively Western) Christianity and a protracted period that was philosophically suspect except for a few thinkers who found sufficient guidance in Aristotle and Plato to try to ground their beliefs in the rational arguments of the Greeks. Modern philosophy as we now know it, however, emerged one fine day in the late 1630s when Descartes walked into his study, formulated his famous cogito argument, and essentially swept away all that had gone before him, especially Aristotelian scholasticism, by creating modern philosophy ex nihilo, not to mention new conceptions of subjectivity, self-consciousness, the self, and so on.

However naïve this is as a story even about Descartes's own account of his discovery—at least to the extent that philosophers had been telling largely similar autobiographical tales of isolated, personal, philosophical discovery ever since the days of Galen[12]—it is even much less plausible as a history of philosophy, although some such view still tends to have widespread effects on scholars working on either side of this putative Cartesian divide. So along with all the "invention" and "discovery" books on one hand, there has been a noticeable turning inward among ancient philosophers who, I think, increasingly view themselves as engaged in a purely scholastic pursuit and who, when push comes to shove, often tend to retreat to arguments based on the supposedly alien conceptual framework that structures ancient philosophical discussions. Of course, one immediate problem is that such a view of a radical break in the conceptual framework between ancient and early modern philosophy would certainly have been news to philosophers like Locke and to his contemporaries, since many of them, like Locke himself, were convinced that Cicero, of all people, was the greatest philosopher they needed to come to grips with. It also seems eminently clear that the philosophical framework and arguments by Hellenistic and Roman philosophers found in a variety of ancient texts not only were thought by a majority of early modern philosophers to provide an entirely congenial framework for thinking about philosophical issues, but also in the case of voluntary action and free will, I would argue, were actually taken to serve as models.

Like many early modern philosophers, Locke does not always go out of his way to flag his intellectual debts in his published writings, even when he is quoting directly, and this perhaps accounts for the fact that if one takes a look, say, at Dan Garber's and Michael Ayer's authoritative *Cambridge History of 17th Century Philosophy*, one finds not even the slightest hint of a connection between Locke's views and those of ancient philosophers. Locke himself, however, often gives evidence of these debts not only in his unpublished writings, journals, and commentaries on ancient texts, but also in his more than 1,200 letters that, not coincidentally, are modeled after Cicero's own.[13] Such evidence, I believe, can be crucial for supporting a particular kind of history of philosophy, one that tries to follow out lines of real historical influence, rather than, say, one that postulates a series of conceptual developments of the philosophical spirit, as it were, without offering any account of the actual relations among historical generations of philosophers and their ideas. However, since this is not the place to present such evidence in detail,[14] I would at least like to flag what the outlines of such an alternative philosophical history might look like, since it can serve as a corrective to the many Hegelian narratives out there as well as help to situate the particular history of the problem of free will among philosophical materialists. Indeed, it was their materialism, I would argue, that was itself responsible in many respects for the particular shape that the problem of free will takes in its most salient and enduring forms.

So in my revised potted history, first you have Plato and Aristotle who are not deeply troubled by these issues for a variety of reasons connected to their teleological views of the world and human action, and, as a consequence, do not formulate questions of compatibilism and incompatibilism with any urgent precision; then follows an upturn with the materialist Stoics and Epicureans who are forced to come to terms with the nature of free human agency in light of their views about universal material causation; in attempting to do so, they ultimately adumbrate what were to become many of the most important philosophical moves in modern discussions of free will; then there is a long period in which questions of human freedom and will are tangled with an authoritative text and a divine personality, until finally, we again get some scattered glimpses of clear Hellenistic light in a variety of early modern philosophers, one of the most important of whom, incidentally, is not Descartes, because he is still committed to the faculty psychology of scholasticism.

With some of these caveats in mind, it is perhaps time to turn to Locke's account. Locke is often taken to hold a straightforwardly deterministic view of human volitions at the phenomenal level. So, for example, he makes the following claim about the nature of voluntary actions:

> 41. *The most pressing uneasiness naturally determines the will.* But we being in this world beset with sundry uneasinesses, distracted with different desires, the next inquiry naturally will be,—Which of them has the precedency in determining the will to the next action? and to that the answer is,—That ordinarily which is the most pressing of those that are judged capable of being then removed...But these set apart, the most important and urgent uneasiness we at that time feel, is that which ordinarily determines the will, successively, in that train of voluntary actions which makes up our lives. The greatest present uneasiness is the spur to action, that is constantly most felt, and for the most part determines the will in its choice of the next action. For this we must carry along with us, that the proper and only object of the will is some action of ours, and nothing else. For we producing nothing by our willing it, but some action in our power, it is there the will terminates, and reaches no further. (*An Essay Concerning Human Understanding* 2.21.41= "Of Power" 41).[15]

In the kind of stimulus/response model that Locke espouses in this passage, human action would appear to be the natural outcome or consequence of prior "uneasinesses", that is, the desires, pains, pleasures, and so on that serve as the causes or motives that determine the operations of the will. Our individual experiences of various feelings of "uneasiness" move the will and determine its choices according to their motive strength. Locke believes, moreover, that everything in the natural world, including human volition, is the product of prior causes. Thus, from passages such as these, one can easily conclude, as most commentators have, that Locke holds a kind of stimulus/response model of human volition in which stimuli causally determine our volitions, which, in turn, cause the actions that flow from them.

Locke, moreover, at times seems to characterize a free action as one that is in accordance with the preference or direction of an agent's mind or will, and thus, accordingly, as that particular power of rational agents that enables them to act or not to act. To many, this has suggested that Locke, like Hobbes, for instance, straightforwardly identifies free with voluntary actions and, like Hobbes, thinks that agents are acting freely insofar as they are voluntarily engaging in what they are doing. I think, however, that it is fairly clear, at least from passages such as the following, that this cannot be the whole story and that although it may be a necessary condition of any free action that it is voluntary, it is not, for Locke, a sufficient condition:[16]

> *Liberty, what.* Of all the actions that we have any idea of reducing themselves, as has been said, to these two, viz. thinking and motion; so far as a man has power to think or not to think, to move or not to move, according to the preference or direction of his own mind, so far is a man *free*. Wherever any performance or forbearance are not equally in a man's power; wherever doing or not doing will not equally *follow* upon the preference of his mind directing it, there he is not free, though perhaps the action may be voluntary. So that the idea of *liberty* is, the idea of a power in any agent to do or forbear any particular action, according to the determination or thought of the mind, whereby either of them is preferred to the other: where either of them is not in the power of the agent to be produced by him according to his volition, there he is not at liberty; that agent is under *necessity*. So that liberty cannot be where there is no thought, no volition, no will; but there may be thought, there may be will, there may be volition, where there is no liberty. A little consideration of an obvious instance or two may make this clear. ("Of Power" 8)

After distinguishing mere volition from liberty, Locke goes on to consider several Frankfurt-style cases in which agents seem to will certain actions or to make voluntary choices that appear to fall short of actions that are fully free and for which they should be held responsible. Thus, identifying or isolating the voluntariness of an action or choice is not sufficient, in his view, to capture the full range of criteria needed to determine whether actions are fully in the power of agents, that is, an expression of their "liberty." To explain this further feature of free actions, Locke introduces the notion of "suspension":

> *The power to suspend the prosecution of any desire makes way for consideration.* There being in us a great many uneasinesses, always soliciting and ready to determine the will, it is natural, as I have said, that the greatest and most pressing should determine the will to the next action; and so it does for the most part, but not always. For, the mind having in most cases, as is evident in experience, a power to suspend the execution and satisfaction of any of its desires; and so all, one after another; is at liberty to consider the objects of them, examine them on all sides, and weigh them with others. In this lies the liberty man has; and from the not using of it right comes all that variety of mistakes, errors, and faults which we run into in the conduct of our lives, and our endeavours after happiness; whilst we precipitate the determination of our wills, and engage too soon, before due examination. To prevent this, we have a power to suspend the prosecution of this or that desire; as every one daily may experiment in himself.

> This seems to me the source of all liberty; in this seems to consist
> that which is (as I think improperly) called *free-will*. For, during this
> suspension of any desire, before the will be determined to action, and
> the action (which follows that determination) done, we have oppor-
> tunity to examine, view, and judge of the good or evil of what we
> are going to do; and when, upon due examination, we have judged,
> we have done our duty, all that we can, or ought to do, in pursuit of
> our happiness; and it is not a fault, but a perfection of our nature, to
> desire, will, and act according to the last result of a fair examination.
> ("Of Power" 48)

It is in passages such as this that we find Locke's most considered views
about the problem of free will. Before continuing, however, it might be
helpful to remember a few facts about the nature of Locke's text. He originally put forward his views on freedom and motivation in Chapter 21 of
the second book of *An Essay Concerning Human Understanding* (1690), which
is titled "On Power." He then revised it extensively for a second edition
that appeared four years later, and over the next twelve years and into a
fifth edition he kept adding new passages, without, however, replacing or
substantially revising any of the material in the second edition. The above
passage about suspension is from the fifth edition and might initially seem
to be at odds with elements in his previous discussions.

On one hand, Locke's arguments seem to give a strong nod to determinism (of the sort we saw in our initial passage) where Locke claims
that volitions are part of a causal chain of stimulus and response, wherein
our voluntary actions are caused by motives and volitions that, in turn,
are responses to the prior stimuli that cause them. On the other hand,
Locke argues that liberty or freedom consists in the "power to suspend the
prosecution of this or that desire," and this creates a series of interpretive
puzzles—puzzles, however, that should immediately strike a chord with
anyone working on Hellenistic and Roman philosophy.

At first glance, it might be tempting to view these two claims as plainly
contradictory and to attribute this inconsistency to the nature of Locke's
methods of composition and his habit of merely adding new arguments
without revising earlier claims. Or, at the very least, we might seem
to have two contradictory pulls in the argument. On one hand, Locke
appears to argue that the will and human volitions are strictly determined;
yet, he also apparently endorses what is often taken to be a kind of liber-
tarian emphasis on our power to suspend volitions, and hence, in some
(admittedly obscure) way, to claim that agents are at any time capable of
suspending the causal force of prior stimuli and of rationally choosing
between two alternative actions. One might argue, of course, that the
appearance of contradiction is just that—merely an appearance—and that
our power to suspend volitions really is just like any other operation of
the will because it, too, is part of the causal mechanisms of nature. Such
a view allows us to absolve Locke of the charge of inconsistency and to

view him as a strict determinist. John Passmore, for example, attributes an account to Locke along these lines—an account that is mirrored by those who have interpreted Hellenistic accounts in a similar manner—by arguing that the way in which we suspend the prosecution of individual desires is entirely dependent on our prior character and preceding causal history.[17] Agents develop their capacities to resist and evaluate desires through habituation and its mechanisms, and such mechanisms both form their characters and ensure that their actions flow from settled dispositions of the mind.

Others, however, view Locke's account of our power to rationally suspend volitions as something more causally suspicious, what Gideon Yaffe calls, for example, "a form of self-transcendence" and a way of "giving oneself over to God, and thereby freeing oneself from bondage to the self."[18] Yaffe is concerned to place Locke in a particular historical context and to acknowledge a precise strand of Christian theological argument that was obviously important in the context of Locke's intellectual commitments. Also, he is keen to find room for Locke in the scholarly conversation about new sources of the self beginning to emerge in the early modern period. Locke's arguments about suspension give us reason to agree with Yaffe that we should not treat Lockean freedom and agency, in Dennett's phrase, as "merely the locus of causal summation for external influences,"[19] I think, however, that it remains a lively question whether Lockean freedom can be viewed as a form of "self-transcendence" that aspires to a theological ideal and that ultimately has its grounding in Christian texts and ideology. I would argue, instead, that we have different and much better evidence that, in this particular case, Locke's models are considerably older and are derived in the main from well-known arguments that arose in debates among Hellenistic and Roman philosophers.

Locke's account of "suspension" suggests, I would agree, not an Aristotelian emphasis on habituation or on the mechanisms that shape individual character. Yet, rather than being grounded in a some notion of transcending the self, the details of his description of rational suspension rely on the account of individual rationality that both Epicureans and Stoics attribute to unitary, rational, non–self-transcending agents. More particularly, it mirrors, on one hand, what Epicurus called *nephon logismos*, or sober reasoning, which he claims "tracks down the sources of every choice and avoidance and banishes opinions that beset souls with the greatest confusion" (*ad Men.* 132);[20] on the other, it invokes a Stoic view of our rational ability to make decisions by giving or withholding assent to various impressions.

Locke summarizes this rational capacity in a way completely consonant with Epicurean and Stoic descriptions of the workings and power of rationality:

This, as seems to me, is the great privilege of finite intellectual beings; and I desire it may be well considered, whether the great inlet and exercise of all the liberty men have, are capable of, or can be useful to them, and that whereon depends the turn of their actions, does not lie in this,—That they can suspend their desires, and stop them from determining their wills to any action, till they have duly and fairly examined the good and evil of it, as far forth as the weight of the thing requires. This we are able to do; and when we have done it, we have done our duty, and all that is in our power; and indeed all that needs. For, since the will supposes knowledge to guide its choice, all that we can do is to hold our wills undetermined, till we have examined the good and evil of what we desire. What follows after that, follows in a chain of consequences, linked one to another, all depending on the last determination of the judgment, which, whether it shall be upon a hasty and precipitate view, or upon a due and mature examination, is in our power; experience showing us, that in most cases, we are able to suspend the present satisfaction of any desire. ("Of Power" 53)

There is obviously much more to say about Locke's account of our power to suspend and how it exactly is meant to fit into his larger account of natural causality, human motivation, and individual responsibility, but for the moment I want to put these questions aside and turn now to the Epicureans and Lucretius.[21]

Whatever their exact relation, we have seen that Locke gives voice to two central commitments. On one hand, he gives an account of voluntary action based on a strictly causal stimulus–response model in which volitions are both the causes of action and the effects of the motivating stimuli that precede them. At the same time, he claims that although such volitions are a necessary condition for free actions, freedom requires the rational scrutiny of every desire to see whether it interferes with our true happiness and misleads us from it, or whether it contributes to it. In my view, one general problem that has puzzled recent Epicurean scholarship has been precisely that the Epicureans similarly seem to offer a strictly stimulus–response and causal account of voluntary action, all the while extolling to almost hyperbolic lengths the power of reason to choose between alternatives, while linking our pursuit of happiness to our ability to scrutinize and cultivate our desires. Scholarship, at least since Gassendi, has not always been clear in marking the difference between these two aspects of the Epicurean account of human agency and it therefore can be very useful, I think, to look at Epicurean accounts from the perspective of their early modern readers, whose lead I will follow.

It will help to begin with a passage in book four of *DRN* that summarizes the Epicurean account of voluntary action. It is perhaps worth mentioning, since it is regularly overlooked, that key features of Lucretius's Latin, such as the critically important notion of *"voluntas"* ("will" or "volition") described here, have no straightforward equivalent in Epicurus's Greek and in fact may be Lucretius's own philosophical coinage. By the same token, the exigencies of his poetic meter and the ambiguities of his poetic syntax and expression can sometimes make it difficult to sort out the exact relation that is supposed to hold between various items in the causal mechanisms he describes. But to set the argumentative context, in the midst of giving material explanations of a series of human functions such as thirst, perspiration, sex, and so on, Lucretius turns his attention to the material mechanisms of voluntary movements, in this case, walking:

> Now I shall tell you—and mark what I say—how it comes about that we can take steps forward when we want to, by what means it is given to us to move our limbs, and what it is that regularly pushes forward this great bulk of our body. First let me say that the images of walking impinge on our mind and strike it, as I explained earlier. After this, volition (*voluntas*) occurs. For no one embarks on any course of action before the mind first has previewed what it wants to do. And an image exists of whatever it previews. So when the mind stirs itself to want to go forwards, it immediately strikes all the force of the spirit distributed all over the body throughout the limbs and frame: it is easily done, because the spirit is conjoined with it. Then the spirit in turn strikes the body, and thus gradually the whole bulk is pushed on and moves forward. (*DRN* 4.877–91. Trans. Long and Sedley, 14E; modified)[22]

Although many commentators have seen in this passage an attempt by Lucretius to characterize spontaneous or uncaused actions (and then to link them somehow to the doctrine of atomic swerves), it seems clear to me that David Furley was right to find in this passage an argument for the fully causal nature of the voluntary.[23] Images, in this case, of walking, strike the mind and appear to it as pleasant. As a result, the mind sets itself in motion in accordance with the image, or more precisely, the mind sets in motion *voluntas* as it decides to move the body forward. This passage supports the view that volitions to act are fully determined by the mind of an individual, and there seems to be nothing in this passage in its own right that is obviously incompatible with the view that volitions themselves are fully determined. At the same time, however, until we know whether Epicureans think that the mind itself is causally determined by the images it receives, it is not clear whether they are committed to a determinist or indeterminist account of human freedom.

On the basis of this passage, however, both Furley and Bobzien conclude, much too hastily, I think, that Epicureans generally believe that our actions can be characterized as free just so long as they voluntarily flow from our characters and are an outcome of the causal mechanisms that have fixed our characters. Furley attempted to bolster this view by placing Lucretius's account in an Aristotelian framework in which actions are held to be free just so long as they causally flow from an agent's prior character. The passage itself, however, says nothing about dispositions, fixed characters, prior causal history, or any of these other Aristotelian concerns. Moreover, there are reasons external to this passage for thinking that Epicureans do not hold any of these Aristotelian tenets. For instance, at *DRN* 3.320–22 Lucretius argues that regardless of the nature of one's inherited inner psychological makeup, by means of *ratio* one can come to live a life worthy of the gods. That is, one can change whether one is naturally inclined to be angry or fearful and the habits that have arisen from these initial natural endowments. This is strictly in keeping with Epicurean rationalism about human action and also with their much-repeated claim that individuals, no matter their condition, can at any instant respond to reasons and to rational argument and transform their lives. Be that as it may, all that this passage claims is that once the mind is struck by an external image, it sets the body in motion by means of *voluntas*. Surely, however, this is compatible with any number of views about the relation of the voluntary and our freedom, especially since Lucretius offers a detailed account of how the mind itself is freely able to select from a welter of images those that move it to action.

When we turn to a much disputed passage on the swerve in Book 2 of *DRN*, we find much the same account of the relation of mind and *voluntas* (2.251–93), but with some further important clarifications:

> Moreover, if all motion is always linked, and new motion arises out of old in fixed order, and atoms do not by swerving make some beginning of motion to break the decrees of fate, that cause should not follow cause from infinity, from where does this free volition (*libera voluntas*) exist for animals throughout the world? From where comes this volition wrested away from the fates, through which we proceed wherever each of us is led by his pleasure, and likewise swerve off our motions at no fixed time or fixed region of space, but wherever the mind (*mens*) itself carries us? For without doubt it is volition that gives these things their beginning for each of us, and it is from volition that motions are spread through the limbs... (269) Thus you may see that the beginning of motion is created from the heart★ (★where the mind is located) and proceeds initially from the mind's volition, and from there is spread further through the entire body and limbs... (289) But that the mind should not itself possess an internal necessity in all its behaviour, and be overcome and, as it were, forced to suffer and be acted upon—that is brought about by a tiny swerve of atoms at no fixed region of space or fixed time. (trans. Long and Sedley 20F)

Lucretius is describing how the mind itself makes a beginning to motion, which is then passed on through the body by means of *voluntas* or *voluntate animi*, the volition of the mind—itself viewed as a kind of material force. Thus, in lines 269ff. we see that it is the mind that begins a motion that passes through the whole body; the role of the swerve as described in lines 289–90 is to keep the mind itself from having an inner necessity in all of its actions. Scholars have latched on to the notion of *"libera voluntas"* in 256–57, but it seems clear that in this account, as in Locke, the will is free only insofar as the mind directing it also is free. That is, *voluntas* is viewed as a material force that conveys the decision of the mind to the limbs and is determined by the mind, so that as Locke notices, calling this capacity or power "free" is actually a loose way of speaking; and in a much-quoted expression Locke says "in an inquiry about freedom, the question is not proper, whether the will be free, but whether a man be free" and "it is as significant to ask whether a man's will be free, as to ask whether his sleep be swift or his virtue square; liberty being as little applicable to the will as swiftness of motion to sleep or squareness to virtue" ("Of Power" 21). Our liberty, that is, consists in our mind's and our reason's capacity to direct the will.

If this picture is right, it allows us to draw two initial conclusions. First, the tradition of scholarship that has tried to link the swerve directly to *voluntas* and a faculty of "free will" has made a kind of category mistake, since as Lucretius claims in this passage, the swerve frees the *mind* from internal necessity, and presumably our freedom in making decisions lies there.[24] Second, Bobzien[25] uses this passage as fodder for her general claim that no Hellenistic philosopher, indeed no one until Alexander of Aphrodisias, several centuries later, ever thought of freedom of choice as a choice between two alternatives. But, of course, this argument, too, is badly misaimed, since her claim that *libera voluntas* in this passage is strictly determined tells us nothing about whether Epicureans think that the freedom of the mind and of our reason is itself similarly determined or whether it is characterized by its ability to choose between two alternatives. In fact, it is just this latter characteristic of rationality and freedom that is driven home again and again in extant Epicurean texts and presumably in such lost texts as *On Choice and Avoidance*. What characterizes the rational pursuit of pleasure and the good life, for the Epicurean, is our evaluating every pleasure and deciding whether to pursue it or not and this depends, as Epicurus writes in the *Letter to Menoeceus*, on the careful comparison (*summetresie*) among pursuits and our rational evaluation, on each and every occasion, of whether something should be pursued or not.

The Epicureans believe, in addition, that in order to explain our ability to reason in this way, they must defend it from a kind of mechanical determinism among the atoms that precludes the possibility of genuine reasoning and of engaging in rational argument.[26] They argue, therefore, that the determinist's conclusions in disputes about the possibility of free human action, if they were actually arrived at through reasoning that is causally necessitated, would fail to be based on genuine reasoning:

> The man who says that everything comes about by necessity cannot even criticize the man who says that not everything comes about by necessity; for he is saying that this is itself something coming about by necessity. (*S.V.* 40)[27]

Epicurus claims that arguments for determinism are self-refuting. It is probably safe to say that this argument is perhaps effective against one extreme form of determinism, namely, fatalism, since only the fatalist is committed to claiming that we must accept the conclusion of an argument simply because we would have accepted it, no matter what. The Stoics try to parry a similar argument and as they claim, such an objection still leaves room for determinists to insist that the truth of propositions will certainly influence in appropriately rational ways the processes and outcomes of their reasoning. In fact, they can easily agree with Epicurus that fatalism precludes rationality, since it fails to show the requisite sensitivity to the merits or truth of particular arguments. However, as long as the causes that fix belief are appropriately sensitive to relations that obtain between the processes and conclusions of our arguments, then such causes do not by themselves undermine the rationality of a belief. Thus, I doubt that Epicurus's argument is effective against all forms of determinism, but why, we might ask, are Epicureans so keen, in the first place, to defend the possibility of rational argument and deliberation from a kind of mechanistic determinism? Certainly one key reason is that they share with Locke the assumption that the rational evaluation of our desires is our most fundamental source of freedom and also the source of our responsibility. They evince, moreover, as opposed to Aristotle, a general optimism about the ongoing power of reason—regardless of the present state of our character, and of the condition of our settled dispositions—to take evaluative attitudes toward our desires at any moment and "to examine the good and evil on every occasion of every choice and avoidance" (*KD* 25).[28] In a sense, the Epicureans come to treat reason as a kind of Archimedean point from which to leverage every aspect of our person and agency despite our prior history of habituation or the nature of our settled beliefs about the good. This raises some difficult questions, of course, as it does for Locke, about how exactly we are to account for and explain these powers of reason in the light of nature's wider causal laws and influences. But leaving those questions aside for the moment, I think that we are now in a better position to see the parallels between Epicurus and Locke. Both allow voluntary actions to be embedded in strictly causal sequences of stimulus and response while ascribing our most important freedom, in Locke's phrase—"the great privilege of finite human beings"—to the ability of our reason to scrutinize and examine alternative courses of action and to judge which of them better promotes our happiness.

Of course, trying to say exactly how this ability of reason grounds our freedom in a world of atoms in motion—that is, how reason is to be naturalized—is a formidable task. For example, because they defend the providential and rational nature of matter itself, the Stoics have a much easier time in making the case that the rationality of human decisions can cohere with the providentially determined movements of a rational material world. It was for this very reason that Gassendi rejected the notion of the swerve and tried to formulate his own version of a divinely providential hedonism. Epicurus, on the other hand, since he thinks of matter itself as having no teleological goals or any properties of rationality, concludes that human rationality must somehow be free from the chains of natural material causality—hence the postulation of an indeterminate atomic swerve. Locke, though he shares a similar model of macroscopic rational human action, has a sufficiently difficult and mysterious account of the ultimate nature of the physical world, that it is hard to know how he might have hoped to defend his particular account of the powers of human rationality. A possible defense had earlier been offered by Gassendi, however, and a concerted group of Gassendi scholars has argued that Locke essentially took over these particular doctrines about the relation of rationality, the voluntary, and God's providence from Gassendi.[29]

Gassendi's argument, at least as articulated in *the Syntagma Philosophicum*, depends on a distinction between *libentia*, voluntary action or willingness, and *libertas*, the free action of a rational agent who is capable of deliberating between alternatives and has the power to refrain from one of two courses of action. He takes himself to be doing exegesis of Lucretius's view (*SP* 2.839ff.),[30] and the parallel with Locke is certainly striking. Moreover, he further attempts to ground this distinction between *libentia* and *libertas* in a naturalistic materialist account of differing kinds of physical motions. He characterizes *libentia* in the deterministic language of Hobbes:

> Just as a stone because it is determined to a downward motion does not possess indifference toward that motion; so the appetite, because it is determined to the good, is not in the same way indifferent toward the good and evil; and the stone by lack of indifference to both motions, is said to move downwards spontaneously (*sponte*), but still not freely; thus the appetite by lack of indifference to good and evil, is said to be inclined willingly (*sponte*), but still not freely to the good. (*Syntagma Philosophicum* 2.823)[31]

Conversely, *libertas* for Gassendi consists in the ability to rationally deliberate and it is that property of an agent that "by its own nature is so pliable, that having the truth as its object, it can judge now one thing, now another about the same object, and it can consider one judgment then another as true" (*SP, Opera* 2.824).[32] In the same passage, Gassendi goes on to explicitly distinguish the free movements of the rational intellect both from the kind of natural motions, like gravity, that determine the movements of inanimate objects and from the causal motions that determine voluntary actions. Voluntary, causal motions (*libentia*) are the sort that characterize the actions of animals generally and small children who have yet to reach the age of rationality. They also are the kind of causal movements characteristic of appetite and desire, whether in animals or rational creatures. *Libentia*, voluntary action, is in Gassendi's account a natural causal movement solely in one direction. Desire or appetite similarly lacks "indifference" and resembles inertial movements: it causally follows or responds to a perceived good, unless reason intervenes to change its direction and thus alter its movement.

Notice, that in this account, voluntary movements are described as being both determined and spontaneous; what they lack are the indifference characteristic of *libertas* and the flexibility grounded in the capacity to deliberate about alternatives and to execute changes of motion accordingly. In order to explain this, Gassendi postulates a particular kind of physical motion that is able to bend, *flectere,* and that in some sense subsumes the Epicurean swerve into the rational movements underpinning human liberty—physical movements that are neither purely inertial nor random. Gassendi's distinction between *libertas* and *libentia* thus corresponds rather neatly to the way that Locke lays down the criteria for freedom of action and the powers of rational agents in the *Essay,*[33] though with less reticence about the actual nature of the material motions that ground them. Locke's reticence here has other interesting Hellenistic precedents among the Skeptics, but it is perhaps time for some conclusions directly relevant to Epicureanism.

Epicurus, Gassendi, and Locke all show hesitations of one sort or another about attempts to naturalize reason—if by that we mean bundling up our explanations of the power of reason to evaluate and direct our desires with our explanations of other varieties of natural physical motions. They are less worried about this, though, when trying to capture actions that are merely voluntary and seem to fall more easily under the aegis of purely naturalistic explanations. But in either case, we might conclude that however benign or arbitrary our overall conception of nature, reason and its various powers offer a particularly difficult obstacle for naturalistic accounts, hence for theories of the will that ultimately depend on our conceptions of rationality.

It has turned out that Epicurean indeterminism rather than Gassendi's specification of different causal atomic movements in the context of a providential nature more closely raises the kinds of larger questions facing contemporary philosophers and scientific worldviews structured by quantum physics—though how explanations are supposed to proceed from atomic indeterminism to human rationality still remains pretty mysterious, which was Lucretius's point in the first place: somehow we and our powers of rationality emerge from the material stuff down there in ways that we are not in a position to trace out; yet the rationality that we observe in the world of macroscopic phenomena has to be grounded in the world of atomic movements that is demonstrated to us by our physical theories, and some of those atomic movements must themselves be undetermined if human reason itself is to remain free. For those committed to free will and quantum events, it seems that the Epicureans have provided what looks like an inescapable blueprint for further sketching out these relations.

My overall point has been, however, that neither the problems confronted nor the solutions proffered in thinking about the will should be seen as being radically different in antiquity and modernity, and that we may sometimes perhaps better understand the scope and goals of later accounts if we see their historical origins. By the same token, we can also sometimes better understand ancient accounts if we understand their historical outcomes. I have only given the barest outlines of the kind of detailed historical work that needs to be done in order to chart the fortunes of Lucretius's doctrine of free agency and its relation to later thinkers. But I hope at least to have cast doubt on the claim that ancient views on issues of human action and freedom are somehow conceptually quarantined from later periods or that Descartes managed to sever the philosophical influence of ancient philosophers with a single argumentative blow. For Locke and Gassendi, Lucretius's arguments about free agency were able to survive Descartes's particular invention of "modernity" mostly untouched. Perhaps in the same way that Descartes never quite managed to show how immaterial souls affect the world of matter, his arguments failed as well to have any palpable effect on materialist traditions of the will. Such a conclusion, at the very least, blurs one entrenched way of drawing a sharp line between antiquity and modernity and between the goals and methods of ancient and early modern philosophers. Although this would probably not have been much news to Locke and his contemporaries, it might be useful to remind ourselves of the particular history of these Epicurean arguments before going on to make larger claims about the nature and genesis of modernity.[34]

Notes

1. Jacques Derrida, "My Chances/Mes Chances: A Rendezvous with Some Epicurean Stereophonies," in *Taking Chances: Derrida, Psychoanalysis, and Literature*, ed. J. Smith and W. Kerrigan (Baltimore, MD: Johns Hopkins University Press 1984), 1–32.
2. See, for instance, Jacques Lezra's discussion of Marx's reflection on *DRN* 2.116 (pp. 129–135).
3. Stephen Greenblatt, *The Swerve: How the World Became Modern* (New York: W. W. Norton, 2011).
4. Not even Don Fowler, perhaps the greatest of modern scholars of Lucretius, in his monumental commentary on Book 2, *Lucretius on Atomic Motion: A Commentary on De Rerum Natura 2.1–332* (Oxford: Oxford University Press, 2002). For an exceptionally clear and nuanced account, see Alain Gigandet, *Lucrèce: Atomes, mouvement physique et éthique* (Paris: Presses Universitaires de France, 2001).
5. A. C. MacIntyre, *Three Rival Versions of Moral Enquiry* (Notre Dame: Notre Dame University Press, 1990), 111.
6. Susan Sauvé Meyer, "Fate, Fatalism, and Agency in Stoicism," *Social Philosophy and Policy* 16 (1999): 250–73. Meyer, unlike Bobzien, is careful, however, to point out continuities among various other features of ancient and modern conceptions of the will.
7. Susan Bobzien, *Freedom and Determinsim in Stoic Philosophy* (Oxford: Oxford University Press, 1999).
8. On which see T. H. Irwin, "Who Discovered the Will?" *Philosophical Perspectives* 6 (1992): 453–73. Irwin argues that Aquinas was able to construct his theory of the

will from materials that he found in Aristotle. Hence, although Aristotle did not consciously formulate a theory of will, he was in a position to do so. This should not be particularly surprising. On one hand, because Aristotle rejected materialism, he was not, as were the Epicureans, forced to try to account for free agency in a world of blind material motions. Nor, on the other, did he have to contend with the determining powers of Aquinas's omnipotent Christian God. Aristotle was able to ground his account of human agency in teleological categories that tend to bypass the kinds of tensions that both Epicureans and Thomists immediately face in explaining our free voluntary movements against a background of externally determined movements stretching back to eternity.

9. Isaiah Berlin, *Four Essays on Liberty* (Oxford: Oxford University Press, 1969).

10. For a detailed account, see Fred Michael and Emily Michael, "Gassendi's Modified Epicureanism and British Moral Philosophy," *History of European Ideas* 21:6 (1995): 743–61. One of Gassendi's most important modifications is to change the Epicurean account of atomic movements to make them compatible with divine providence, but his phenomenal account of free choice strictly follows Lucretius's account.

11. For one of the very few recent attempts to address this problem, see *Hellenistic and Early Modern Philosophy*, ed. Jon Miller and Brad Inwood (Cambridge: Cambridge University Press, 2003).

12. Stephen Menn, "*The Discourse on the Method* and the Tradition of Intellectual Autobiography," in Miller and Inwood, *Hellenistic and Early Modern Philosophy*, 141–91. Although Menn is unable to provide any direct historical evidence that Descartes knew these earlier accounts, he raises the interesting possibility of viewing Descartes as writing within a particular philosophical genre.

13. For detailed evidence of Locke's preoccupation with Cicero and ancient philosophers, see John Marshall, *John Locke: Resistance, Religion, and Responsibility* (Cambridge: Cambridge University Press, 1994). I set out some of the evidence for Locke's reliance on Cicero's *De Officiis* in Phillip Mitsis, "Locke's Offices," in Miller and Inwood, *Hellenistic and Early Modern Philosophy*, 45–61.

14. See notes 10 and 13.

15. John Locke, *An Essay Concerning Human Understanding*, ed. Peter H. Nidditch (Oxford: Clarendon Press, 1975). Hereafter cited parenthetically as "Of Power" followed by the section number.

16. See the discussions of Peter A. Schouls, *Reasoned Freedom: John Locke and the Enlightenment* (Ithaca, NY: Cornell University Press, 1992), 117–44, to which I am much indebted throughout this discussion, and more recently, Patricia Sheridan, *Locke: A Guide for the Perplexed* (New York: Bloomsbury, 2010). Among those who view Locke as an indeterminist, Vere Chappell takes the changes that Locke made to the fifth edition of "Of Power" to signal a repudiation of this conception of volitional intentionality and argues that Locke's correspondence with Limborch, in 1701–02, was the catalyst. V. C. Chappell, "Locke on Suspension of Desire," *Locke Studies* 29 (1998): 23–38; cf. V. C. Chappell, "Locke on the Freedom of the Will," in *Locke's Philosophy: Content and Context*, ed. G. A. J. Rodgers (Oxford: Oxford University Press, 1994), 101–121. Schouls argues, however, that the most significant change is Locke's adoption of the notion of "suspension," which appears as early as the second edition. I am more inclined to this latter view.

17. John Passmore, "The Malleability of Man in Eighteenth-Century Thought," in *Aspects of the Eighteenth Century*, ed. E. R. Wasserman (Baltimore, MD: Johns Hopkins University Press, 1965), 21–46.

18. Gideon Yaffe, *Liberty Worth the Name: Locke on Free Agency* (Princeton, NJ: Princeton University Press, 2000), 6.

19. Qtd. from Schouls, *Reasoned Freedom*, 118.

20. *Epicuro: Opere*, ed. Graziano Arrighetti (Turin: Einaudi, 1960).

21. The question of the respective influence of Epicureanism and Stoicism on Locke's theory is complicated. I try to sort out some of this in "Locke on Pleasure and Law as Motives," in *Motive*, ed. Iakovos Vasiliou (Oxford: Oxford University Press, forthcoming). Here I only argue that Locke takes aboard a conception of reason that mirrors Stoic claims about assenting and withholding assent. His further talk in this passage about reason determining the will is what I focus on in the comparisons with Epicureanism.

22. A. A. Long and D. N. Sedley, *The Hellenistic Philosophers*, 2 vols. (Cambridge: Cambridge University Press, 1987).

23. David Furley, *Two Studies in the Greek Atomists* (Princeton, NJ: Princeton University Press, 1967).

24. Although I agree with Pamela Huby that the Epicureans first formulated the free will problem, I disagree with her about how to conceive of their theory, since she thinks that freely willed actions are directly correlated with indeterminate atomic swerves. See Pamela Huby, "The First Discovery of the Freewill Problem," *Philosophy* 42 (1967): 353–62.

25. Suzanne Bobzien, "Did Epicurus Discover the Free-Will Problem?" *Oxford Studies in Ancient Philosophy* 19 (2000): 287–337.

26. Here I summarize arguments from my *Epicurus' Ethical Theory: The Pleasures of Invulnerability* (Ithaca, NY: Cornell University Press, 1988), esp. Ch. 4.

27. In *Epicuro*, ed. Arrighetti.

28. Ibid.

29. See note 9 and the magisterial and wide-ranging discussion in Lisa T. Sarasohn, *Gassendi's Ethics: Freedom in a Mechanistic Universe* (Ithaca, NY: Cornell University Press, 1996): 168–207, to which I am greatly indebted in what follows.

30. Sarasohn, *Gassendi's Ethics,* 140–41.

31. Cited and translated by Sarasohn, *Gassendi's Ethics,* 127.

32. Qtd. from Sarasohn, *Gassendi's Ethics,* 128.

33. "This discussion so nearly duplicates Gassendi's analysis of voluntary freedom (*libentia*), and freedom (*libertas*), in the 'Ethics,' that it is difficult to believe that Locke did not have it in mind when he wrote it": Sarasohn, *Gassendi's Ethics*, 188.

34. I am grateful to audiences at New York University, City University of New York, Cornell, University of Paris—Sorbonne, Toronto, Queens University, and the American Philosophical Association for comments on earlier versions of this chapter.

CHAPTER SEVEN

On the Nature of Marx's Things

JACQUES LEZRA

This *potestas*, this *declinare* is the defiance, the headstrongness of the atom, the *quiddam in pectore* of the atom; it does not characterize its relationship to the world as the relationship of the fragmented and mechanical world to the single individual.

As Zeus grew up to the tumultuous war dances of the Curetes, so here the world takes shape to the ringing war games of the atoms.

Lucretius is the genuine Roman epic poet, for he sings the substance of the Roman spirit.

[Diese *potestas*, dies *declinare* ist der Trotz, die Halsstarrigkeit des Atoms, das *quiddam in pectore* desselben, sie bezeichnet nicht ihr Verhältnis zur Welt, wie das Verhältnis der entzweigebrochnen, mechanischen Welt zum einzelnen Individuum.

Wie Zeus unter den tosenden Waffentänzen der Kureten aufwuchs, so hier die Welt unter dem klingenden Kampfspiel der Atome.

Lukrez ist der echt römischer Heldendichter, denn er besingt der Substanz des römischen Geistes.]

Karl Marx, *Notebooks on Epicurean Philosophy*, 4

"It goes without saying that but little use can be made of Lucretius" [*Es versteht sich, dass Lucretius nur wenig benutzt werden kann*].[1] So, by way of preface or prophylaxis, opens the fourth of Marx's *Notebooks on Epicurean Philosophy*, composed around 1839 as Marx was preparing his doctoral dissertation. A long list of citations from *De Rerum Natura (DRN)* follows, and then Lucretius is put to use—as Plutarch's antagonist, in the long battle over the Epicurean tradition. In these early, informal notes by a young dissertator the reception of Lucretius hangs in the balance; what Althusser refers to as an "underground current" of the materialism of the encounter surfaces and is soon, over the course of the next 15 years, rechanneled or resubmerged.[2] An account of mediation at odds with the mechanics, the economics, of *use* presents itself here, to be translated, never entirely successfully, first into the great Hegelian lexicon that the young Marx and his preceptors were unfolding, then into the languages of political economy. What sorts of use can be made of a thing? In what respects is Lucretius something to be *used*?

This is how Marx puts it:

> As nature in spring lays herself bare and, as though conscious of victory, displays all her charm, whereas in winter she covers up her shame and nakedness with snow and ice, so Lucretius, fresh, keen, poetic master of the world, differs from Plutarch, who covers his paltry ego [his "small 'I'": *sein kleines Ich*] with the snow and ice of morality. When we see an individual anxiously buttoned-up and clinging into himself, we involuntarily clutch at coat and clasp, make sure that we are still there, as if afraid to lose ourselves. But at the glimpse [*Anblick*] of an intrepid acrobat we forget ourselves, feel ourselves raised [*erhaben*] out of our own skins like universal forces [*allgemeine Mächte*] and breathe more fearlessly. Who is it that feels in the more moral [*sittlich*] and free state of mind—he who has just come out of Plutarch's classroom, reflecting on how unjust it is that the good should lose with life the fruit of their life, or he who sees eternity fulfilled, hears the bold thundering song of Lucretius?[3]

These are marvelous lines—rich and complex, evocative, precise. Marx's enthusiasm for Lucretius's "bold," "acrobatic" verse, for the "infinitely more philosophical" interpretation of Epicurus he offers than we find in the wintry Plutarch—this shines through. We admire the "poetic master of the world"; we "forget ourselves"; at the glimpse of Lucretius's verse what was "small" about our "I" is forgotten, and expands to fill the vertiginous air below the acrobat. Lucretius's verse dances dangerously above the world of things, Marx says: here, at this circle, standing as it were by the seaside, Marx describes not (as Lucretius does in the poem) a vessel's catastrophe but a world of things and states of affairs, and a world above it, a world of poetic turns and propositions made philosophically as well as poetically, concerning and corresponding to that world of states of affairs and things. How will Marx make use of Lucretius, use of a discursive realm whose figures turn in paths parallel to the wintry tracks of things below, enskied things above in correspondence with those below, some force drawing them together, the poet's art pulling them apart; gravity (or whatever norm "gravity" stands for here: let's call it "reference," or "correspondence," or "continuity," or the rule of "parallelism," always bearing in mind that each of these terms works in its own lexical-philosophical frame, as well as in relation to the other terms here), "gravity" threatening always to plunge the acrobat, or the poet, or the Lucretian philosopher, from the air in which he spins toward things below?[4]

One answer to this question is obvious enough. On reading Lucretius, Marx seems licensed by the vigor and intelligence of the poet's verse to spread his own literary wings, and to treat himself to climatological antitheses, mythologies, analogies, anthropomorphisms, and epic similes: "As nature in spring lays herself bare," he writes, "and, as though conscious of victory, displays all her charm, whereas in winter she covers up her shame and nakedness with snow and ice, so Lucretius, fresh, keen, poetic master of the world, differs from Plutarch." Marx trots out a small stable of poetical and rhetorical tricks that echo the invocation of Venus at the opening of *DRN*, where the *Aeneadum genetrix* is said, as you will remember, to be acclaimed by nature *simul ac species patefactast verna diei,* "as soon as the vernal face of day is made manifest" (1.10).[5] But these lines also express a degree of anxiety. The acrobatic thrill of flying with Lucretius, of catching a glimpse of nature's ravishing and seductive nakedness, of forgetting ourselves—all these mark the philosophically familiar experience of feeling upraised, *erhaben,* sublimated. For this early Marx, to read Lucretius is to come across that which elevates-exposes us and threatens us with a loss of self that is correlative to the expansion of our "small I" into the space between the acrobat and the ground, between the world of poetic figures and the wintry ground of things. We may feel "like" universal forces when we come across Lucretius's verse, but only when we have forgotten that we *are* not; spring's victory always slips into winter's grasp, and back out again. We purchase a certain sort of moral disposition—*Sittlichkeit*—and a feeling of increased freedom on the coin of this sublime and sublimating exposure, and on the back of a necessary forgetting that is brought about by Lucretius's boldness. Just what sort of moral disposition this is, and just what sort of freedom is contingent upon sublime forgetting, and what, beyond our "small I" and "paltry egos," we must forget in order to achieve a free moral disposition—these questions are themselves momentarily forgotten, in the thrill of Lucretius's victory over Plutarch.

But only momentarily, and never entirely. Manifestly, Marx approaches *DRN* in the epic-poetic mode that Lucretius's verse puts at his disposal, but also through or against the elevating, sublimating lexicon of Kantian aesthetics—among others. At this level, "forgetting" does not obtain. Marx's readers—and, as these lines are private notes, intended for Marx's own use alone, the only "reader" of interest here is Marx himself—Marx's readers, Marx himself, are invited to recall the artifice of Lucretius's verse, and the long tradition, epic as well as philosophical, that it engages. At "the glimpse [*Anblick*] of an intrepid acrobat," then, we may well "forget ourselves," but at the glimpse of Marx's summary account of the experience of reading Lucretius we recall that when we then, and consequently, "feel ourselves raised [*erhaben*] out of our own skins like universal forces [*allgemeine Mächte*] and breathe more fearlessly," we are rejoining an aesthetic tradition, and a tradition of writing about aesthetics, that places us in our own skin again, wraps us back into a philosophical surface on which the lexicon of our experience is detailed. Here, in short, the determining laws of mediation draw Marx the reader toward Marx the writer of these note-books, just as the epic simile with which Marx opens this notebook draws him into analogy with the epic poem of nature itself, draws Marx into contact with Lucretius. Here, then, the philosopher's "little I" coincides with itself, as the writer of these notebooks coincides with their reader, when it glimpses itself in the shape of the Roman poet, in the skin of the Kantian aesthetician, who people the element in which the dance of poetical figures and of philosophical propositions corresponds, mediately, to the world of things and states of affairs.

If this sounds rather imprecise, it is because Marx is treading on very tricky ground indeed, and—although recognizing perhaps how inad-equate his largely Hegelian frame is to the stubborn, poetic matter before him—prefers obscuring his argument to abandoning his frame (we are many years away from *Capital*). Marx is careful to leave the "glimpse" that Lucretius affords him at just that—a glimpse. The domain of the acrobat (*Luftspringer* is the wonderful word Marx uses: the air-jumper) remains the pastoral world of the circus, set aside from the humdrum, workaday world in the same way that the sublime experience serves more as an interruption, an epochal punctuation, than a part of the fabric of our "paltry" lives. Spring, the appearance of Venus, the reading of Lucretius's poem, these are radically heterogeneous with respect to the wintry, encloaked body of the paltry I, the world where the mere "usefulness" of one or another experience is the measure of its worth—for example, the "experience" of reading Lucretius. And vice versa; my glimpse of the acrobat is nothing at all like the way I see the shivering, Plutarchan mor-alist; the acrobat is as different from Plutarch as spring's female charms are from winter's harsh grasp. But the circus and the sublime landscape are also inextricably connected with the world from which they escape. Even Marx's strange analogies tell us as much: nature remains the same—same in name, same in continuous substance—beneath the exposure of her springtime victory or the huddled mantle of winter; I may forget myself on glimpsing the acrobat, but I gaze at him with the same eye that has seen the shivering Plutarch. Lucretius's verse is at one and the same time "of little use" in understanding the difference between the Democritean and Epicurean systems, and indispensable, inasmuch as it provides the point at which I, Marx-the-writer and I, Marx-the-reader, coincide, where the forgetting that Marx-the-writer demands shows itself to be correlative to the remembering that Marx-the-reader exemplifies. Winter and spring, the flight of the acrobat, and the pedestrian tread of the schoolteacher: these are accidents of nature or of the "small I" or the "paltry ego," mere *eventa*, circumstantial and disseverable properties; and they are also *coniuncta*, non-severable and constitutive properties "which without destructive dissolution can never be separate or disjoined" from substances, *id quod nusquam sine permitiali discidio potis,* in the words of the poem (1.451). The world of things and the world of statements about things remain correspondent, parallel, symmetrical; and they lean in, collapse, fall, decline into each other.

One imagines, as a result, two destinies, two uses, for Lucretius, encoded in these letters that the young Marx sends to himself, in these notebooks in which he sketches for himself the outlines of the Epicurean tradition. These uses, these destinies for Lucretius, set the pattern to which Marx will make other forms of thought conform. On one hand, we imagine a line of thinking stressing the sublime, indeed unbreachable difference between the world of things, and the lofty, *Luftig*, world of statements about things. The acrobatic figures of *DRN* are, on this description, the epitome of what Marx will call, in the First of the "Theses on Feuerbach," "all hitherto existing materialism," inasmuch as in this circus-world "the thing, reality, sensuousness, is conceived only in the form of the *object or of contemplation*, but not as *sensuous human activity, practice*, not subjectively."[6] In the "Theses," such Feuerbachian, conceptually defective materialism leads to the *idealization* of "things" rather than to their being understood as the result of, or under the aspect of, practice. Feuerbachian "things" are, for Marx, "things" imagined as objects, objects-for-consciousness or for thought, and in a specular and parallel determination, Feuerbachian "thought" becomes, in the "Theses," the contemplation of objects-for-thought alone. The correlation of thought and object, the adequation of thought to object-for-thought and vice versa, expresses the fantasy of a pure, unthought immediacy of thought to itself. On the other hand, one imagines the collapse of the plane of figures onto that of "things." On this side, we find a materialism of a different sort—even of a different national lineage, an antimetaphysical, British materialism, a materialism of cases for which no figure is to be found. This Marx describes elsewhere, also quite famously, as Baconian, based in the senses, experimental, nominalist.[7] Things, on this side, imagined as for-themselves alone; the work of thought, producing hypotheses about things alone to be tested in the event; thought, an activity of a consciousness alone among things, a thing among other things; relation, which might be construed as an abstract figure corresponding to the plane of things in themselves, demoted, fallen to earth, a further thing among things; the pure, unthought immediacy of the thing to itself.

These two declensions of Marx's early encounter with Lucretius appear to mark the outside limits of Marx's thought on materialism, and in particular on the status of things in and for thought. (Are mental objects material? In what sense?) But already at this stage of Marx's career this description is inadequate—inadequate to Marx's understanding of things, inadequate to his reading of Lucretius.

Let me now turn to a third, decisive aspect to Marx's earliest encounters with Lucretius. Marx gives a fairly straightforward—though not for that less interesting—Hegelian account of *declinatio*. It begins by asserting that "the straight line, the simple direction, is the negation of immediate being-for-self, of the point; it is the negated point; the straight line is the being-otherwise of the point."[8] Steps follow—Marx walks his reader, in summary form, through Lucretius's argument in Book 2, insisting on the difference between what Marx calls the spatial law according to which atoms fall primitively, in parallel, and the different law, Marx's word in both cases is indeed *Gesetz*, followed by the declining or swerving atom. Concerning the first, the law of spatiality, the term that Marx uses to designate the subsisting path from which the atom swerves is *Voraussetzung*, the law or track that is laid out before the atom, the precondition or presupposition of its path, but with a strong play on the root, *Ge-setz*. That atoms follow the path that is presupposed or preposed, *Setzen*, for them, the path that is set-out-before-them, this is the law, *Gesetz,* of spatiality— indeed, this is the definition of space that Marx offers: the collection or set of paths-to-be-followed; in other words, the unfolding of what is set out as potentiality for the atom-in-motion. The term *Voraussetzung* preserves a foot in colloquial usage, but it also carries the more technical sense of a logical *premise* that we would expect of an argument or a note in which Marx "expresses" himself, as he says, "in terms of logic," or indeed of the *Logic*. For in these pages in which Marx discusses Lucretius he is not only adopting the lexicon of Kantian aesthetics, he is referring quite directly to the sections of Hegel's *Encyclopedia* and of the *Science of Logic* in which the concept of "Measure" is discussed, where, Hegel says in *Science of Logic*, "there is a sudden interruption of merely indifferent relations which do not alter the preceding specific reality or do not even form any such, and although the succession is continued quantitatively in the same manner, a specific relation breaks in *per saltum.*"[9] It would take me too long to consider in detail the nature of this strange, early but far-reaching meeting of Lucretius with Hegel in Marx's notebooks, but it should be clear that for Marx there is a dramatic and informing line leading from Lucretian *declinatio* to Hegel's description of the "jump" from quantitative to qualitative relations, the seeming action-at-a-distance by means of which the quantitative relation makes the acrobatic jump into the qualitative, while also preserving-eliminating its mere quantitativity—thus giving rise to the dialectically more ample concept of measure. Hegel (who has in mind Leibniz's account of what comes to be called the Principle of Continuity: *natura non facit saltum*, from the 1704 *Nouveaux essais*) describes these "jumps" as knots or nodes in otherwise straight number-lines or arithmetically sequential number-sets, and he has in mind something like the mathematics of recursive functions, which make manifest second-order relations among numbers in arithmetic series in which numbers seem to bear to each other exclusively what one might call first-order relations, relations that flow from their definition as quanta. Still, it should be clear as well that this dramatic and informing line leading from the *Luftspringer* to Lucretius's account of *declinatio* to Hegel's account of the "jump" from quantitative to qualitative relations is importantly *discontinuous*. The persistent uncertainty of Lucretian *declinatio* is not of the same order as the retrospective understanding of the potentiality of other-than-arithmetic relations that we are afforded by the "jump" in order of relations that Hegel describes, a jump that is nothing but the law of the unfolding of the premises according to which quanta, or atomic propositions, establish themselves as such in relation to other such.

What, then, is Marx's purpose in passing Lucretius through Hegel, if to do so is to bend together into a seeming identity two merely parallel, merely analogous swerves or jumps?

Consider this brief, rather dense passage from the Fourth of the *Notebooks on Epicurean Philosophy* in which Marx describes the principle of atomic movement in *DRN*:

As the atom swerves away from its premise [*Wie das Atom von seiner Voraussetzung ausbeugt*], divests itself of its qualitative nature and therein shows that this divestment, this premiseless, contentless being-enclosed-in-self exists for itself, that thus its proper quality appears, so also the whole of the Epicurean philosophy swerves away from the premises; so pleasure, for example, is the swerving away from pain [*Schmerz*], consequently from the condition in which the atom appears as differentiated, as existing, burdened with non-being and premises. But the fact that pain exists, etc., that these premises from which it swerves away exist for the individual—this is its finiteness [*seine Endlichkeit*], and therein it is accidental...One swerves away from determinism by elevating [*erhoben*] accident, necessity and arbitrariness to the level of the Law; God swerves away from the world, it is not for him, and therein he is God.[10]

[Wie das Atom von seiner Voraussetzung ausbeugt, seiner qualitativen Natur sich entzieht und darin nachweist, daß dies Entziehn, dieses voraussetzungslose, inhaltslose Insichbeschlossensein für es selbst ist, daß so seine eigentliche Qualität erscheint, so beugt die ganze epikureische Philosophie den Voraussetzungen aus, so ist z.B. die Lust bloß das Ausbeugen vom Schmerze, also dem Zustande, worin das Atom als ein differenziertes, daseiendes, mit einem Nichtsein und Voraussetzungen behaftetes erscheint. Daß der Schmerz aber ist etc., daß diese Voraussetzungen, denen ausgebeugt wird, sind für den einzelen, das ist seine Endlichkeit, und darin ist er zufällig. Zwar finden wir schon, daß an sich diese Voraussetzungen für das Atom sind, denn es beugte nicht der graden Linie aus, wenn sie nicht für es wäre. Aber dies liegt in der Stellung der epikureischen Philosophie, sie sucht das Voraussetzungslose in der Welt der substantialen Voraussetzung, oder logisch ausgedrückt, indem ihr das Fürsichsein das ausschließliche, unmittelbare Prinzip ist, so hat sie das Dasein sich unmittelbar gegenüber, sie hat es nicht logisch überwunden...Dem Determinismus wird so ausgebeugt, indem der Zufall, die Notwendigkeit, indem die Willkür zum Gesetz erhoben wird; der Gott beugt der Welt aus, sie ist nicht für ihn, und drin ist er Gott.][11]

This is a considerable reformulation both of the Lucretian passage that Marx is commenting on, and of the Hegelian lexicon into which he is translating it. It becomes a crucial element in a number of ways. The link between pain and the law or premise from which the Epicurean pleasure principle is to swerve is not to be found in these terms in Hegel—not, at any rate, in the way that this "persistence" is imagined, as the finiteness of the number or the unity of the number, as it were. This affect of the point, as it can be called, is at the same time an expression of its finiteness, that is, it designates the point as a point, it is the condition of its arithmetic, atomic relation-to-itself and also of its first-order relation-to-other-points; and also it is an expression of the in–itself-as-finite of the point. *Schmerz* is a swerving away from pain, and pain is the characteristic of the punctual rain of atoms. "Pain" is the term that Marx employs to express *both* the condition of uncertainty that in Lucretius forms the juncture of the four-part system, atom and motion, void and declination, *as well as* the condition of disclosable potentiality that characterizes the arithmetic relation in Hegel. Marx's term is, we might say, a compromise-formation, or a symptom.

Marx's symptomatic "pain" is useful on three further levels. The first is conventional: using the concept of "pain" in this way, Marx swerves from the onto-epistemological level to the ethical one, and translates the atomic register at which he has been proceeding, the map of the actualization or the coming-together of the atoms according to the *declinatio*, into the consideration of the Epicurean freedom to choose pleasure over pain. Using "pain" in this way *also* allows Marx to import a lexicon that is of particular interest to him in these years, and that remains connected with his discussions of Epicurus for the next decade or so. This is Marx's description of *matter* in *The Holy Family*, his polemic, written toward the end of 1844 with Engels, against the Young Hegelians:

> Induction, analysis, comparison, observation, experiment, are the principal forms of such a rational method. Among the qualities inherent in matter, motion is the first and foremost, not only in the form of mechanical and mathematical motion, but chiefly in the form of an impulse, a vital spirit, a tension—or a "Qual", to use a term of Jakob Böhme's—of matter. The primary forms of matter are the living, individualizing forces of being inherent in it and producing the distinctions between the species.[12]

> [Unter den *der Materie* eingebornen Eigenschaften ist die *Bewegung* die erste und vorzüglichste, nicht nur als *mechanische* und *mathematische* Bewegung, sondern mehr noch als *Trieb, Lebensgeist, Spannkraft*, als *Qual*—um den Ausdruck Jakob Böhmes zu gebrauchen—der Materie. Die primitiven Formen der letztern sind lebendige, individualisierende, ihr inhärente, die spezifischen Unterschiede produzierende *Wesenskräfte*.][13]

Böhme's *qual*, which means *cruciatus*, *tormentum*, as Grimm's diction-
ary tells us, stamps matter with a "force of being," a *Lebenskraft*: *qual* is,
Böhme tells us, "the mobility, boiling, springing and driving of a thing"
[*Qualität ist die Beweglichkeit, Quallen oder Treiben eines Dinges, als da ist die
Hitze, die brennet, verzehret und treibet alles, das in sie kommt, das nicht ihrer
Eigenschaft ist.*][14] This individuating *Lebenscraft* inheres in matter, and supports the distinction between mechanical and mathematical movement.
In Marx's physics, the primitive "force or might of being" is a form of
suffering or torment proper to matter, and it is the condition upon which
matter becomes mathematized and mechanized—*qual* is the condition
under which undifferentiated matter swerves, at uncertain times and in
uncertain places, into differential relation, forming organized bodies; and
it is the condition under which merely arithmetic relations "jump" into a
qualitative relation, revealing an always-already operating law of measure
retroactively.[15]

There is a third, remarkable aspect, rather subterranean, of Marx's
approach to Lucretius in these lines. In the dense and poetic paragraph I
have cited, in which Marx reads Lucretius through Kant, through Hegel,
and now, we see, through Böhme, the language of the *swerve* takes on different, overdetermined, and symptomatic shapes and functions. Among
these, the term and the little lexicon to which it is now associated come to
describe a metaphilosophical maneuver in Marx's own writing—as when
he uses the same, rather unusual word, *Ausbeugen*, to describe, not only the
swerving of the atoms, their *declinatio*, but also a significant swerve in the
historiography of philosophy.[16] There is physical *declinatio*—the swerve of
atomic *minima*; traditionally, though controversially, Epicureanism understands what we are accustomed to call the exercise of moral freedom on
the model of *declinatio* as well, the individual's election of pleasure over
pain not being given in advance, but always only recognized after the fact
as having occurred. Finally, for Marx the history of philosophy moves
per saltum, according to *declinationes*, among schools and forms of thought
appropriate to times and sets of thoughts or mentalities. Thus determinism is said to swerve into something else; Epicureanism moves suddenly
away from the principle of pain, *Schmerz*, and toward pleasure. Hegel, in
the sections of the *Logic* from which Marx is borrowing, makes a point
not dissimilar from this when he speaks of the task of "the historian of
philosophy," to whom, Hegel says, "it belongs to point out more precisely
how far the gradual evolution of his theme coincides with, or swerves
from, the dialectical unfolding of the pure logical Idea." The word that
Hegel uses to designate this "swerving" is not *ausbeugen* but the rather
different *abweichen* [*Während es nun der Geschichte der Philosophie überlassen
bleibt, näher nachzuweisen, inwiefern die in derselben stattfindende Entfaltung
ihres Inhalts mit der dialektischen Entfaltung der reinen logischen Idee einerseits
übereinstimmt und andererseits von derselben abweicht*]. The result of this repetition, on different levels, of the lexicon of "swerving" and *declinatio* is to
split the object of Marx's argument, or to double it: he is no longer writing

about Lucretius alone, but also about the uses to which Lucretius can be put—in, for instance, the history of philosophy, including in Marx's own contributions to that history. These are not, however, symmetrical objects or corresponding discourses, one mappable onto or translatable into the other according to an algorithm, a principle of abstraction, or an established lexicon; we are not dealing with the topographer's view of surfaces, with the Idealist philosopher's map of a numinous world of forms to which phenomena relate, or more generally with geometry, that late development of British materialism, as Marx has it in *The Holy Family*. The distinction between a discursive and a metadiscursive position is also susceptible of *declinatio*; a *Qual* internal to the discourse turns it metadiscursive, and vice versa. What sort of dialectic is at hand when we cannot establish firmly whether something is occurring on a discursive level or on a metadiscursive level—and thus what sort of finiteness is appropriate to the object, and which to the subject? This is the point, rather a sort of nodal crossing that occurs by virtue of *declinatio*, at which Marx the student of philosophy swerves from Hegel's path. Writing to himself, hoping to furnish himself with a professional identity, with a sublime perspective on his object of study and his subject matter, Marx shows himself that it is not possible to tell whether the nature of philosophical writing is to correspond to a world of things above which it floats, or to have these touch—any more than it is possible to tell whether the principle of correspondence is a principle of uncertainty or a principle that reveals the recursive law of their potential touching. This uncertainty means that it is equally unclear at what points his own language is of the order of discourse or of the order of metadiscourse—that is, he does not know, and cannot firmly know, whether he, the "little I" or "paltry ego" writing these notebooks to himself, belongs to the order of things or to the order of statements concerning things, of the order of the acrobat who swings above them. Knowing that these two touch, but that they touch painfully *both* in uncertain times and at places, *and* where the law of their touching reveals itself, as the force of gravity does only in the fall of the acrobat, the *Luftspringer*.

In this complex approach to the nature of things, and to his own nature as a thing, Marx proves himself an acute reader of Lucretius. Marx was especially struck at the almost Empedoclean strife that obtains in the poem at both levels, both in its descriptions of the tormented or turbulent interaction of atomic *minima* in the cosmological as well as the physical sections, and in the verse-form itself. Martial analogies abound, of course; so does recourse to the term *turba*, as a way of describing the violence of the sea as well as the small turbulence caused by *declinations* broadly.[17] This irreducibly *turbulent*, unexpected, and unlocalizable aspect of Lucretian and Epicurean cosmology runs precisely against the affective or dispositional attitude to which the philosopher aspires, where the *suavitas* and equanimity of katastatic pleasure undergird the moral or ethical "paltry I." The battle between Mars and Venus, in brief, is both the subject of *DRN* and its abiding consequence: the philosopher is the ground on which that battle represents itself, and on which it is fought—or rather, the status of philosophical language, of philosophical statements about things in a world of things, is that battleground itself. Or rather, the philosophical *text* is this ground and battleground on which it is impossible to decide, for a class of predicates, whether they are accidental or non-disseverable properties of substances, and thus escape the bivalent logic that Lucretius seems on one level to require, when he says that all things that are named or called [*cluent*] must either be *eventa* or *coniuncta* of void and bodies, *inane* and *corpora*. Or, to be even more precise, it is *at* the place, and *as* the place, where the philosophical text confronts the problem of its *use*, that this battle takes place.

When I say the "philosophical text," I am taking an obvious and notorious liberty. For it is just where Lucretius's great poem looks *least* like a classical "philosophical" text—like what has come to be called a "philosophical text," perhaps in an effort to evade what is most radical about a work like *DRN*—which is to say precisely where the matter of how things are called or named, and in what sorts of matter this calling or naming takes place, that the problem of *use* arises formally. Tmeses, paronomasias, all sorts of anagrammatic devices that go into the so-called alphabetical paradigm—these are where the poem's *value* as a vehicle for the exposition of a philosophical doctrine is decided.

Take the lovely image of the motes of dust, the privileged "simulacrum et imago" that Lucretius recalls for Memmius at the opening of Book 2 (2.116). The sun's rays show a great dance or battle of dust particles, just where we thought there was nothing. "You will see," Rouse's translation goes, "many minute particles mingling in many ways throughout the void" [*multa minuta modis multis per inane videbis corpora misceri radiorum lumine in ipso*]. For Marx, these lines show that "the formation of combinations of atoms, their repulsion and attraction, is a noisy affair. An uproarious contest, a hostile tension, constitutes the workshop and the smithy of the world. The world in the depths of whose heart there is such tumult, is torn within... Even the sunbeam, falling on shady places, is an image of this eternal war" [*Das Hervorgehn der Bildungen aus den Atomen, ihre Repulsion und Attraktion ist geräuschvoll. Ein lärmender Kampf, eine feindliche Spannung bildet die Werkstätte und Schmiedestätte der Welt. Die Welt ist im Innern zerrissen, in deren innerstem Herzen es so tumultuarisch zugeht. Selbst der Strahl der Sonne, der in die Schattenplätze fällt, ist ein Bild dieses ewigen Krieges.*][18] "Lucretius," wrote Paul Friedländer about these lines some time ago, "has a queer inclination for the old-fashioned phrase *multis modis* or *multimodis*... Not through the nature of the sound but through the associative force of alliteration do the *m*'s become for Lucretius a badge of the atoms." After listing other examples of the alliterative use of /*m*/, Friedländer concludes a delicate analysis of the sunbeam lines remarking how Lucretius moves from the atomic /*m*/ toward "the unique and beautiful *concilia et discidiis exercita crebis*, the opposites *con*- and *dis*- joining with almost the identical root words *−ciliis, −cidiis* which by their very sound and rhythm tickle the ear as the motes glitter in the eye."[19] Friedländer's rather Baroque conceit (sound and rhythm tickling in the same way, or at the same time, in rhythm with, the glittering of sun-motes in the eye) might be rendered a little more formal, queered even further. In these verses the remarkable alliteration of the /m/ in *multa minuta modis multis* meshes with the chiasm, *multa . . . multis, minuta . . . modis,* a formal dance that is cross-hatched by the contradictory coupling of the two pairs of endings, which do not line up chiasmatically: *multa minuta,* whose *–ta* ending contrasts with the doubled *–is* ending of *modis multis.* This sort of lexical dance-and-polemic is supposed to instantiate, at the very smallest level, the great movement of thought that the passage paints for us: the analogy illuminates the movement of the atomic minima, and the component parts of the analogy, Lucretius's own poetic materials, reflect, capture, and repeat that movement. We read his verse: the sun's light picks out for us the parallel paths that letters take as they fall into order, into sense and out of it. This is indeed how Lucretius ends his description of the dust-mote analogy, saying: "So far as it goes, a small thing may give an analogy of great things, and show the tracks of knowledge" [*dumtaxat rerum magnarum parva potest res exemplare dare et vestigia notitiai*] (2.123–24). The point is methodological (this is how we should read the poem: with an eye to the *formal,* even lexical, iteration of thematic or semantic points vestigially made at the level of the verse's component elements; we should be what has come to be called *atomologists*) as well as philosophical (writing is subject to the same laws as nature—and vice versa), and it echoes Lucretius's methodological instruction to Memmius in Book 1, *verum animo satis haec vestigia parva sagaci sunt, per quae possis cognoscere cetera tute* [for a keen-scented mind, these little tracks are enough to enable you to recognize the others [other proofs] for yourself] (1.402–3).[20] Lucretius's atomic alphabetism seems even to survive translation: "Many minute particles mingling in many ways," writes Rouse; who would not admire the skill the translator shows in rendering Lucretius's alliteration?[21]

But matters immediately get ticklish. The hunting metaphor in these verses is carried through *DRN*, and speaks to the strange doubleness of the term *vestigia,* trace, footprint. The philosophical hunter finds his quarry, the truth, hidden from him, thanks to these *vestigia.* Lucretius follows the *vestigia signis* of Epicurus, at the beginning of Book 3: the fundamental philosophical use of signs is then triple: the search for the truth, the imitation of the great model, and the movement within the text from small to large. The use and *value* of poetic form lie in its practical enactment of this theory of the philosophical sign: an enactment that produces pleasure, *voluptas,* at the service of understanding, an enactment that leads from pleasure to contemplation, which flushes the truth from the thicket of false attachments and desires. Finally, the ability to track *vestigia* is what unites the philosophical text with the world of things: the poem carries the traces of the truth printed upon it as tracks are printed upon the earth, but also as motes swirl in the air, to be disclosed by slanted sunlight and attentive reading.

The term *vestigia*, however, as is already clear from these examples, is closely tied to two other circumstances, both of them threatening methodologically as well as conceptually. In the first place, *vestigia* are almost always also vestiges of certain sorts of violence. We saw the hunting metaphor; nowhere is the term the subject of greater pathetic investment than further in Book 2, where Lucretius unfolds the term with the greatest delicacy and precision. He is talking about the natural capacity—shared, he says, by "the race of men," *genus humanum*, with all other animals—to recognize differences, even within a *genus*:

> Often in front of the noble shrines of the gods a calf falls slain beside the incense-burning altars, breathing up a hot stream of blood from his own breast; but the mother bereaved wanders through the green glens, and seeks on the ground the prints marked by the cloven hooves, as she surveys all the regions... nor can tender willowgrowths, and herbage growing rich in the dew... give delight to her mind and rebuff her sudden care, nor can the sight of other calves in the happy pastures divert her mind and lighten the load of care.

> [nam saepe ante deum vitulus delubra decora
> turicremas propter mactatus concidit aras
> sanguinis expirans calidum de pectore flumen;
> at mater viridis saltus orbata peragrans   355
> novit humi pedibus vestigia pressa bisulcis,
> omnia convisens oculis loca, si queat usquam
> conspicere amissum fetum, completque querellis
> frondiferum nemus adsistens et crebra revisit
> ad stabulum desiderio perfixa iuvenci]

Vestigia, the traces that the truth leaves as it withdraws into the shelter of the thicket, the spoor followed by the active spirit, the minimal evidence left, in the material of the poetic work, of the philosophical argument it hides—these *vestigia* are (or can be) also traces of utter and irremediable loss, marks of the absence of what cannot have a substitute, that for which nothing will substitute, the utterly particular that draws our care as Narcissus does Echo's when she hopelessly follows him, *ubi Narcissum per deuia rura uagantem uidit et incaluit, sequitur uestigia furtim* (*Metamorphoses* 3.370–71).[22]

There is a second sense in which Lucretian *vestigia* hold a sort of methodological threat. Ovid again can help us to understand it, when he describes in Book 4 of the *Metamorphoses* the tracks of the wild beast, then the "thin cloaks" found by chance, first by the lioness that Thisbe flees, then by Pyramus, who *uestigia uidit in alto*, "sees hanging in the tree these signs" of his beloved's death (4.105). Lucretius has not lost sight of this double function of *vestigia* in his construction of the *value* of his work. To dwell too long on the interrupted, anaphoric /m/ in the verse I cited (2.116), *minuta modis multis*, to attend with excessive care to the literal *vestigia* that truth leaves in the text, is to suffer the fate that Pyramus will suffer, when he confuses the fate of the cloak with the fate of his beloved: one never escapes from the example, one is caught in contemplation of the "small things" and unable to reach the truth. *Not* to attend to such *vestigia*, however, means losing track of the occulted truth, or, in the lexicon that both Lucretius and Ovid employ, it means not *loving*, refusing the care of the unsubstitutable, not following the trace of the beloved, not spelling out the name of the friend or the patron in the letters of the work addressed to him. Here, for instance, a reader or a listener, Memmius, for example, who hears in the anaphoric /m/ in *multa minuta modis multis* the echo of the many /m/s in the name of the poem's addressee, Memmius, a reader or a listener who thus recognizes himself in the lexical *vestigia* of the poem, but cannot allow the pleasure of that recognition to arrest him there, to keep him attached to the mere echo of his name or to its mere lexical vestige, lest he suffer the fate of Ovid's characters, of Narcissus, for example. Here, as in all things in this poem, a suddenly ungrounded criterion applies: to attend just enough, but not too much, to the *vestigia* literally left at the level of the letter throughout *DRN*. To take pleasure in the recognition of the pedagogical function of the work—but not too much. To see just enough of oneself in its *vestigia*, but not too much.

Just enough—but not too much. This is plainly unsatisfactory as a principle of interpretation just here: how, for instance, do we read Marx's own comments regarding the dust-motes—*Selbst der Strahl der Sonne, der in die Schattenplätze fällt, ist ein Bild dieses ewigen Krieges?*[23] Is the repetition of the /s/ here another admirable case of *good* translation or good interpretation, inasmuch as it captures the repetition of the letter in Lucretius's original? Perhaps, but without also capturing the possible swerve of the letter toward the letters in the name of the poem's patron, Memmius—or toward the letter opening the name of the *Notebooks'* writer, a certain Marx. What criterion would we apply to ascertain whether a translation had or had not occurred, just here, literally?

Just enough—but not too much. The *via media* has some appeal in the domain of a certain Aristotelianism, in which measure, as μεσότης, applies to the moral virtues and vices by analogy to the quantitative measure to which mechanical forces are subject. The middle path is a weak, but plausible, description of an impoverished form of dialectical reasoning, in which a mean is set out in advance by the quantitative difference between the extremes that it negotiates.[24] In the latter case "measure" is the resultant of a "jump" whose middle path is revealed as the premise, the preexisting potentiality of quanta and qualia as such. It is the path of Daedalus, of technology, of machine translation, of mediation that puts nature at the service of civilization.

But the middle path between the firmament and the ground, between discursive and metadiscursive elements, between things and their discursive correspondents, is not the path that Lucretius draws, and neither is it the one that Marx will slowly develop and follow.

Let me return, in conclusion, and in order to suggest how Marx's early encounter with Lucretius will shape the nature of Marx's things, to his early remarks about Lucretius—that grand gesture of disavowal ("It goes without saying that but little use can be made of Lucretius," *Es versteht sich, dass Lucretius nur wenig benutzt werden kann*), the almost immediate use to which the philosopher is put. I am tempted to see here a sort of joke, if not a kind of performance: in and through Marx's reading, Marx tells us, and tells himself, Lucretius, the corpus of Lucretius's poem, the *interpretation* of the poem, will swerve just the slightest bit from what the understanding lays out before us as self-evident and self-understood, *sich verstehende*, the philosophical-poetic understanding of *DRN*, the established understanding of the work. "Little use" can indeed be made of Lucretius by the "little I," a "little I" that understands itself and what it lays out for itself in advance. (As if one said: "I, Karl Marx, am setting out for myself in these *Notebooks on Epicurean Philosophy* what was already given to me by the history of philosophy and what I am merely rediscovering—and I settle my identity, the small professional 'I' to be rendered me *by* the philosophical establishment, after I flush out from the thickets what I already know to be there, waiting, withdrawn, that 'thing' that philosophy already calls 'Lucretius.'") The "small I": when the understanding understands itself, when it makes of itself the reflexive object to which it devotes itself, when the understanding follows the spoor of a truth it recognizes in advance, a truth the understanding already grasped, which has merely withdrawn for a time from the understanding—at this sight, as at the reading of Plutarch the moralist (but *not* of Lucretius the poet), as "when we see an individual anxiously buttoned-up and clinging into himself, we involuntarily clutch at coat and clasp, make sure that we are still there, as if afraid to lose ourselves."

We can now be clearer on what this rather allegorical description might mean. For the earliest Marx the experience of "losing oneself" is simultaneously constitutive of thought, and Lucretian through and through. Lucretius is put to use in the *Notebooks* as *a way* of registering how the philosopher's "little I" fails to coincide with itself, how the writer of the notebooks swerves away from their reader, how the philosopher's "little I" fails to find what it expected as it tracks the *vestigia* of truth into the thickets, or finds what it did not expect, or finds something where it did not expect to find its quarry. We would be tempted to say that this failure expresses, in the affective register, a structural discontinuity—that neither the dance of poetical figures nor the march of philosophical propositions can be translated into or shown to correspond to, however mediately, the world of things and states of affairs. But this not correct, and not sufficient. Marx takes from his reading of Lucretius both the contingent dynamics of the poem (the register of *declinationes* that crosses theme and form in *DRN*) and the poet's persistent figuration of matter, including the matter of his poetic expression, as a substance constituted in the first place by the *Qual* of this contingent dynamics. From where I stand I can look tropically down the avenues of Marx's career and observe the transformation, or the translation, of the *Qual* of contingent dynamics into the value-form of labor. Here, too, or especially here, I will want to proceed carefully. I am at a circus again; at the glimpse of Marx's intrepid reading of Lucretius's poem I subject the principle of translation, translated this time *from* the domain where I have been tracking it *to* the historical, even biographical level, I subject the principle of translation to the contingent dynamism that Marx takes from *DRN*. I no longer face, in Marx, even in Marx's name, the spurious choice between the speculative logic of self-recognition, and the hermetic isolation of language from the world of things. I note that Lucretius is put to use in Marx's *Notebooks* as a *thing* that at once registers and produces effects of translation, without becoming a regulative *principle* of translation (or an axiom of continuity, of correspondence, of identity). I conclude: Marx first glimpsed in Lucretius, in that contingently dynamic thing—"Lucretius"—that the poem affords him, literally and formally, the nature of things wrought and to be wrought, including that "I" he would fashion over the next 40 years.

Notes

1. Karl Marx, *Notebooks on Epicurean Philosophy*, in *Marx/Engels Collected Works* (New York: International Publishers, 1927), vol. 1. The German is from *Epikureische Philosophie*, in *Marx-Engels Werke* (Berlin: Dietz Verlag, 1968), B. 40, 145. Marx reads Lucretius in the 1801 Lepizig edition, *De rerum natura libri sex*, ed. H. C. A. Eichstädt (Leipzig: Wolf, 1801), which was based on Gilbert Wakefield, Richard Bentley, and Roscoe Pound, eds., *Lucretii Cari De rerum natura libros sex, ad exemplarium mss. fidem recensitos, longe emendatiores reddidit* (London: A. Hamilton, 1796).
2. Louis Althusser, *Philosophy of the Encounter: Later Writings, 1978–87*, ed. François Matheron and Oliver Corpet, trans. G. M. Goshgarian (New York: Verso, 2006).
3. Marx, *Notebooks*, 468; *Epikureische*, 154.
4. The bibliography of works concerning Marx's reading of Lucretius is not short—and the publication of Althusser's essays on the so-called materialism of the encounter has served to complicate and considerably deepen the scholarship on the subject. I have in mind, among others, the work of Antonio Negri; in this line, I have found particularly useful a recent essay by Melinda Cooper, "Marx beyond Marx, Marx before Marx: Negri's Lucretian Critique of the Hegelian Marx," in *Reading Negri: Marxism in the Age of Empire*, ed. Pierre Lamarche, Max Rosenkrantz, and David Sherman (Chicago, IL: Open Court, 2011), 127–49. See especially Cooper's remarks on 144: "Marx's early dissertation and notebooks on Lucretius contain his most eloquent philosophical riposte to the Hegelian philosophy of time. In the Hegelian tradition, time is always mediated by the quantitative measures of space and can therefore only account for the linear fall of atoms in space—it is for this reason, contends Marx, that Hegel is unable to respond to the shock of the *clinamen*, and ultimately refigures it

in terms of the dialectic of space and time. In Lucretian philosophy, Marx discovers something that resists the very terms of Hegel's analysis—the *clinamen* introduces a swerve in the fall of atoms, a movement of absolute deviation through which time is able to diverge from the mediations of space. The *clinamen* thus allows Marx to refigure resistance in nondialectical terms, as the affirmation of an absolute and prior difference—a difference without possible mediation...Marx however (like Negri) is not satisfied with theorizing this purely disruptive notion of resistance. Once we have discovered the *clinamen* as difference without possible mediation, he insists, we need to get *beyond* here to a positive philosophy of time and constitution...we need to discover how the *clinamen* itself can become constitutive of its own world." Cooper, who focuses on the temporal aspects of *declinatio*, is in dialogue here with Francine Markovits, *Marx dans le jardin d'Epicure* (Paris: Editions de Minuit, 1974), among the most influential works on Marx's reading of Lucretius.

5. For the Latin text, see Lucretius, *Titi Lucreti Cari De Rerum Natura Libri Sex*, 3 vols., ed. Cyril Bailey (Oxford: Oxford University Press, 1947). English translations of Lucretius are generally taken from *De Rerum Natura*, trans. W. H. D. Rouse, trans. revised Martin Ferguson Smith (Cambridge, MA: Harvard University Press, 1992), with occasional modifications.

6. The standard translation of the "Theses on Feuerbach" is by William Lough, in *Marx/Engels Selected Works*, vol. 1 (Moscow: Progress, 1969), 13–15. For a searching account of the concept of "species being" that the Theses develop, see Etienne Balibar, "From Philosophical Anthropology to Social Ontology and Back: What to Do with Marx's Sixth Thesis on Feuerbach?" *Postmodern Culture* 22:3 (2012). A more extensive version of Balibar's essay appears as "Anthropologie philosophique ou Ontologie de la relation? Que faire de la 'VI Thèse sur Feuerbach'?" as a "Complément" added in 2014 to the reedition of his *La philosophie de Marx* (Paris: La Découverte/Poche, 2014), 193–250.

7. "Materialism is the born son of Britain. Even one of his great schoolmen, Duns Scotus, asked himself 'whether matter cannot think.' In performing this wonder, Duns had recourse to God's omnipotence, that is, he made theology itself preach materialism. He was, moreover, Nominalist. Nominalism is one of the main elements of the English materialists, as it is indeed the first expression of materialism in Christian Europe." ["Um dies Wunder zu bewerkstelligen, nahm er zu Gottes Allmacht seine Zuflucht, d.h. er zwang die *Theologie* selbst, den *Materialismus zu* predigen. Er war überdem *Nominalist*. Der Nominalismus findet sich als ein Hauptelement bei den *englischen* Materialisten, wie er überhaupt der *erste Ausdruck* des Materialismus ist."] "England and Materialist Philosophy," in "Further Selection from the Literary Remains of Karl Marx," trans. and annotated by Max Beer, *Labour Monthly* (August 1923): 105–13; *Aus dem literarischen nachlass von Marx und Engels*, ed. F. Mehring, vol. 2 (Stuttgart: J. H. W. Dietz, 1902), 225–40.

8. Marx, *Notebooks*, 473.

9. G. W. F. Hegel, *The Science of Logic*, trans. A. V. Miller (London: Allen & Unwin, 1969), 369. At the time when Marx is writing, the question of *declinatio* has an additional value, inasmuch as the categorical jump from quantity to quality we find in Hegel also echoes the leap or jump of faith that becomes requisite in the so-called *Spinozastreit*, in Jacobi, Mendelssohn, and others. The differences with Lucretius are notable; the most important for my purposes is the voluntarist register into which Jacobi translates what in Lucretius, and even in Leibniz, is a condition of matter and of statements regarding matter.

10. Marx, *Notebooks*, 473.

11. Marx, *Epikureische*, 163.

12. Karl Marx, *The Holy Family*, in *Marx/Engels Collected Works* (New York: International Publishers, 1927), vol. 4, 128.

13. The German is from *Marx-Engels Werke* (Berlin: Dietz Verlag, 1962), B. 2, 135. Compare from "England and Materialist Philosophy": "Of the qualities inherent in matter the foremost is motion, not only as mechanical and mathematical motion, but more as impulse, vital force, tension, or as Jacob Boehme said, pain of matter. The primitive forms of the latter are living, individualising, inherent, and essential forces, which produce specific variations."

14. Jakob Böhme, as cited in Ludwig Feuerbach's *Geschichte der neuern Philosophie von Bacon von Verulam bis Benedict Spinoza*, Ansbach, 1833, S. 161. Böhme's work has recently been enlisted in the service of philosophical environmentalism; see, for example, Joel Kovel, "A Materialism Worthy of Nature," *Capitalism Nature Socialism* 12:2 (2001): 73–84.

15. Engels underscores Marx's use of Böhme's concept as well. Here is the note he writes to the English edition of *Socialism: Utopian and Scientific* of 1892: "'Qual' is a philosophical play upon words. *Qual* literally means torture, a pain which drives to action of some kind; at the same time, the mystic Bohme puts into the German word something of the meaning of the Latin *qualitas*; his 'qual' was the activating principle arising from, and promoting in its turn, the spontaneous development of the thing, relation, or person subject to it, in contradistinction to a pain inflicted from without." Trans. Edward Aveling, in *Marx/Engels Selected Works*, vol. 3 (Moscow: Progress, 1970), 95–151.

16. For comments about Marx's translation of *declinatio* as *ausbeugen*, see Carl Schmitt, *Frieden oder Pazifismus?: Arbeiten zum Völkerrecht und zur internationalen Politik 1924–1978*, ed. Günter Maschke (Berlin: Duncker & Humblot, 2005), 934.

17. For Lucretius's use of military analogies in this part of the poem, see Phillip De Lacy, "Distant Views: The Imagery of Lucretius 2," in *Oxford Readings in Lucretius*, ed. Monica R. Gale (Oxford: Oxford University Press, 2007), esp. 148–53.

18. Marx, *Notebooks*, 472; *Epikureische*, 154. The edition that Marx uses draws a comparison between this verse and Seneca's *Natural questions* 5.1.2, "quod ex hoc intellegas licet: cum sol in aliquem clusum locum infusus est, uidemus corpuscula minima in diuersum ferri" (Seneca, *Natural Questions, Books 4–7*, trans. Thomas H. Corcoran [Cambridge, MA: Harvard University Press, 1972]). The difference with Lucretius's verses is striking. For a comprehensive discussion of this section of the poem, see Don Fowler, *Lucretius on Atomic Motion: A Commentary on De Rerum Natura 2.1–332* (Oxford: Oxford University Press, 2002), 195.

19. Paul Friedländer, "Pattern of Sound and Atomistic Theory in Lucretius," *The American Journal of Philology* 62:1 (1941): 16–34. I cite from pp. 27–28. For Memmius's role in the poem, see Gavin. B. Townend, "The Fading of Memmius," *The Classical Quarterly*, New Series, 28:2 (1978): 267–83.

20. An unimpeachable reading of the Epicurean bases of the sun-mote-*vestigia* system leads H. S. Commager Jr. to conclude that "Lucretius is committed to the discovering of *vestigia notitiai* (2.123) in every imaginable physical phenomenon," in "Lucretius's Interpretation of the Plague," in Gale, *Oxford Readings in Lucretius*, 189n. The best account I know of Lucretius's so-called atomology is Brooke Holmes's excellent "Daedala Lingua: Crafted Speech in *De Rerum Natura*," *American Journal of Philology* 126:4 (2005): 527–85. Holmes is entirely right "not to concede so readily the subordination of the phonic materiality of the word [in *De rerum natura*] to its power to provoke images and thought" and to seek to show how the "intransigence" the poem

demonstrates in "sustain[ing] a sense of synesthesia rather than a sense of coherence" itself has philosophical implications, not to mention implications for what we might call Lucretius's philosophy of language (579–80). I differ with Holmes only on the consequences of this "intransigence," which I take to be associated with a perhaps stronger account of contingency than she does.

21. In his "Repetition in Lucretius" (*Phoenix* 25:3 [Autumn 1971]: 227–36), Wayne Ingalls reviews traditional understandings of the function of repetition in the poem, especially the repetition of words—rather than letters. He argues that lexical repetition in *DRN* flows most proximately and directly from Ennius.

22. *P. Ovidi Nasonis Metamorphoses*, ed. Richard J. Tarrant (Oxford: Oxford University Press, 2004).

23. Marx and Engels, *Werke*, supplementary volume (*Ergänzungsband*) (Berlin: Dieter Verlag, 1968), 154.

24. Here, for instance, are the well-known words in which the *Nicomachean Ethics*, vol. 2.6, 1106b–1107, makes the point. The translation is Ross's: "Virtue, then, is a state of character concerned with choice, lying in a mean [μεσότης], i.e. the mean relative to us, this being determined by a rational principle, and by that principle by which the man of practical wisdom would determine it. Now it is a mean between two vices, that which depends on excess and that which depends on defect; and again it is a mean because the vices respectively fall short of or exceed what is right in both passions and actions, while virtue both finds and chooses that which is intermediate. Hence in respect of its substance and the definition which states its essence virtue is a mean, with regard to what is best and right an extreme." Aristotle, *Nicomachean Ethics*, trans. W. D. Ross (Oxford: Clarendon Press, 1908).

CHAPTER EIGHT

All Sense-Perceptions Are True: Epicurean Responses to Skepticism and Relativism

K A T J A   M A R I A   V O G T

Epicurean epistemology is infamous for the claim that all sense-perceptions are true.[1] This is how Lucretius puts it: what is perceived by any of the senses at any given time is true (*De Rerum Natura* [*DRN*] 4.499). This claim—which I shall call SPT—seems deeply misguided. It appears obvious that sense-perception can err. The plan for this chapter is to show that SPT is a sophisticated philosophical proposal and, what is more, a proposal that aims to capture the truth in relativism.[2]

SPT is presented in the midst of a series of anti-skeptical arguments.[3] And yet the skeptic is not the only opponent Lucretius has in mind. As I see it, much of the background for his position lies in Epicurean engagement with relativism. According to its best-known formulation in antiquity—in Plato's *Theaetetus*—relativism embraces the view that all sense-perceptions are true. Epicurean epistemology, as I shall argue, aims to depart from relativism while preserving its insights.

The most difficult question in interpreting SPT is how to understand 'true.' In which sense do Epicureans employ the predicate 'true' when they say that all sense-perceptions are true? Scholars currently tend to favor a propositional reading: 'true' is used in SPT as it is used when propositions are evaluated as true or false. They tend to reject an existential reading, according to which 'true' means something like 'existent.' By drawing on the comparison with relativism, I argue that both readings are misguided. SPT, I propose, is the claim that sense-perception is *factive*. Before I defend my reading (sections titled "Truth," "Perception Is Factive," and "The *Theaetetus*"), an outline of Lucretius's arguments is needed (sections titled "Lucretius's Anti-Skeptical Arguments" and "The Criterial Argument and the Parity Argument").

Lucretius's Anti-Skeptical Arguments

SPT is part of an extended anti-skeptical argument in Book 4 of *De Rerum Natura*.[4] The passage occurs within a section that can plausibly be said to begin at 4.469:

> If then someone holds that nothing is known, he also doesn't know
> whether this can be known, for he acknowledged to know nothing.
> Against him then I give up to fight about this matter,
> who has placed himself with his head in his own footprints. (4.469–72)

Lucretius's skeptic says, quite naively, that nothing can be known. This claim is inherently problematic.[5] An unqualified assertion is plausibly understood as implying that the speaker takes herself to know what she is saying. So how can she claim that nothing is known? She would invite the question of whether she knows this—that nothing can be known.[6] Perhaps Lucretius assumes that in some commonsensical way one can conceive of the skeptic as someone who says "nothing can be known," or perhaps he does not care whether any particular thinker indeed holds this view. Whatever the case may be, Lucretius does not respond to the skeptic by arguing that, insofar as there is sense-perceptual knowledge—or some other kind of knowledge—there is knowledge. Instead he defends sense-perception as a basic kind of access to the world. This is a serious project, whether or not the skeptic who is invoked is a straw man. SPT, the claim I am interested in here, is put forward as part of it. Let me thus go through Lucretius's arguments, asking whether any of the points he makes help to explain and defend SPT.

Notions Argument (4.473–79): Lucretius argues that if we could not trust the senses, then we would not even have the notions of truth and knowledge.[7] He asks the skeptic how, if she has never seen anything true, she knows what knowing and not-knowing are (474–75). As Lucretius sees it, the notion of truth was first created by the senses.

Impossibility Argument (4.479): In the same vein, Lucretius suggests that it is, in principle, impossible to conceive of any attempt to refute the senses. Our access to the world is primarily and fundamentally via the senses—the idea that we could attempt to step outside of this is absurd. Life is so deeply rooted in sense-perception that the very idea of calling sense-perception into question is ultimately incomprehensible.

Priority Argument (4.483–85): Sense-perception is the beginning of cognitive activity, and thus the root of thinking. Thinking derives from or stems from sense perception (483–84). Thus, if sense-perceptions are not true, how could thinking be true (485)?

Parity Argument (4.486–98): Each sense—vision, hearing, and so on-has its own domain and power (*potestas, vis*), and insofar as it does, the senses cannot interfere with each other. Similarly, Lucretius argues that no sense can correct itself; that is, for example, no particular vision can correct another vision. All sense-perceptions have the same standing. SPT is presented as following from this consideration (499).[8] Here is the quote, together with the preceding lines:

> And therefore it is necessarily the case
> that the senses are not such that they can compel each other.
> Nor will they be able, each for itself, to correct itself,
> for one must always have equal trust.
> Therefore what is perceived by one of them at a given time is true.
>   (4.498–99)

Criterial Argument (513–21):[9] Lucretius ends his series of anti-skeptical arguments by appealing to the criterial role of sense-perception. This is a core Epicurean commitment: sense-perceptions are criteria of truth. If the senses were false, Lucretius argues, our cognitive situation would resemble a house that is built with crooked measuring sticks and ill-adjusted scales. If such tools are used while the foundations of the building are erected, the whole building will be a mess, in danger of collapsing.

What do these arguments, from the immediate context of SPT, achieve? Lucretius describes the senses as our primary kind of access to the world, so much so that it is not even clear what it would mean to call them into question. However, one might hold this view without holding the claim that every *particular* sense-perception is true. One could agree with the Epicureans that sense-perception is basic to concept-formation and our ability to think. And one could argue that concept-acquisition is such as to secure access to the world, so that knowledge is possible. This line of argument is widespread in Hellenistic philosophy, shared by the Stoics and Epicureans. SPT goes beyond it in characterizing every single sense-perception as true. Lucretius's anti-skeptical arguments do not seem to offer much explanation of this far-reaching claim. Or, at least, they are so condensed that they need unpacking. As I see it, the Parity Argument and the Criterial Argument contain the seeds of a rationale for SPT, but they need to be explained further for this to become clear.[10]

The Criterial Argument and the Parity Argument

Consider first the Criterial Argument. Sense-perception, Lucretius says, must play the role of a criterion. According to Epicurean doctrine, sense-perceptions are criteria of truth (DL 10.31).[11] Notably, they do not serve to assess each other. Instead, our judgments are to be assessed in their light. A theory that agrees with sense-perception gains support; a theory that is in conflict with sense-perception must be dismissed. Sense-perception can play this criterial role because it is arational (DL 10.31). Perceptions are thought of as deliverances of the senses. We are aware of them, and in that sense they are 'in the mind.' But they do not involve the cognitive activity of judging. This is of great importance to SPT: error or falsity is germane to judgment or belief-formation.[12] The claim that the senses are arational in the sense of not involving any judgment-activity translates into a further claim, namely, that the senses are truthful: they do not lie. The senses are mere receptacles and reporters of content.[13] They are passively affected and do not 'add' or 'subtract' anything to the perception: they do not lie insofar as they do not alter the perception.[14]

And yet, the Epicureans locate sense-perception in the sense organs. Put somewhat crudely, this means that the eyes see and the ears hear, rather than the cognizer seeing with her eyes and hearing with her ears. To understand the upshot of the Epicurean position, it is helpful to compare it to two views discussed in Platonic dialogues—views that I here present in a highly schematic fashion, setting aside any number of controversial interpretive questions about the relevant passages.

First, one might think that the sense organs are responsible for perceiving. Qua bodily organs, they are deficient tools: their physicality negatively affects the quality of the input. This idea is discussed in the *Phaedo* (64–68).[15] The eyes, here, are described as windows that the soul uses to glance at the outside. But, figuratively speaking, larger windows made from clearer glass would afford better vision. Human eyes have a particular physiology. This physiology not only shapes how we see, but also affects it in such a way as to 'blur' things by its very physicality. Second, one might go to the other extreme and argue that it is misguided to place sense-perception in any important way in bodily organs. They are tools, but the real activity lies with the mind. Sense-perception consists in sense-perceptual judgments, and it is thus a form of thinking. This view is discussed in the *Theaetetus* (184a–186e).[16] The Epicurean account of the senses as non-falsifying deliverers is, as it were, in between. It ascribes the central role in sense-perception to the senses rather than to thought, but it does not see the senses as sources of alterations—it views them as neutral messengers.

Add to this that, according to the Parity Argument, there is no context that alters perception such as to make it erroneous. Consider external circumstances, say, of one's position vis-à-vis an object: one can be far away from a tower or nearby. Being far away, the Epicureans argue, is not a falsifying circumstance. To think so, they say, is to make the very mistake that one would make if one thought that one could not hear the sound of a bell properly because one did not climb inside the bell (SE M7.206–10, LS 16E). This comparison strikes me as particularly helpful in understanding the gist of the Epicurean proposal. The bell example suggests that, in ordinary life, we assume that things will look differently from different angles and sound differently from different distances. We find this rather obvious and unproblematic. It is not a reason to consider any of these perceptions false.[17] We still think that there are, say, better and worse 'viewing conditions' or 'hearing conditions.' But it is not as straightforward as one might suspect to explain what 'better' and 'worse' mean here. In one context— say, the acoustics of a concert hall—audio conditions are better if a certain ideal of musical sound can be achieved. In another context—say, wanting to judge whether a tower is round or square—viewing conditions are best when we stand at a distance that allows us to see the object as a whole (not too close) and still sharply (not too far away).[18] None of this, however, disputes the Epicurean proposal. The music does sound off in a room with bad acoustics; still, the sound is real and perceived as what it is. It is true that the tower looks round from a distance, and that is a relevant fact about it.[19] Things look, sound, etc., differently from different angles, distances, and so on. These different perceptions are not such that one would ideally identify the one that is best. Instead, all of them provide us with information about the object—for example, how it looks when you look at it from a distance, or how it looks when you come so close that you no longer see the object as a whole.

Consider next 'internal circumstances,' states of the cognizer and their potential effect on her perceptions. Lucretius and Epicurus accept an idea that is already formulated in Plato's *Theaetetus*: dreams and the visions of sick or mad people do not count as examples of false perceptions.[20] In the *Theaetetus*, this view is developed as a component of relativism. The relativist finds it arbitrary to prefer one state (say, being awake or healthy) over another (say, being asleep or sick). Similarly, dream-images and hallucinations are simply perceptions in Epicurean epistemology, on par with other perceptions. As Epicurus puts it, Orestes's perception when he seemed to see the Furies was true, for he was moved by images that really existed. His mind jumped to a false belief, namely, that the Furies were solid bodies, but his perception was true (SE M 8.63).

Lucretius's anti-skeptical arguments, if unpacked with the help of other evidence on Epicurean epistemology, defend the claims that all sense-perceptions are on a par and that, thereby, they serve as criteria of truth. However, it is one thing to say that sense-perceptions are criteria of truth, and another thing to say that they (themselves) are true. We need to hear more about the sense in which Lucretius calls sense-perceptions true.

Truth

How should one understand the predicate 'true' in the claim that all sense-perceptions are true?[21] Gisela Striker, Stephen Everson, and Elisabeth Asmis see the puzzle as follows: truth-predicates cannot attach to sense-perceptions. Truth-predicates, it is assumed, must attach to something like propositions. Accordingly, the puzzle would be resolved if the Epicureans talked about the truth of propositions. Absent any texts that explicitly support this, scholars are content with a related idea: the truth-predicates could be applied to representational states, on the assumption that representational states have propositional counterparts.[22] It is arguably not far-fetched to assume that, in Hellenistic epistemology, perception is thought to involve representational states.[23] Suppose we envisage such states and corresponding propositions, say "this looks like a round tower to me now." And suppose that, according to the Epicurean proposal, the corresponding proposition is the bearer of the truth-value. Then, it is argued, the problem is resolved. We have found a respectable bearer of the value 'true.'

Interpreters readily admit that the sources are ambiguous and that there is a competing reconstruction. Their proposal stipulates (what can be called) a propositional sense of 'true' in SPT. A widely recognized alternative to this view is an existential sense of 'true.' Epicurus's core argument is that perceptions are true insofar as each impression is the product of something existent (M 8.63).[24] An existent atomic image causes the perception. Moreover, and interpreters also grant this point, there is a Greek usage that takes 'true' in an existential sense, so that 'true' means 'real' or 'existent.'[25] A version of the existential reading—the version that, for example, Everson engages with—formulates it as follows: SPT means that sense-perceptions exist. Call this the simple existential reading. It does not satisfy interpreters, and rightly so. Arguably, no one denies that sense-perceptions exist: the simple existential reading does not generate a controversial thesis. SPT, however, is put forward and responded to as highly controversial.

Interpreters also advance a positive argument for the propositional reading. As Everson points out, the Epicureans hold two theses: "all perceptions are true" and "beliefs are true or false" (M. 7.210).[26] Everson, Asmis, and Striker argue that the Epicureans employ 'true' in the same sense in both domains. The existential reading, however, does not allow for a plausible understanding of "beliefs are true or false." It must be concluded, so the argument proceeds, that the Epicureans employ 'true' as one of two truth-values, true and false, which attach to something like propositions. This is presumably the only reading that makes sense of the claim about beliefs. Interpreters conclude that therefore 'true' must also be employed in a propositional sense in SPT. That is, according to widespread scholarly views, the existential reading—or what I call the simple existential reading—is to be dismissed as generating an uninteresting thesis, and the propositional reading is accepted as making sense of the comparison between sense-perceptions and beliefs.

However, though Epicurus compares sense-perception and belief, it is implausible that 'true' is used in precisely the same way in both contexts.[27] If this is the interpretive suggestion, the argument is in danger of turning the debate on its head. In the thesis that beliefs are true or false, 'true' is a success-term. In forming a belief, one aims to form a true belief. If one's belief is, in fact, true, then one has succeeded in doing so. It is crucial to this enterprise that one could also fail, thus forming a false belief. In claiming that beliefs are true or false, the Epicureans are pointing to the activity of judgment, which, in their view, can add to or subtract from the perception, thus introducing falsity (M 7.210).

In discussing propositions or representational counterparts of propositions, interpreters move away quite significantly from the discussion of belief. The truth and falsity of propositions are, arguably, studied in logic or philosophy of language. If beliefs are characterized as true or false, this tends to be part of what we today call normative epistemology.[28] It is part of a discussion of *how to think*—how to judge and not to judge, which criteria to employ in forming judgments, and so on. These kinds of questions are a central preoccupation of Hellenistic epistemology, including Epicurean epistemology. Contrary to what recent interpreters assume, with respect to belief, truth is not well explained as the notion one uses when speaking about truth-values of propositions. Instead, the relevant notion of truth includes the idea of truth as an *aim*.

The currently widespread reading is thus doubly problematic: it does not offer a compelling analysis of the claim that beliefs are true or false, and its assumption that 'true' is used in the same sense in SPT and in "beliefs are true or false" is misleading. If this were the case, it would imply that sense-perceptions can be false, which is denied in SPT. Moreover, to understand 'true' in the sense in which it attaches to propositions moves rather far away from the pervasive references in the relevant texts to the existence of atomic images and the perceptions they cause. Accordingly, a third interpretive option is needed, one that goes beyond the simple existential reading and that does not stipulate that 'true' is used as a success-term in SPT, as it is in "beliefs are true or false."

Perception Is Factive

To find such an option, consider the question of whether there are other things that are characterized as true even though each instance is true and could not be false. There is an obvious candidate: knowledge. Knowledge is unerring, as Plato puts this premise in the *Theaetetus* (186c–e). The claim arguably goes back as far as Parmenides, who associates being, knowledge, and truth: knowledge is of what is, and "truth accompanies knowledge."[29] This is a deep insight about knowledge, one that has not been disputed since. If one knows that p, it follows that p is true. One cannot know something that is not the case: what is known is a fact. This idea is today sometimes expressed as the thesis that the verb 'to know' is factive.

To say that knowledge is factive is to use a formulation that avoids the perplexity of assigning the truth-predicate to something that could not be false. The thesis "all pieces of knowledge are true" is one that, as far as I can see, no one holds—not because people think that knowledge can be false, but because people think that the relevant intuition is better expressed by saying "knowledge is unerring" (Plato) or "truth accompanies knowledge" (Parmenides) or "knowledge is factive" (contemporary epistemology). In colloquial terms, one may perhaps say that all knowledge is true. But after philosophical reflection one would reformulate this claim, saying, for example, that knowledge by its very nature is factive.

Perhaps Lucretius is putting forward the claim that perception is factive. SPT might be reconstructed as saying that every sense-perception is *of what is* and therefore is *true*. This is my proposal: 'true' in "all sense-perceptions are true" means 'factive.'[30] To see the advantages of this view, return to the simple existential reading, according to which SPT means that all sense-perceptions exist. This reading neglects what Epicurus says, namely, that perceptions are true insofar as each impression is the product of something existent (M 8.63). That is, Epicurus says here that the cause of perceptions exists, not that perceptions exist. A more sophisticated reading that takes seriously Epicurean concern with 'what is real' must begin with the question of what precisely exists: the sense-perception? its cause? or both?

To answer this question, turn to Epicurus's explanation of the truth of pleasure and pain, which he claims is analogous to the truth of sense-perception. Pleasure and pain "come about from certain agents and in accordance with these agents," pleasure from pleasant things and pain from painful things (M 7.203). There exist things that are productive of pleasure and others that are productive of pain. The former necessarily produce pleasure, the latter pain. The same applies to sense-perception. "That which produces each of them is always perceived entirely and, as perceived, cannot bring about the perception unless it is in truth such as it appears" (M 7.203).[31] Accordingly, the answer must be "both": the cause of the sense-perception exists and the sense-perception exists. Together, this accounts for the truth of sense perceptions. Every sense perception is caused by something that exists, and it is of that which causes it. This is, I submit, precisely the thought that sense-perception is factive. A sense perception is generated by some atomic image, and it is this atomic image that is perceived.[32]

The factive reading of 'true' meets several constraints of interpretation. First, it reads 'true' in such a way that what is characterized as true is not thereby something that could also be false. Second, it makes sense of the comparison with beliefs. "All perceptions are true" translates into the claim that perception is factive; "beliefs are true or false" can translate into the claim that belief is not factive. Third, it takes seriously Epicurean concern with the 'real' or 'existent.' Fourth, it generates a significant epistemological thesis—as significant as the analogous claim about knowledge. Fifth, it fits well with the upshot of the Parity and Criterial Arguments that Lucretius discusses. Sense-perceptions are the starting points of cognitive activity; judgments and theories are to be tested by whether they are in agreement with them. If sense-perception is factive, it plausibly supplies us with such starting-points.

The *Theaetetus*

To assess further whether the factive reading is compelling, I turn to Hellenistic engagement with Plato's *Theaetetus*. The *Theaetetus* has long been recognized as a text that influenced Hellenistic epistemology greatly.[33] It offers a host of arguments that became crucial to Hellenistic discussions about perception and that relate immediately to the questions discussed above. Accordingly, it seems rather plausible that Epicureans engage with some of Plato's arguments, if not as readers of the *Theaetetus* then as participants in debates about the ideas that are discussed in the dialogue.

In Part I of the *Theaetetus*, the interlocutors discuss the hypothesis that knowledge is perception, an idea that is of obvious relevance to my proposed line of thought. If every instance of perception is an instance of knowing, so the argument goes in the *Theaetetus*, then an account of perception must be formulated on which every perception is true. If perception is knowledge, Socrates says, "then, [it] is always of what is, and unerring" (152c).

In Plato, "perception is knowledge" is taken to be a thesis that interprets Protagoras's claim that "man is the measure."[34] That is, "each perception is true" is seen as a component of the larger proposal that every appearance—every case of "it appears to A that p"—is true, and this larger proposal counts as relativism. Now, one possible reaction to Plato's *Theaetetus* is the following: one could argue that Plato, by extending "each perception is true" to "each appearance is true" arrives at an unpalatable position, global relativism, a position that he goes on to reject. But suppose one were to stop at the initial intuition captured by the well-known Cold Wind Example: when I am cold, then there is a fact of the matter—a fact about how the wind feels to me—and my perception is true by virtue of this fact.[35] Is not this an insight about perception worth holding on to, even though the larger relativist perspective is flawed? Moreover, this example may lead one to think about the two components mentioned earlier: my state of being cold is real, and if it is, then it would appear that it must be *of* something real—perhaps a 'cold-wind-for-me'—that causes it. This is one of the ways in which Plato thinks through the implications of relativism.[36] As I see it, this cluster of ideas is precisely the motivation behind SPT.

SPT offers an alternative to relativism that, nevertheless, aims to capture the insights expressed in the Cold Wind Example. It says that all perceptions are true, not that all perceptions are knowledge. By claiming that perception is arational, Epicurean epistemology denies one move that is crucial to relativism, namely, that access to the truth implies *knowing* the truth. It is one thing to have a perception that, qua perception, is true; it is another thing to formulate a judgment and know the content of the perception. That is, Epicurean epistemology aims to capture the insight expressed in the Cold Wind Example without thereby accepting that, in such cases, anything is known.

At one point in the discussion of Protagoras's Measure Doctrine, Plato toys with an interesting concession to relativism. As a theory about all appearances or all judgments, relativism fails in multiple ways. But Socrates temporarily grants that there might be some truth to it. The claim that "what seems to A is true-for-A," he suggests, might be plausible for sense-perceptions in the present tense (171d–172c and 177c–179c).[37] It seems to be true for "things like hot, dry, sweet," and so on, but not insofar as the future is concerned. It seems true only insofar as we consider what seems hot, dry, sweet, and so on, to a given cognizer now. In this context, Socrates introduces a notion that gains much importance in Hellenistic philosophy, and it is Epicurus who is credited with making it central: the notion of a *kriterion* ("criterion," 178b). Socrates says that Protagoras's doctrine seems to hold for white and heavy, and so on, as perceived in the present. In these cases, he says, people have the *kriterion* in themselves. Indeed, it seems as if Epicurus could have lifted this claim directly from the Platonic text.

A restricted relativism might hold for present-tense sense-perception. Or perhaps, given this restriction, the relevant position might not be properly described as relativism; it might instead be best described as a forerunner of Epicurean epistemology. Lucretius's claim, that "every sense-perception at any given time is true" (SPT) contains the temporal qualifier from Socrates's proposal in the *Theaetetus*. Sense-perceptual judgments about the future—say, "the sound of the trumpet will be loud"—are already a different matter. Such judgments are, indeed, judgments, not perceptions, and they can be false. But "this sound is loud [to me, now]" cannot be false if thought or uttered sincerely. If limited to the domain of present tense sense-perception, the claim that each perception is true is a candidate for being taken seriously.

For Plato, the point that relativism might hold for present-tense perceptions is only a preliminary concession. In the *Theaetetus*, it does not hold up to scrutiny. It fails because it misconstrues perception as if perception were a nonrational activity, something taking place between objects and sense-organs, rather than objects and cognitive faculties. That is, its rejection hangs on Plato's rejection of a general picture of sense-perception as arational. But as we have seen, Epicurean epistemology embraces precisely this picture: for Epicurus and Lucretius, sense-perceptions do not involve any judgment-activity, and it is crucially for this reason that every present perception is true.

Conclusion

From the point of view of Epicurean philosophy, the insight that each perception is factive—what is perceived is the case and thereby the perception is true—is too important to be glossed over. In the *Theaetetus*, this insight motivates relativism. Relativism goes too far, according to both Plato and the Epicureans. Still, from the point of view of Epicurean epistemology, relativism justly takes an interest in the kind of phenomenon that the Cold Wind Example captures. When I say "the wind is cold," I say something that is true; and implicitly, I mean it to refer to me qua cognizer and to the present tense—"the wind is cold for me now." Present-tense perceptions are interesting because they occur in such a way as to make talk about them being true plausible, *and* in such a way as to make talk about them being false implausible. This, I think, is the Epicureans' truth in relativism.

The factive reading has the great advantage of recognizing Lucretius's argument as a rather good one. Recall that leading up to SPT Lucretius explains how all sense-perceptions are on a par, the point I called the Parity Argument. This point turns out to be crucial to the more complicated story in the background of the Epicureans' commitment to the truth of all sense-perceptions. All sense-perceptions are deliverances of the senses, and all of them are of something that is; this is why they are factive, and in that sense true.[38]

Notes

1. Important discussions of this claim include Gisela Striker, "Epicurus on the Truth of Sense-Impressions," *Archiv für Geschichte der Philosophie* 59 (1977): 125–42, reprinted in Gisela Striker, *Essays in Hellenistic Epistemology and Ethics* (Cambridge: Cambridge University Press, 1996), 77–91; David Sedley, *Lucretius and the Transformation of Greek Wisdom* (Cambridge: Cambridge University Press, 1998); Elisabeth Asmis, *Epicurus' Scientific Method* (Cornell: Cornell University Press, 1984) and Elisabeth Asmis, "Epicurean Empiricism," in *The Cambridge Companion to Epicureanism*, ed. James Warren (Cambridge: Cambridge University Press, 2009), 84–104; David K. Glidden, "'Sensus' and Sense Perception in the 'De rerum natura,'" *California Studies in Classical Antiquity* 12 (1979): 155–81; James Warren, "Lucretius and Greek Philosophy," in *The Cambridge Companion to Lucretius*, ed. Stuart Gillespie and Phillip Hardie (Cambridge: Cambridge University Press, 2007), 19–32; Stephen Everson, "Epicurus on the Truth of the Senses," in *Epistemology*, ed. Stephen Everson (Cambridge: Cambridge University Press, 1990), 161–83; Fritz Jürss, *Die epikureische Erkenntnistheorie* (Berlin: Akademie-Verlag, 1991); C. C. W. Taylor, "'All Perceptions Are True,'" in *Doubt and Dogmatism*, ed. Malcolm Schofield et al. (Oxford: Oxford University Press, 1980), 105–24; Paul Vander Waerdt, "Colotes and the Epicurean Refutation of Skepticism," *Greek, Roman and Byzantine Studies* 30 (1989): 225–67.
2. I borrow this phrase, the "truth in relativism," from Bernard Williams's famous paper "The Truth in Relativism," *Proceedings of the Aristotelian Society* 75 (1974–75): 215–28. The expression can serve as a catchphrase for critical responses to relativism, responses that, nevertheless, concede that relativism makes some philosophically worthwhile proposals or addresses philosophically perplexing phenomena.
3. Throughout the chapter, I will be concerned with a subsection of Book 4 in Lucretius's *DRN*, 4.469–521. Other contributors to this book, most notably Jacques Lezra and Philip Mitsis, explore the reception of Lucretius among modern philosophers such as Locke, Marx, and others. My chapter aims to take this one step further, asking how Lucretius's views about sense-perception relate to contemporary discussions in epistemology. I hope to demonstrate that the relevant portion of *DRN* contains arguments about sense-perception and relativism that we can take seriously. Like the modern philosophers referenced in other essays, philosophers today have reason to turn to Lucretius's writings.

4. I agree with David Sedley's outline of the sections of Book 4 (Sedley, *Lucretius*, 150); 26–238: existence and mobility of images; 239–468: vision, truth, and falsity; 469–521: refutation of skepticism; 522–721: the other senses; 722–822: thought; 823–57: critique of teleology; 858–1287: nutrition, motion, sleep, dreams, sex. For the Latin text, see Lucretius, *De Rerum Natura*, 3 vols., Books 1–4, commentary by Cyril Bailey (Oxford: Oxford University Press, 1947). All translations, unless otherwise noted, are my own.

5. It is so obviously problematic that it was already improved upon by the Pre-Socratic Metrodorus of Chios, a student of Democritus. Metrodorus says at the beginning of his book *On Nature*: "None of us knows anything, not even this, whether we know or we do not know; nor do we know what 'to not know' or 'to know' are, nor on the whole, whether anything is or is not" (Cicero, *Acad.* 2.73, trans. Mi-Kyoung Lee, "Antecedents in Early Greek Philosophy," in *The Cambridge Companion to Ancient Scepticism*, ed. Richard Bett (Cambridge: Cambridge University Press, 2010), 13–35, 19 = DK 70B1 [H. Diels, and W. Kranz, eds., *Die Fragmente der Vorsokratiker*, 3 vols. (Berlin: Weidmann, 1996). [= DK; hereafter cited as DK]; SE M 7.48, 87–88 [*Sextus Empiricus: Against the Logicians*, ed. and trans. R. Bett (Cambridge: Cambridge University Press, 2005). [=SE; hereafter cited as SE or Sextus]; Eusebius, *Praep. evang.* 14.19.9 [*Eusebius Werke, Band 8: Die Praeparatio evangelica*, ed. K. Mras. *Die griechischen christlichen Schriftsteller*, vols. 43.1 and 43.2 (Berlin: Akademie Verlag, 1954 [43.1], 1956 [43.2]).

6. If Lucretius intends to address the skepticism of those who wrote during the second and first century BC, he fails. Here are some dates that may help situate Lucretius: Pyrrho (360–270); Epicurus (341–270); Arcesilaus, the first Academic skeptic (316–241); Aenesidemus, a major Pyrrhonian skeptic (first century BC); Lucretius (99–55). In general, I suspect that skepticism develops more in exchange with Epicurean epistemology than it is standardly assumed. But Epicurus does not yet have sophisticated skeptics as interlocutors. Skepticism was significantly advanced by the need to reply to Epicurean and Stoic challenges. At the time when Lucretius writes there are sophisticated kinds of skepticism to respond to.

7. "You will find that by the senses was first created / the notion of truth; and that the senses cannot be refuted." [*Invenies primis ab sensibus esse creatam / notitiam veri neque sensus posse refelli.*] (478–79); *notitiam veri* is ambiguous: it could mean "notion of truth" or "acquaintance with truth." The context suggests that Lucretius wants to cover both ideas. This argument is in line with what appears to be an Epicurean argument against skepticism, namely, the charge that skeptics cannot have concepts and accordingly cannot think. Cf. Katja Maria Vogt, "Skepticism and Concepts: Can the Skeptic Think?," Chapter 6 in K. M. Vogt, *Belief and Truth: A Skeptic Reading of Plato* (New York: Oxford University Press, 2012), 140–57.

8. Sextus ascribes SPT to Epicurus (M 8.63), but there is no explicit version of it in the surviving letters.

9. I skip some famous lines, because they are, for current purposes, a distraction. They contain an Apraxia Argument (500–12): Lucretius asks his reader to suppose that an object looks square from nearby and round from a distance. Even if one were to make a false judgment, ascribing one's perception of the distant object to a false cause—a round object causing the perception—one would be better off, in Lucretius's view, than if one were to generally mistrust the senses. Life and safety depend on trust in the senses.

10. Cf. Epicurus's defense of the truth of sense-perceptions: "All sensation, he says, is arational and does not accommodate memory...Nor does there exist that which

can refute sensations: neither can like sense refute like, because of their equal validity nor unlike unlike, since they are not discriminatory of the same things; nor can reason, since all reason depends on the senses; nor can one individual sensation refute another, since they all command our attention. And also the fact of sensory recognitions confirms the truth of sensations. And our seeing and hearing are facts, just as having pain is...The figments of madmen and dreaming are true. For they cause movement, whereas the non-existent does not move anything"] (DL 10.31–32 [Diogenes Laertius, *Lives of Eminent Philosophers*, with an English translation by R. D. Hicks, 2 vols. (Cambridge, MA: Harvard University Press; London: Wm. Heinemann, 1958–59); vol. 1, 1959 [=DL; hereafter cited as DL]; trans. LS 16B [A. A. Long, and D. N. Sedley, eds. and trans., *The Hellenistic Philosophers*, 2 vols. (Cambridge: Cambridge University Press, 1987) [=LS; hereafter cited as LS].

11. Asmis, "Epicurean Empiricism" focuses on Epicurean criteria of truth. Cf. Epicurus, *Principal Doctrines* 23 [=LS 16D]: "If you argue against all your sensations, you will then have no criterion to declare any of them false."

12. Epicurus says: "There is no error in sense-perception" (SE M 8.9).

13. Lucretius uses the same word, *sensus*, for sense-perception in general, for sense-organs (physiologically conceived), and for their deliverances (the perceptions); cf. Glidden, "'Sensus' and Sense Perception," 155. Accordingly, it is not always evident that "all sense-perceptions are true" and "the senses are truthful" are two theses—but they are. It is likely that Epicurus can be credited with the view that the senses never lie (*Lucullus* 26.82; Cicero, *Akademische Abhandlungen Lucullus*, ed. and trans. Christoph Schäublin [Hamburg: Felix Meiner Verlag, 1998]). Moreover, it is likely that Epicurus took that claim to be immediately related to another claim, one that is rather close to SPT, namely, that if one perception were false, then none would be true. According to Cicero, Epicurus says, for this reason, that all of the senses give a "true report" (*De natura Deorum* 1.25, 70). Cicero, *De Natura Deorum. Academica*, with an English translation by H. Rackham (London: William Heinemann, 1933).

14. Everson argues that, for Epicurus, this point provides the rationale for SPT: "What allows Epicurus his confidence in the truth of all perceptions is the fact that the processes involved in perception are such that external objects 'imprint their natures' on the senses: what perception is produced is entirely determined by the nature of the external object which gives rise to it by affecting the sense-organ" ("Epicurus on the Truth of the Senses," 173–74).

15. *Plato: Complete Works*, ed. John M. Cooper (Indianapolis, IN: Hackett, 1997).

16. Cf. Michael Frede, "Observations on Perception in Plato's Later Dialogues," and John Cooper, "Plato on Sense-Perception and Knowledge (*Theaetetus* 184–86)," both in *Plato 1: Metaphysics and Epistemology*, ed. Gail Fine (Oxford: Oxford University Press, 1999), 355–76 and 377–83.

17. Cf. Lucretius 4.379–86 on shadows and light (LS 16H).

18. The claim that all sense perceptions are true is compatible with the claim that, for a given purpose, there are good viewing (hearing, etc.) conditions. The sound of a bell does not, *simpliciter*, sound right from a given distance, though it can sound right for calling people to lunch, or for patients in hospitals calling a nurse when they need assistance, and so on.

19. Architects tend to design buildings such that, from different angles and distances, they generate different 'vistas.' This is not a misleading side effect, occurring when viewers are not in the 'right' place vis-à-vis the building; it is essential to good architecture.

20. Epicurus was firmly committed to this view. Cf. DL 10.32 [= LS 15F] and Plutarch *adv. Col.* 1109B; 1121 D, E; 1124 B. Plutarch, *Reply to Colotes in Defense of the Other Philosophers*, in *Plutarch: Moralia*, vol. 14, trans. Benedict Einarson and Phillip H. de Lacy (Cambridge, MA: Harvard University Press, 1967), 151–315.

21. Asmis argues that there is a correspondence between the appearance (as a mental representation) and the influx of atoms ("Epicurean Empiricism," 94, n.19). Asmis writes: "All perceptions are true in that they correspond to something from the outside; in addition, we are able to perceive enduring external objects" ("Epicurean Empiricism," 85), and "whatever appears in perception corresponds to something that enters us from outside; in every case, therefore, we perceive something from the outside as it really is" ("Epicurean Empiricism," 95).

22. Say, if the tower looks round to me, Striker thinks that a proposition corresponds to it, namely, "this looks like a round tower" ("Epicurus on the Truth of Sense-Impressions," 90). This kind of proposition—that is, one that refrains from judging how things are, merely capturing what Epicurus calls *to paron*, what is 'present'— might plausibly always be true.

23. For example, Stoic impressions (*phantasiai*) seem to be of this sort. For current purposes, the question of how precisely representational states are thought of in Epicurean epistemology need not be pursued.

24. At M 8.9, Sextus says that, according to Epicurus, it makes no difference whether you call something "true" (*alêthes*) or "existent" (*huparchon*).

25. Rist argues that "a real event takes place in the act of sensing" (John M. Rist, *Epicurus: An Introduction* [Cambridge: Cambridge University Press, 1972], 19–20). Striker, "Epicurus on the Truth of Sense-Impressions," says that the interpretation that "true" means "real" is, at the time, the standard view in the literature.

26. Everson, "Epicurus on the Truth of the Senses," 167. Cf. SE M 7.203.

27. If the report in Sextus Empiricus is to be trusted, Epicurus says that sense-perception and belief are 'two corresponding things' (Ἐπίκουρος δὲ δυεῖν ὄντων τῶν συζυγούντων ἀλλήλοις πραγμάτων, φαντασίας καὶ [τῆς] δόξης) (M 7.203). However, this need not mean more than that they are to be compared with each other, and that there is a sequence and connection to explore: sense-perception comes first and belief, which is in danger of adding or subtracting something, second.

28. On this distinction, cf. Vogt, "Why Beliefs Are Never True: A Reconstruction of Stoic Epistemology," Chapter 7 in Vogt, *Belief and Truth*, 158–82.

29. "But come, I will tell you—preserve the account when you hear it— / the only roads of enquiry there are to be thought of: / one, that it is and cannot not be, / is the path of persuasion (for truth accompanies it)" (B 2.1–4, trans. Jonathan Barnes, ed., *Early Greek Philosophy*, 2nd ed. [New York: Penguin Books, 2001], 80, with changes) [εἰ δ' ἄγ' ἐγὼν ἐρέω, κόμισαι δὲ σὺ μῦθον ἀκούσας, / αἵπερ ὁδοὶ μοῦναι διζήσιός εἰσι νοῆσαι· / ἡ μὲν ὅπως ἔστιν τε καὶ ὡς οὐκ ἔστι μὴ εἶναι, / Πειθοῦς ἐστι κέλευθος (Ἀληθείηι γὰρ ὀπηδεῖ)]. Assuming that "persuasion" is the domain of knowledge, the opening lines in Parmenides's poem associate *truth, knowledge,* and *what is.* Knowledge is true and 'of' what is. I am glossing the relevant idea about knowledge and truth as "truth accompanies knowledge."

30. Today, many philosophers assume that, while perceptual experience is non-factive, perception is factive. Cf. Tim Crane: "I assume the now standard terminological distinction between perceptual experience, which is non-factive or non-relational, and perception, which is both factive and relational." ("Is Perception a Propositional Attitude?," *The Philosophical Quarterly* 59 [2009]: 452–69.)

31. I am here adopting Everson's translation of the passage ("Epicurus on the Truth of the Senses," 166–67).

32. Note that this is not a proposal about correspondence, as if the pleasure (or pain or perception) was true by virtue of corresponding to its cause. The relevant relation is one of production. Cf. M 7.205.

33. Everson, "Epicurus on the Truth of the Senses" also draws on the *Theaetetus*, though not to the extent that I do.

34. "Man is the measure of all things, of things which are, that they are, and of the things which are not, that they are not." (*Theaetetus*, 152a2–5; this is a quote from Protagoras's book *Truth* (*Alêtheia*); cf. SE M 7.60). "That as each thing appears to me (*emoi phainetai*), so it is for me (*estin emoi*), and as it appears to you, so it is for you." (152a2–5, 152a7–9). Later in the dialogue the Measure Doctrine is rephrased in terms of what we might call Truth Relativism (cf. 157e): what seems to A is true-for-A and what seems to B is true-for-B.

35. Here is how the Cold Wind Example is introduced (152b): The same wind is blowing. One of us feels cold, the other does not. The wind is cold for the person who feels cold, and not cold for the other person.

36. *Theaetetus* 153d–160e.

37. Socrates suggests that the Measure Doctrine might hold for *two* domains: present-tense sense-perceptions and the law as it applies to the present. The latter, however, is irrelevant for present purposes (though obviously there are interesting questions about the interrelations between both domains).

38. I am grateful to Jacques Lezra for inviting me to present this chapter at a conference on *Lucretius and Modernity*, and to the other speakers and audience for lively discussion. Jens Haas contributed extensive feedback on several versions of the chapter.

PART IV

Following Lucretius

C H A P T E R   N I N E

From Clinamen to Conatus: Deleuze, Lucretius, Spinoza

WARREN MONTAG

In 1961, Gilles Deleuze published a short essay titled "Lucrèce et le natu-ralisme" in the journal *Études philosophiques*.[1] At the end of the sixties, a version of the essay, approximately two pages longer, which included the entirety of the earlier version (with the exception of a diagram) appeared as one of five appendices to *The Logic of Sense*.[2] It was presented under the heading "The Simulacrum and Ancient Philosophy" where it was pre-ceded and, in a certain sense, introduced by an essay on Plato, "Plato and the Simulacrum," also a revised version of an earlier essay originally pub-lished under the title "Renverser le platonisme" ("To Reverse Platonism") in the *Revue de métaphysique et de morale* in 1967.[3]

This history will help us situate Deleuze's essay on Lucretius and per-haps allow us to note certain subtle but important differences between the first and second versions that are revealing of Deleuze's philosophical trajectory. The first version was composed in the context of Deleuze's major text on Nietzsche, while the second appeared shortly after *Difference and Repetition*, and perhaps most decisively, *Expressionism in Philosophy: Spinoza*.[4] I say most decisively because Deleuze in the second version of his text on Lucretius adds Spinoza's name to that of Nietzsche (whose name appeared alone in the first version) as a descendant of Lucretius (who was, in turn, a descendant of Epicurus), a genealogy similar, if not exactly identical, to Althusser's notion of the underground current of the materialism of the encounter. Most decisively also, and perhaps even more importantly, because Deleuze will apply Spinoza and Spinoza's concepts to what is arguably the central theoretical problem or puzzle of *The Nature of Things*, a problem that has occasioned enormous speculation and debate: the problem of the clinamen. The fact that of these concepts, it is that of the conatus, itself the subject of numerous and often incompatible inter-pretations, that Deleuze uses to explicate one of the most difficult passages in Lucretius's text, means that far from clarifying, not to say simplifying, the clinamen by translating it into Spinoza's concept as if the latter were its fulfillment or completion, Deleuze removes both concepts and both philosophers from their respective places in the chronology of the history of philosophy, and situates them in a single conjuncture, half revealing and half interpolating a dialogue between them. Deleuze thus permits us to grasp the fact that Lucretius may prove as acute a reader of the *Ethics* as Spinoza is of *The Nature of Things*.

We might begin by questioning the very title of Deleuze's essay: why naturalism instead of, say, realism or materialism? Naturalism, for Deleuze, is the "first philosophy": it speaks of nature, "rather than the gods."[5] It does so not simply by passively ignoring what Deleuze elsewhere calls, following Lucretius, "religion," but by actively preventing the introduction into philosophy of any "myth" that will deprive it of its "positivity," knowing that the inescapable affects of fear and desire tend to convert nature into the mere appearance of something more real: "Being, the One, the Whole," the objects of "a false philosophy completely filled with theology."[6] These are figures of the negative, the negation of difference, and the negation of a positive infinity whose right to speak in philosophy naturalism works to deny. By eliminating the negative from philosophy, an elimination that can never be final or definitive but must be continually undertaken, naturalism makes visible and thinkable its true object: that "infinite sum" whose elements cannot be totalized or united into a whole. If the object of naturalism is nature, nature must be understood not in opposition to the Divine as its degraded emanation, or in contrast to nomos or techne as a more proximate expression of a god or gods.

It is precisely this theme that explains Deleuze's pairing of Lucretius with Plato in the final section of *The Logic of Sense*: *On the Nature of Things* can best be understood as the, or at least an, original "reversal of Platonism." While the concept of the simulacrum is key here, its importance lies less in the technical function of the specific term in Lucretius as opposed to Plato, than in the very concept of *natura* or nature in the work of the former. For Plato, argues Deleuze, the activity of philosophy consists of making distinctions and of sorting and separating. The theory of the Forms or, as Deleuze staying closer to the Greek writes, the Ideas, necessitates a registering of the difference between "essence and appearance, the intelligible and the sensible, the original and the copy, the model and the simulacrum."[7] For the world consists of good copies and bad, the icons and the phantasms: "copies always well founded and simulacra always engulfed in dissimilarity."[8] The objective of philosophy for Plato must be then to "assure the triumph of copies over the simulacra, to repress the simulacra, to keep them chained below, to prevent them from rising to the surface and 'insinuating' themselves everywhere."[9] It is in this sense that Lucretius succeeds in reversing Platonism. By severing the world from the dictate (rather than the pact or treaty) of fate or destiny, the *foedera fati* (2.254), by placing the gods outside of the *foedera naturae* (2.302), the pact of nature,

Lucretius has made the world a simulacrum in Deleuze's sense, no longer a derivative or degraded version of the something more primary, but rather the site of a power that denies any distinction between the original and the copy, between the model and its reproduction.[10] Deprived of any hierarchy of being, the world is the site of events rather than representations, of effects rather than similitude. Nature, for Lucretius, does not unify its products into the form of the One or Being and the copy ceases to be reducible to its origin: it "is not attributive, but conjunctive; it is expressed in 'and,' not in 'is.'"[11] Nature "must be thought as the principle of the diverse and its production"[12] rather than a process of reconciling or bringing into the proximity of resemblance the singularities previously thought as copy and original, or essence and appearance.

It is at this point that the notion of the simulacra (as explicated in Book 4 of *The Nature of Things*) assumes its importance for Deleuze. Lucretius begins by recapitulating Epicurus's theory of the *eidola* (εἴδωλα) (which he translates into Latin as *simulacra*, although he will also use other terms such as *effigies* and *imago*), images of very fine texture that are shed like a membrane from solid bodies whose shape they resemble, as stated in the Letter to Herodotus (46–47).[13] The simulacra flow continuously from the object that exudes them and enter our organs of sensation, for example, the eyes, causing us not only to see the original objects but also to think of their shapes. Epicurus will argue that because the *eidola* (εἴδωλα) are a part, albeit an infinitesimal part, of the body from which they are continuously detached, they can never be the source of error. As Spinoza, clearly drawing on Epicurus and Lucretius in *Ethics* II, puts it, we have true ideas, thereby displacing the age-old philosophical quest for truth and for the conditions of attaining truth, in favor of the long-forgotten question raised by his forbears: how do we come to have false ideas?

Here Deleuze points us to a passage from *On the Nature of Things* 4.130–32: "But that you may not think that only simulacra detached from things are in motion, there are those that generate themselves (*quae sponte sua gignuntur*) and constitute themselves (*et ipsa constituuntur*) in this sky that is called air." Deleuze comments: "These are phantasms that enjoy a high degree of independence with respect to objects, an extreme mobility, an extreme inconstancy in the images they form (since they are not renewed by the constant emissions of the object). It seems therefore that here the image takes the place of the object itself."[14] In particular, Deleuze argues, the images that are formed spontaneously in the sky that we call air are theological phantasms, responsible for the erroneous belief that giants exist in the sky who inhabit a world out there. Here he cites Hume concerning the origin of the belief in the gods. Other phantasms are formed of the simulacra shed by existing things, but selected and recomposed by the mind to produce its own beings: centaurs and other mythical creatures. Finally, there are erotic phantasms, determined by the impossible desire to possess the very body of the beloved instead of mere simulacra, the experience of which emphasizes the irreducible separation of human bodies.

Thus it appears that Lucretius, following Epicurus himself, has appro-priated Plato's practice of making distinctions or, to use Althusser's phrase, drawing lines of demarcation that separate simulacra detached from and therefore resembling real bodies and capable of instilling a kind of know-ledge of these bodies, from simulacra that generate themselves and produce illusions, as well as the images in the mind determined directly by the body that sheds them from the recompositions created in the mind. For Deleuze all these distinctions are mobilized to produce the distinction that may be said to be fundamental to Lucretius in that it is the point at which his phys-ics and ethics converge: the distinction between the true and false infinite. Out of the simulacra that Deleuze has called phantasms there emerges a specular structure of illusion in which the freedom of the gods dancing through the heavens both mirrors the perpetuity of erotic desire in which illusions of infinite pleasure alternate with those of infinite pain, and pro-duces a vacillation of the mind between "the cupidity and culpability so characteristic of the man of religion."[15] If the false infinite "troubles the soul," a "rigorous distinction of the true infinite and a correct apprecia-tion of times enclosed one within the other and of the passages to the limit which they imply," that is, a sense of the infinite chain of finite modes, to use Spinoza's language, would mean that "men could see that there is fixed limit (*certam finem*) to their sorrows" and thereby "might have the power to stand against the scruples of religion and the threats of seers" (1.107–10). Delivered in this sense from the torment of the false infinite and its prom-ises of everlasting pleasure and threats of everlasting pain, we would even be allowed to delight in the very phantasms that once so perturbed our mind. Spinoza was surely referring to Epicurus and Lucretius when he argued that "if the mind, while imagining that things that did not exist were present to it, knew, at the same time, that these things did not exist, it would certainly attribute this power of imagining to a strength rather than to a defect of its own nature" (*Ethics* II, P17, Scholium).[16]

The import of these positions, thus, is as practical as it is speculative and it is here that Deleuze in a phrase added to the second version of the essay tells us that "for Lucretius, as for Spinoza later on,"[17] anxiety and guilt trouble the soul, elevating suffering and denouncing pleasure, con-taminating life with death and nature with nothingness. The religious man fears death when alive and fears that he will live after death. The ideas of another world and another life thus not only deprive nature of its positivity in a speculative sense, but also produce a practical orientation to mortification and renunciation of the body and the sensations of pleasure that increase its power, leading to a violence against both self and other. But that rigorous distinction of the true infinite necessary to our happi-ness and to our deliverance from the terrors that religion threatens and the crimes to which it leads is not easily achieved. The problem of conceiving the infinite without submitting it to the dictates of destiny or confining it to the One or Being, that is, to return to Deleuze's primary theme, to conceive of nature as "the principle of the diverse and its production," will

lead to some of the most difficult and elliptical passages in the entirety of
On the Nature of Things.

It is here, in attempting to think about this principle that naturalism
both requires and yet has not entirely elaborated, that Deleuze's later text
differs most from the earlier version, adding nearly a page on the question
of the clinamen and calling upon Spinoza (whose name does not appear
in the earlier version) to help confront some of the problems posed by
Lucretius: "Naturalism needs a powerfully structured principle of causality that accounts for the production of the diverse, but accounts for it as
compositions, as diverse and non-totalisable combinations between the
elements of nature."[18] What is interesting here and throughout the essay
is Deleuze's insistence that the great theoretical object of Naturalism is
a concept of "causality" as opposed to both contingency (understood as
indetermination) and destiny, or to use Spinoza's language both miracle
and providence. What does Deleuze mean when he says that such a concept, a concept that is simultaneously necessary but absent, still to be
elaborated, must be "powerfully structured" (*fortement structuré*)? What
follows in the text suggests that the principle of causality that accounts for
the production of the diverse is itself diverse, not a coherent and therefore
unified set of propositions about a reality to which it must be external as
a condition of its making this reality intelligible, but a mode of thought
that is structured by the power of the diverse itself, as if thought could not
be separated from it.

Accordingly, Deleuze begins his exposition of this "powerfully structured principle" with an examination of the relation between thought
and atom, as discussed briefly by both Epicurus (Letter to Herodotus,
58) and Lucretius (*DRN* 1.749–52): "The atom is what must be thought
(*doit être pensé*), what can only be thought. The atom is to thought what
the sensible object is to the senses: the object that is addressed essentially
to it, the object that gives to thought (*qui donne à pensée*) as the sensible
object is given to the senses (*se donne aux sens*)."[19] We can understand
from our previous discussion how the simulacra emitted by bodies affect
the senses; we can even, using Deleuze's slightly Heideggerian language,
understand the emission of simulacra as a body "giving" or "addressing"
itself to our senses. But what exactly does it mean for that which is "not
sensible and cannot be," that which is "essentially hidden,"[20] to "give"
itself to thought? The phrase "essentially hidden" is perhaps key here. For
the senses there is a "sensible minimum that represents the smallest part
of the object." Deleuze here insists that "by analogy" that atom represents
that smallest part of that which can be thought: "The atom is endowed
with thought parts (*parties pensées*)...The indivisible atom is formed by
thought minima (*minima pensés*)."[21] Later in the essay he adds that, according to Epicurus, the atom "moves as swiftly as thought."[22] The atom can
only be thought: does this mean that as a "thought minimum" the atom is
constituted by thought as an "ideal" object? Such a position is impossible
from the perspective of Epicurus and Lucretius given that the mind or

the soul is not "incorporeal," consisting of a different substance from the bodies that address themselves to it, but on the contrary is itself made up of atoms and has no existence apart from the body that, in fact, constitutes it.[23] As Pierre François Moreau has shown, Lucretius never fully theorizes the corporeality of the *anima*, nor does he fully acknowledge the far-reaching theoretical consequences of such a position.[24] He has, however, conducted us to a theoretical threshold on the other side of which perhaps only Spinoza (absent from this part of Deleuze's exposition) can serve as a guide. At the risk of leaping over a whole set of theoretical differences and problems, it is possible to argue that the concept of the atom and the idea of the corporeality of the soul are coextensive: the idea of the atom is the same thing as the atom itself; the limit of thought is the limit of the thing. As Deleuze remarks of "ancient atomism" in *Difference and Repetition*, ideas were "conceived as multiplicities of atoms, atoms being the objective elements of thought."[25] If we cannot conceive of a further division of the atom, it is not because of a failure in thought, but because the atom itself cannot be further divided.

Of course, we must note that starting from the same assumptions, Spinoza himself would arrive at the opposite conclusion: that the composition of things extends to infinity without minimum or maximum. It is perhaps, above all, the concept of God that allows or compels him to do so. Further, as Deleuze reminds us, Lucretius's infinity differs from Spinoza's in that the void is essential to it: the sum of atoms "would not be infinite if the void were not itself also infinite. The void and the plenum are interwoven and distributed in such a way that the sum of the void and the atoms is itself infinite. This third infinite expresses the correlation between atoms and the void."[26] And yet there is something in Deleuze's account that suggests a more complicated relation between Lucretius and Spinoza than simple opposition. In fact, no passage in the *Ethics* exhibits a greater Epicurean influence than EII, P13. The union of mind and body, itself an Epicurean theme, requires a discussion of the human body, which in turn necessitates a discussion of the nature of bodies as such. What is striking about Spinoza's account of bodies in motion or at rest, colliding and being deflected, or, on the contrary, moving at the same speed, communicating their movements to each other in such a way that they together form a single body or individual and continue as such indefinitely, is that nowhere in the entire of P13 and its demonstrations, corollaries, scholia, axioms, lemmas, and postulates does he specify or name that in which or through which bodies move. Of course, earlier in the *Ethics,* Spinoza argues against the existence of a vacuum: "Because therefore there is no vacuum in nature (about which see elsewhere), but all its parts must concur (*concurrere*—that very Lucretian term) in such a way that there is no vacuum or void" (EI, P15, Scholium). The parenthetical phrase, "about which see elsewhere (*de quo alias*)" has puzzled more than a few readers. The only other explicit (and equally brief discussion) of this question appears in his *Principles of Cartesian Philosophy* where, nominally explicating Descartes's rejection of the concept of the void, he writes that "bodies between which nothing lies must necessarily touch one another and also to that nothing there belong no properties" (II, 3). To this he adds: "Space and body do not differ in reality" (2.4).[27] From this follows Spinoza's postulation near the end of his discussion of bodies in EII, P13 of nature as "one single individual whose parts, that is, all bodies vary in an infinite number of ways without changing the individual as a whole" (EII, P13, Scholium).

At stake here is not a restoration of the privileges of the One or the Whole that would represent precisely the totalization that would impose an imaginary unity on the infinitely diverse (given that Spinoza rejects such a totalization as vehemently as Lucretius and cites the concept of the irreducible atom as a resistance to the infinite) but a theory of encounter without the void, a theory of the encounter that no longer requires the void to render intelligible the causal series arising from an infinity of encounters between bodies. Of course, the void in Spinoza's time did not belong to the realm of natural science alone, any more than it had in the time of Lucretius. In the seventeenth century, the void, in opposition to its function in *On the Nature of Things*, was a sign, the sign, of an absence or a concealment, God's absence, or the empty place left behind, perhaps from the beginning, when he turned away and withdrew from the world. The empty spaces that interrupted what was otherwise the eternity and infinity of matter served to remind us of a transcendence so absolute that it eluded human comprehension and could only be understood as absence.

Encounter, collision, deflection, conjunction: just as these themes required conceptual innovation on Lucretius's part, so they led Deleuze to the most significant revisions of the first version of the essay in which he stages an encounter between Lucretius and Spinoza around the notion of the clinamen. Deleuze begins by citing Lucretius's summary in 2.225ff. of Epicurus's discussion in the Letter to Herodotus of the fact that bodies move with equal speed through the void insofar as it continually "gives way" (2.237). The fact that they all move with equal speed further implies that no body by virtue of its movement will collide with any other body and, Lucretius notes, from such a scheme no world could ever be created: atoms would move through the infinite void without ever encountering each other. Hence, another principle must be found to explain the existence not only of nature (or the infinity of worlds), but even of a single composite thing. Thus, Deleuze comments, "we must conceive an originary direction for each atom, as a synthesis that gives to the movement of the atom its first direction, without which there would be no collision."[28] This "synthesis" is, Deleuze tells us, precisely the clinamen.

Here, he not only has departed from Lucretius's text, but insists on adding to the question of the clinamen a dimension nearly absent from the section in which it appears: that of time. It is not only that the swerve takes place "in a time smaller than the minimum of continuous time, that is, smaller than the time of the atom's movement which is the minimum of continuous time,"[29] but also, perhaps even more importantly, that the swerve, which Deleuze repeatedly insists must be understood as a "synthesis," and thus as composition and a conjunction, does not come after the fall or movement of the atom; it does not arrive secondarily to "modify its vertical fall."[30] Rather, this synthesis "is present for all time": an original synthesis, a synthesis that precedes the elements that are synthesized, to determine from the outset the direction of the atom's movement.[31] It is at this precise point in the revised version of the essay that Deleuze will turn to Spinoza to help explain the originary synthesis of deviation: "It is a kind of conatus, a differential of matter and by that fact a differential of thought."[32] The application of this term to the clinamen is at least as illuminating for Spinoza as for Lucretius.

First, Deleuze's insistence that the conatus can be identified with that which "modifies a vertical fall" severs the conatus from the notions of instinct, inclination, and interest (with which it was indentified since the time of the Stoics—the most recent representative being Hobbes), and therefore from its exclusive tie to animate, as opposed to inanimate, matter. This is particularly important given the tendency of Spinoza's readers to see conatus as pertaining to animate existence and in the human world, serving as a synonym for self-interest. Deleuze also allows us to read the propositions concerning the conatus in EIII P4–8 as a continuation of the discussion of bodies in EII, P13, where Spinoza argues that in order to have an adequate knowledge of the human body (which is, in turn, "the object of the idea constituting the human mind"), we must speak not only of the idea of the human body, but also necessarily of the idea of "any thing whatever (*de conjuscunque rei*)." Hence, EIII, P6, in which Spinoza introduces conatus in the verbal form ("*conatur*"): "Each thing (*res*), to the extent that it is in itself, endeavors (*conatur*) to persist (*perseverare*) in its being (*in suo esse*)." Note that Spinoza does not say "living thing" and clearly affirms in the demonstration to the proposition that he refers here to all singular things (*res singulares*) whatever, each of which expresses the power by which God is and acts (*qua Deus est, et agit*). The misreadings of this passage, the persistent tendency to see in the things of which Spinoza speaks, an exercise of the will or at least instinct in the conatus, which, after all, means effort or endeavor, and further the exercise of the will to achieve an end, that of "self-preservation," are perhaps inevitable from Spinoza's own perspective (see especially EI Appendix), but it cannot be said that he himself does not repeatedly attempt to forestall them. Thus, in EIII, P7, "the effort (*conatus*—here in the nominal form) by which each thing endeavors (*conatur*) to persist in its being is nothing other than the actual essence (*actualem essentiam*) of that thing itself." Here actuality is no longer opposed to an essence of which it would represent merely a partial realization, but is identical to it. There can be no passage from essence to existence: the essence and actual existence of a singular thing are one and the same. The thing has no essence other than its present existence or, better, the power or conatus (*potentia, sive conatus*) by which it, "alone or with others" exists. Further, its existence, as Spinoza explains, is not finite, but indefinite: "If it is not destroyed by an external cause it will always continue to exist by the same power by which it now exists" (EIII, P8). In a sense, Spinoza has thus appropriated Lucretius and translated the language of atoms moving through the void into his own idiom, simultaneously temporal and spatial, of singular things continuing to exist by the power that enables them to be what they are.

Let us recall that for Lucretius the clinamen serves two theoretical functions: first (2.220–24), it explains how atoms, which otherwise would fall at equal speeds through the void without ever impinging upon each other, in fact, have from eternity and through infinity, swerved from this only ever hypothetical trajectory to collide, repel, and conjoin with each other. Out of such conjunctions, when atoms become hooked or interlocked, bodies and worlds are born. Secondly (2.251–55), just as nature as such can only emerge out of the very encounters that determine that there is not nothing, so these encounters prevent the consolidation of an everything, a Whole or a One that would impose the reign of destiny. The swerve or clinamen is that which shatters the decree of fate (*fati foedera rumpat*), opening nature to an infinite multiplicity of divergent causal series. Here Deleuze is insistent that in breaking the pact of Destiny, in rejecting final causes, neither Spinoza nor Lucretius have, as some of their critics have charged, abandoned causality as such to embrace mere indeterminacy. If the will is free according to Lucretius, its freedom cannot be understood as self-determination by which the will would will itself without prior cause: "Nothing is created out of nothing" (2.287). Thus, if it is true that the movements of the limbs initiated by the heart "first proceed from the soul's will (*ex animique voluntate*)" (2.269–70), this sequence cannot be understood as arising from the soul or mind as a first cause that would be itself uncaused. On the contrary, "the mind has no necessity within" (2.289–90); if it is free in the sense that it can resist the decrees of fate or the command of first and final causes, its freedom is created by the swerve, that original and disjunctive synthesis, and, in a larger sense, by the infinite plurality of divergent causal series. The mind's decisions, argues Spinoza, are nothing but its desires, which vary according to the disposition of the body itself determined by another body and so on ad infinitum (EIII, P2, Scholium). But in the human world of servitude and coercion, as in nature itself, bodies no more reach their destination than they do their end and destiny: diverging, swerving, joining, and dividing, they jostle thought and upend desire. These bodies in movement know themselves in their flight like escaped slaves crossing into freedom, who by evading death stumble onto life.

The search for the concept of causality adequate to Lucretius's discovery led Deleuze from Lucretius to Spinoza and back again, in a decade whose encounters and conjunctions had made such a concept imperative, as if he could discern in these thinkers past the barest signs, not of destiny, nor even the future, but of a present still to be known.

Notes

1. Gilles Deleuze, "Lucrèce et le naturalisme," *Études philosophiques* 1 (1961): 19–29.
2. Gilles Deleuze, *The Logic of Sense*, trans. Mark Lester (New York: Columbia University Press, 1990).
3. Gilles Deleuze, "Renverser le platonisme (Les simulacres)," *Revue de Métaphysique et de Morale* 71 (1966): 426–38.
4. Gilles Deleuze, *Difference and Repetition,* trans. Paul Patton (New York: Columbia University Press, 1995); Gilles Deleuze, *Expressionism in Philosophy: Spinoza*, trans. Martin Joughin (New York: Zone Books, 1992).
5. Deleuze, *Logic of Sense*, 323.
6. Ibid.
7. Ibid., 295.
8. Ibid., 257.
9. Ibid.
10. Lucretius, *De rerum natura libri sex*, The Latin Library, accessed October 31, 2014, http://www.thelatinlibrary.com/lucretius.html (my translation).
11. Deleuze, *Logic of Sense*, 267.
12. Ibid., 266.
13. Epicurus, "Letter to Herodotus," in *Lives of Eminent Philosophers*, by Diogenes Laertius, Perseus Digital Library, accessed October 31, 2014, http://www.perseus .tufts.edu/hopper/text?doc=urn:cts:greekLit:tlg0004.tlg001.perseus-grc1:10.1 (my translation).
14. Deleuze, *Logic of Sense*, 275.
15. Ibid., 277.
16. Baruch Spinoza, *Ethica*, The Latin Library, accessed October 31, 2014, http://www .thelatinlibrary.com/spinoza.ethica1.html (my translation). See also Baruch Spinoza, *Complete Works*, trans. Samuel Shirley (Indianapolis, IN: Hackett, 2002).
17. Deleuze, *Logic of Sense,* 273.
18. Ibid., 277.
19. Ibid., 268.
20. Ibid.
21. Ibid.
22. Ibid., 274.
23. Pierre-François Moreau, *Lucrèce. L'ame* (Paris: Presses Universitaires de France, 2002), 29.
24. Moreau, *Lucrèce*, 30.
25. Gilles Deleuze, *Difference and Repetition*, 184.
26. Deleuze, *Logic of Sense*, 269.
27. Baruch Spinoza, *Renati Descartes, Principia Philosophiae*, Spinoza et nous, accessed October 31, 2014, http://spinozaetnous.org/wiki/Renati_Descartes_Principia _philosophiae (my translation).
28. Deleuze, *Logic of Sense*, 269.
29. Ibid., 270.
30. Ibid., 269.
31. Ibid.
32. Ibid.

CHAPTER TEN

Notes on Leo Strauss's
"Notes on Lucretius"

ALAIN GIGANDET

According to Leo Strauss, the question of Lucretius's modernity can be answered without any ambiguity, and we should read the Roman poet as a prominent representative of a way of thinking that lays the very foundations of modernity.[1] Reading Lucretius should thus introduce us to the true meaning of the word "modernity," and, at the same time, make us realize how problematic the concept happens to be. Now, this set of concerns is obviously the central point of Strauss's global meditation on modernity.

From the first works on Spinoza to the late theorizing of Natural Right, Strauss's interest in Epicurus and Lucretius remains constant. In his early work *The Critique of Religion in Spinoza*, Strauss introduces a very specific claim concerning the meaning of Lucretius's poem, both historical and philosophical, summed up in the concept of "Epicureanism." The later "Notes" confirm that he never changed his mind on this topic.

On March 17, 1949, Strauss writes to Eric Voegelin: "At the moment I am studying Lucretius. I have the desire to write freely and frankly on the meaning of his poem, that is, without footnotes, assuming that there is some prospect of publishing an essay of this sort. As far as Lucretius is concerned, the classical philologists are again remarkably blind."[2] Yet, we must wait for a letter to Alexandre Kojève of June 1965 to find the Lucretius project again and get a clearer sense of the genesis of the "Notes." After announcing the conclusion in the near future of his current philosophical agenda, Strauss concludes with the wish of starting soon his work on Lucretius.[3] "A note on Lucretius" is published two years after, as a contribution to a collective volume honoring Karl Löwith.[4] One year later, in 1968, "Notes on Lucretius" reproduces this essay as the first part of a complete commentary of Lucretius's poem.[5] Strauss *appears* to have delayed confronting Lucretius directly, though the encounter was, nevertheless, required by his earlier work. One might ask why it was finally published in a rough draft form, as simple "notes." Did Strauss really consider this version definitive?

Refutation of Religion

Let us start now with two preliminary questions concerning the general orientation of Strauss's commentary.

As regards *De Rerum Natura*'s (*DRN*'s) form and Lucretius's style, we find in "Notes on Lucretius" this notable methodological remark about the anti-Presocratic polemics of Book 1: "One cannot begin to study how Lucretius read Empedocles before one knows how Lucretius wrote." What Strauss suggests here, to all appearances, is that the principles of what he elsewhere calls the "art of writing" are relevant for a global inter-pretation of the *DRN*.[6] We may in consequence ask: What? Why? How? What is the purpose, the "motive" or the *motif* (the word that Strauss uses in his writings on Spinoza and religion), that is, the hidden meaning of Lucretius's poem? What could Lucretius's reasons be for choosing such an equivocal manner of writing? What devices are characteristic of this man-ner? For Strauss, answering these questions is the only way of understand-ing the true philosophical design of Lucretius's poem.

Now our second question—bearing this time on the poem's *content*. What does Lucretius's "motive" actually consist of? Let us return to the beginning. From *The Critique of Religion in Spinoza*, Epicurus and Lucretius are mentioned as giving rise to a philosophical criticism of religion that provides modernity with its basis.[7] This observation is made in the name of truth, and has at its base a scientific purpose; at the same time, however, this scientific purpose is prompted by an "originary heart interest" (these are Strauss's words), that is, it is conceived of as the only appropriate way to happiness. And this goal alone can make it fully understandable. The reader will observe that the "Notes on Lucretius" are based on the same claim.

Connecting both questions gives rise to a difficulty: How can Strauss claim that the refutation of religion is Lucretius's key, but covert, pur-pose, when every reader of Lucretius will find this purpose strongly and openly expressed from the very beginning of the poem and methodically brought into play in every part of it? We may guess that Strauss's implicit answer is based on three considerations. In the first place, the question of religion cannot be separated from Lucretius's guiding design: to bring a non-Epicurean Roman (Memmius) around to Epicurus's doctrine, that is, to bring Memmius over to Athens and to Greek thought. Second, the question of religion is not only the driving force of the Lucretian project as a whole: it moves each and every particular part of Lucretius's argu-ment, and runs especially strongly through the arguments regarding the physical makeup of nature; consequently, the question of religion is far from limited to its treatment in explicit passages: one must learn to identify it where it is only implicit, or where it works allusively, that is, almost everywhere in the poem. Finally, the true meaning of religion and of its refutation are neither enunciated straightaway in the poem nor given a relevant expression in the most explicit passages (e.g., the first eulogy of Epicurus,[8] or the scene of Iphigenia's sacrifice).[9] Quite the contrary is the case. The true meaning of religion and of its critical treatment in the poem are revealed in a progressive and indirect way, by means of successive shifts, displacements, and corrections that can be detected only by a well-informed reader.

Why Did Lucretius Write? Rome and Athens

If one wants to understand *how* Lucretius writes, one has first to understand *why* Lucretius writes. In his letter to Voegelin of April 15, 1949, Strauss points out what, in his opinion, makes for the high philosophical interest of the *DRN*, and adds: "As for Lucretius' 'personality'? I do not believe it matters. Nor does his Romanness: his poem tries precisely *to be free from* 'Romanness' (among other things): *primum* [sic] *Graius homo*—this means *not* the Romans."[10] Nearly 20 years later, Strauss's commentary on the hymn to Venus in *DRN* gives him the opportunity to make this judgment clear.

For Strauss, the opening hymn becomes intelligible if it is understood as the first step in a process aimed at bringing the reader forward from Rome to Athens: "After having turned to Venus, the ancestress of the Romans, the Roman must turn to Greeks, to men belonging to a foreign people now enslaved by Rome, in order to become free."[11] The first stage thus leads from the hymn to Venus to the eulogy of Epicurus by means of a series of associations: Venus, the Romans' mythical ancestor, is given privilege over Mars. Strauss is unequivocal: "Venus, not Mars, is the link between Romanism and Epicureanism."[12] The foundation of Rome is the result of Eneas's flight from Troy. Since, however, the Trojan War itself originated in an impious action—Iphigenia's sacrifice—Lucretius's reader is prompted to conclude that there must be an ethical truth that is higher than this Roman genealogy: *primus Graius homo* ("first a Greek"). This higher truth comes from Greece. It is to be found in Epicurus's doctrine: "It was a Greek who won the greatest of all victories, a victory surpassing all Roman victories."[13]

Religion, of course, underlies the whole sequence: "Lucretius," Strauss writes,

> leads Memmius from Rome via Venus to the victorious Greek. In the remote past the Greeks defeated and destroyed Troy, protected by Venus, through religion, that is, the sacrifice of Iphigenia; this victory leads to the founding of Rome, which defeated Greece, but

did not altogether destroy it. At their peak some Greeks won through
philosophy the most glorious victory possible.[14]

When Lucretius apologizes for the "poverty" of his "paternal speech,"
Strauss suggests, his expression should be considered together with the
patria praecepta ("paternal precepts") of Epicurus:[15] "Lucretius has two
fathers or fatherlands, one by virtue of language (or blood) and another by
virtue of the mind; the precepts which bind or guide him stem exclusively
from the latter."[16]

From this beginning forth, the further reappearances of the goddess
in the poem, either explicit or implicit, will be considered by Strauss as
symptomatic of a correction, a rectification, of the primitive scenario.
Clearly enough, this "autocorrection" will be a prominent device of
Lucretius's "art of writing." Lucretius's text often hints at such corrections
of the meaning or significance of a topic by making a visible contradiction
or incoherence that plays the role of a sign. (A good example would be the
six "theological verses" at the end of the hymn to Venus,[17] which puzzle
Lucretius's reader by describing gods who do not care about human affairs
at the very moment when the poet is asking Venus's help in composing
his poem.)

The next step is taken in the ontological passage where Lucretius
draws the dictinction between *coniuncta* ("properties") and *eventa* ("accidents"), and offers the elements of a theory of time.[18] Strauss points out
that all the examples of *eventa* concern the Trojan War. Paris, Venus's
favorite (just like Memmius), is the cause of the Greek's victory: is the
DRN the Trojan Horse of Greek thought in Rome? In opposition to the
poem's Prelude, this passage suggests the radical relativity of Roman as
well as Greek affairs: both, like all human events, belong to the class of
accidents. How might we understand this passage as a "rectification" (in
Strauss's own words) of the hymn to Venus? Inasmuch as it carries out
a displacement from the field of cultural and historical representations
(where Memmius's conversion is at stake) to the basic level of physical
truth, the truth of atoms and void (it is at this level, too, that the possibility of Memmius's conversion will be decided). We have reached a
key question in Strauss's interpretation: what is the connexion between
the "pedagogic" and "psychagogic" processes that underlie the poem,
and the very "nature of things," this physical truth that is the core of its
teaching?

We understand now that the principle revealed by Strauss's interpretation is supposed to apply generally. The totality of the poem, in
its rhetorical fashioning, shows itself as a gradual correction, taken in
stages, of its own first beginnings. From this standpoint, Lucretius's
next goal is gradually to convince his reader that the physical truth he
teaches cannot be identified with Venus's law. The key passage, then,
is the one that establishes the eternity of atomic movements through

the Democritean analogy of the "ceaseless struggle" of specks of dust watched in a sunbeam.[19] Even if, to some extent, "the likeness sweetens the likened," since it presents in full light a movement that, in fact, takes place in the dark, the reader's mind is, nevertheless, led to the ultimate truth about the nature of things: toward understanding the "blind blows which the blind atoms inflict on one other."[20] In short, this truth falls not on Venus's side, but rather on Mars's. This understanding was anticipated by the second Book's prelude, which replaced the spring rut of animals (Venus's side) by storm and war (Mars's).

From this point forward, the main question that Strauss will ask is: Can Lucretius make this physical truth acceptable, and if so, how? The first echo of the question is found in Lucretius's own apology for his poem: it is not only the obscurity of the Epicurean doctrine, the poet argues, but also the fact that "it often appears off-putting to those who have not experienced it," which justifies the use of "the sweet honey of the Muses."[21] Consequently, for Strauss, the movement that leads from error to truth does not cause any joy in itself: quite the opposite. After following this thread out, one should conclude that the final picture of the plague in Athens stands for the definitive rectification of Venus's Prelude. And all the more so since, in the prelude of Book 6, we were reminded that Athens "in former days first imparted the knowledge of corn-producing crops to suffering mortals and remodeled their lives and established laws"; and, much more importantly, gave birth to Epicurus, who brought "suffering mortals" the remedy to the worst pain: the fearful disease of the soul.[22]

What real impact can philosophical truth be expected to have upon the reader? Does philosophy actually bring "the sweet consolations of life"— Lucretius's explicit goal?[23] What is the true meaning of the "progress" from Venus to the nature of things, a movement that at last proves to be as destructive as it is creative? Strauss goes so far as to speak of "an ascent followed by a descent."[24]

Seen in this light, Lucretius's "main motive" seems more problematical. According to Epicurus, understanding the nature of things has one use only for humankind: it serves to help humans free themselves from the fear and anxiety caused by religion. But since the truths of this knowledge are not as comforting as we are promised they will be, we may begin to suspect that what they are supposed to fight against is also more complex than it seemed. In other words, Strauss's commentary will rest on a gradual complication of the religious problem in DRN.

Lucretius's project, then, revolves around Venus, but the meaning and function of this divine figure gradually change as the poem proceeds. Two main topics are involved here: (a) the formal question of poetry, linked to the difficulty of making physical truth ethically acceptable; and (b) as regards *content*, the central topic of religion and theology, the ambiguity of which should gradually be disclosed to the reader's eyes.

The Lucretian "Motif": The
Religious-Theological Problem

The "theologico-religious motif," in Strauss's opinion, pervades the whole poem, and particularly its physical explanations of the nature of things. In addition to this line of interpretation, Strauss advances the hypothesis that the most indirect and allusive occurrences of the *motif* are also the most significant. Such a reading allows Strauss to propose a revisited version of some of the key passages of Lucretius's poem. Here are some significant examples, drawn from across the poem.

As concerns Book 2, the description of Cybele's cult (*DRN*, 2.600–60) must be connected with the refutation of belief in the divine creation and government of the world, at the beginning of Book 2.[25] Conclusion: the questions of the gods and of providence underlie the entire physical problem of atomic combination. Now, as regards Book 3, among the numerous arguments supporting the claim of an indissoluble link between body and soul (so that they necessarily perish together), Strauss focusses on the principle that "the place where each thing may grow and exist is fixed and determined."[26] When Lucretius concludes from this principle that an immortal entity cannot be linked to a mortal one, Strauss reminds his readers that for an Epicurean, only three types of immortal entities are real: atoms, void, and the Universe. Lucretius's argument, he observes, is thus part of a strategy that aims at making the reader think of the gods by evoking immortality, without mentioning them in any way: immortality without explicit mention of divinity. Lucretius might even be alluding precisely to the *intermundia* ("interworlds"), which were supposed to protect gods' bodies from destruction. "At any rate, the central part of Book 3 begins and ends with allusions not so much to the gods as to the problem of gods."[27]

Concerning the subtle physical nature of the mind we find in Book 4 of *DRN*, Strauss associates this topic with the mental perception of divine images in Book 5. But, doing so, he does not hesitate to reverse the explanation's obvious order: "We understand this section better if we look forward to the fact that 'the nature of the gods is subtle and far removed from our senses,'" he says, quoting Lucretius.[28] This statement looks typical of his reading method: Lucretius's text is, as it were, brought out of center, so as to confirm that an essential development on a quite different subject, the mechanics of thought, actually revolves around the theologico-religious question. The same symptomatology is used again in Book 4 to reinterpret (and maybe overinterpret) the explicitly antifinalist theory of psychophysical functions: "More important, it is the only criticism of teleology occuring in the work which contains no reference whatever to the gods. The poet desires to remain silent on the gods in the present context. But not to mention the gods is not the same as not to think of them."[29]

From the very nature of this method, it follows that the exposition of the various results of Strauss's interpretation of religion (that is, the true status of religion according to Lucretius) lacks any systematic order (justifying his title: "Notes"). So let us merely try to follow one prominent thread.

"Disillusion" is a recurrent term used by Strauss to specify the meaning of Lucretius's global argument. He calls "ascent" this movement that leads from an attractive divine figure to the terrifying image of the gods' power as seen in the mirror of religion. The *DRN* soars from there to the principles of nature (blind movement of atoms, arid void), the knowledge of which—though unattractive in itself—allows us to reach true pleasure. This reconstruction reaches its peak in Strauss's commentary of the prelude to the Second Book. *Suave mari magno* ("It is sweet, when the sea is stormy") means that watching the greater evils we escaped from is the most delightful sight: "The sad is necessary as a foil for the sweet, for sensing the sweet."[30] Does the happiness of a few people require others' unhappiness, insofar as "nature will not be the source of happiness if it is not also the source of unhappiness"?[31] Is the Sage's existence linked to the existence of "stupid" or "ignorant people," the *stulti*? Obviously, these considerations are deeply connected with the elitist dimension of Strauss's own thought. And let us not forget that Epicurean wisdom relies on the knowledge of the most arid, inhuman, reality: blind atoms and void. "Nothing is more alien to wisdom than that with which wisdom is above everything else concerned." No model, no example for mankind is to be expected from this.

The next step, according to Strauss, is taken when the *theologoumenon*, "the religious theme," swerves into a cosmological, then psychological perspective.

The first shift, to a cosmological perspective, occurs when the source of religious fear moves from the consideration of gods to the consideration of the world. The end of Book 2 introduces this change as a consequence of the infinity of the Whole.[32] It is an unexpected and altogether difficult and repulsive truth, which must be assumed only because it *is* the truth: "(Lucretius) seems to be less concerned with making (Memmius) an Epicurean than with liberating him from fear of the new as new."[33] Once having connected the infinity of the Universe with the existence of our limited world, Lucretius concludes that there must be an innumerable number of worlds, all different—a claim that "destroys our importance" and makes humankind appear as a single individual among an infinite crowd of other individuals. A remedy to this uncomfortable truth, however, is immediately suggested: if the Whole, the Universe, is so, then it cannot be ruled by such "arrogant despots" as mythological gods are. "The infinity of the world, however unattractive in another respect, is a small price to pay for the liberation from religion."[34]

Another consequence of the infinity of the Whole is the simultaneous growth and decline of the world and (in parallel) of its creatures. "The planter of the old shriveled vine" is forced to conclude that the earth gradually becomes exhausted. "By generalizing the experience of old peasants about the decay of agriculture and piety into the doctrine of the decay of the world, Lucretius may even be said to sweeten the sad doctrine in accordance with the feelings of the true Romans: the decay or end of Rome is the decay or end of the world."[35] But Strauss immediately clarifies this statement: in Book 5, "Lucretius takes away this scaffolding." He can explain to Memmius, now at a more advanced stage on the way of true knowledge, that the world is still young: and that, actually, some arts are still making progress rather than declining, namely, philosophy, which, thanks to the *DRN*, is now entering Rome.

The upshot is that Lucretius is mindful of revealing the truth as if it were a medical prescription, paying great attention to the appropriate dose. The world is condemned to perish: this verdict is cautiously pronounced after the disturbing revelation of the infinity of the Universe. Let us turn to the methodical demonstration of the same statement at the beginning of Book 5: in no way does it free us from fear—quite the contrary. It could rather lead us into the temptation to come back to the protection of gods, even though they behave like arrogant despots. That is probably why Lucretius, at that very moment, argues that the imperfections of the world refute the claim that it could be governed by gods. In Strauss's opinion, at any rate, Lucretius "has tacitly shown that religion is comforting, for on his own showing religion asserts that man is the end or purpose of creation or that man alone, at least among the earthly beings, is akin to the highest beings."[36] Epicurus's truth—that gods have no interest at all in human affairs—is much harder. These aporias underlie Lucretius's explicit argumentation.

The cosmological dimension of the religious question reappears in Book 5, with the explanation of the origins of religion.[37] Strauss stresses the difference between what Lucretius actually does, that is, provide an etiology of religion, and a theological explanation of the existence and the nature of gods. According to Strauss, the first cause of religion, as pointed out by Lucretius (a mental vision, in a dream, of divine *simulacra* ["images"], then corrupted by a strain of false judgments and opinions), offers a fully satisfying explanation for religious phenomena. Why, then, does Lucretius add a second cause that has nothing to do with human dreams: the incomprehensible sight of heavenly phenomena? This is indeed an allusion to the fundamental Epicurean *theologoumenon* ("the religious theme"): gods are not concerned with the world and its inhabitants. But, in a more indirect way, the reader is asked to assume the consequences of this claim in the dramatic circumstances evoked at the end of the passage: thunder, storm, earthquake, "it all goes to show that there is some invisible force that tramples on human ambitions and similingly treads underfoot the glorious rods and grim axes of high office, and treats them as its playthings."[38]

A careful interpretation will detect here a confession: there is actually a cosmological fear, prior to the belief in gods. It is a fear of real dangers, but Lucretius's theory aims at connecting it to the fear of gods, and it can do so by means of the mental vision of divine simulacra.

Such an ambiguity, Strauss argues, reappears in the theory of earth-quakes, expounded in Book 6.[39] These natural disasters are "directly linked with the poet's fundamental concern; they offer the most massive proof of the possibility of the death of the world; they give as it were a foretaste of that death."[40] Tacitly again, the fear of gods shifts and is even reversed into the fear that gods might abstain from protecting the world. Following this line of argument, the reader should rephrase the etiology of the belief in gods:

> It is this fear for the world, that is, for this world, for everything that is for a man's own or his nation's own, which gives rise to the belief in gods and therewith also to the fear of the gods; the fear of gods is not the fundamental fear. The fundamental fear gives rise in the first place to fear of that very fear, to fear of the most terrible truth. The poet, having exposed himself to the fear of the terrible truth, can calmly face that truth. His courage is not in need of support by belief in social progress between now and the death of the world or by other beliefs.[41]

It is notable that, according to Strauss, the earthquake theory of Book 6, if rightly understood, constitutes Lucretius's concluding message about the religious question. The excerpt's conclusion indeed suggests a progressive revelation, in a dramatic mood, of this essential truth:

> So let people imagine that heaven and earth will remain imperishable, entrusted to eternal safety. And yet from time to time the influence of immediate danger applies on some side or other a goad of fear that the earth may suddenly be snatched away from under their feet and swept into the bottomless abyss, that the aggregate of things, utterly deprived of its foundation, may follow, and that the world may be reduced to a chaotic ruin.[42]

Might such a truth, Strauss asks, be considered as a sufficient reward for the amount of efforts required to understand it? The paradoxes in the Lucretian text on this topic seem to indicate an inner debate about the utility of religion as a remedy for human anxieties. Further analysis will strengthen this suspicion.

The second shift takes place in the analysis of the psychological perspective, the starting point of it being Strauss's commentary on Book 3. Here, the fear of death, together with anxiety about eternal punishments, seems to bring the fear of gods to a climax. Strauss first turns to the original theory that takes criminal passions to be "nourished in no small degree by dread of death,"[43] an implicit response to the traditional objection that breaking with the fear of gods means giving free rein to men's criminal violence. Matters are quite the opposite: Lucretius claims that freeing mankind from the fear of death and eternal punishments should help to abolish criminal thoughts. Now, there dawns in the reader's mind "the suspicion that prior to Epicurus, and in Rome even prior to Lucretius, religion served a good purpose. Given the fact that many men, nay, almost all men, will always refuse to listen to the Epicurean teaching, religion will always serve a good purpose."[44] And especially as Lucretius, when putting forward men's refusal of death as a proof of the mortality of the soul (if our soul were obviously immortal, we should not care about dying), induces his reader to guess that the fear of death, though it may appear quite unreasonable, is altogether fully natural.

The suspicion is strengthened when considering the link between the origin of political organization and religion suggested by Lucretius on several occasions. The first time Lucretius makes this link occurs in the allegorical interpretations of Cybele's cult mentioned in Book 2.[45] Many of them adduce a sociopolitical background for the cult: domestic obligations and taboos, patriotic duties, and so on. Through this investigation of its cultural symbolical function, "religion thus appears to be a human invention which serves the purpose of counteracting the indifference of the whole to man's moral and political needs, for not all men are or can be philosophers; this is to say nothing of the question as to whether philosophy, that is, Epicurean philosophy as Lucretius understood it, enjoins patriotism and gratitude to parents."[46] If it is so, then breaking with religion should have heavy consequences. Strauss connects them with the inaugural "Roman project" of *DRN*.

The second link between the origins of political organization and religion is forged in the "etiological" passage upon religion of Book 5, immediately following the story of the transition from prepolitical to political society.[47] Now, the best guarantee against the contraventions of the law, Lucretius explains, is the fear of punishment, human as well as divine, with an ambivalent result, the price to pay for security and civil peace being that "ever since that time fear of punishment has poisoned the blessings of life."[48] Strauss hardens the difficulty by recalling Epicurean abstention from political life, which is condemned by the law: he who ignores the law will suffer permanent anxiety. The conclusion itself is ambivalent: when Lucretius says that gods *could* witness human crimes and punish them, he certainly refers to a belief that may be beneficial under certain circumstances, but he altogether means that, for him, "religion is of a utility which is not altogether negligible."[49]

Let us try to clarify Strauss's hermeneutical intentions. For him, the progressive exposition of the nature and function of religion in the *DRN* goes along with an implicit process of rehabilitation. Step by step, Strauss argues, the "hideous face" defeated by Epicurus in Book 1[50] gradually takes on a better appearance, until it becomes more the mirror than the proper cause of the fears and torments that are philosophy's main target. There is no doubt that, according to Lucretius, the arid truth about atoms and void should replace, with great ethical benefit, the perverse illusion of religion. Strauss unequivocally affirms this thesis: "His poem is the purest and most glorious expression of the attitude that elicits consolation from the utterly hopeless truth, on the basis of its being only the truth."[51] Here is the mark of the Roman poet's philosophical courage. On the other hand, on Strauss's account, it is doubtful that Lucretius actually judged that this rational development was valuable for everyone, that it was possible and desirable for everyone to adopt it. Once again, the March 17, 1949 letter to Voegelin announced this essential topic: "There is no idea of the use of the hopeless, godless truth for some social purpose, as is almost always the case with other fashions and trends."[52]

Lucretius turns out, in consequence, to be doubly involved in the origins of "enlighted" modernity. He conceives its fundamental principles and design, but, at the same time, lucidly foresees the difficulties and limits of that design. One might identify here, of course, Strauss's main hobbyhorse against the "Moderns." Their central mistake, in his view, is to imagine that they can so easily get rid of religion, both for an intrinsic motive (that reason cannot refuse the possibility, at least logical, of Revelation) and for an extrinsic one: given that the sociocultural gap between elites and common people cannot be filled in, the conviction that rational truth could be profitably substituted for faith is naïve and irresponsible. Lucretius's superiority over Modern Enlightment rests on his supposed clear-sightedness concerning the necessary distinction between elites and common people, and the choice of an "art of writing" based on this distinction.

Conclusion

Let us conclude just as we started, with questions of form, returning to Strauss's reasons for composing his commentary in the form of "notes." Did he intend, doing so, to warn his readers that the underlying truth of *DRN* should not be conceived of as a systematic whole, intended to provide a counterweight to the strict Epicurean dogma, but rather as corrections, complements, or alternative indications? Perhaps so, but this does not explain Strauss's own elliptic, allusive, and ambiguous style, as if the indirect truth of *DRN* could only be revealed in an indirect way.

This formal choice is enigmatic. Strauss, of course, was aware of the antique rhetorical device called "teaching through example," which makes the writing as such formally mimic the described object. Did he have in mind to practice a "teaching through example," as it were, gradually accustoming his reader to the posture he wants readers to assume toward Lucretius's poem, that is, gradually training his reader to read between the lines, and to be able to identify the poem's underlying *motifs*? But can such a device resolve the latent contradiction of the "art of writing," since it aims both at concealing and at teaching?

In any case, one may remain puzzled by the "politic design" with which Lucretius is credited, on the fringe—so to speak—of his ethical commitment as a disciple of Epicurus. Strauss always had an idea of philosophy as a perilous activity and of its "art of writing" as a way of putting into practice the necessity for philosophers to be cautious. But such a hypothesis hardly fits Lucretius's historical and cultural background. One might rather incline to consider it as an expression of Strauss's deeply elitist and hierarchical conception of the "economy of truth" (the way truth should be disclosed), which opens his interpretation to the suspicion that it may, not infrequently and always questionably, give way to Strauss's own imaginary projections and identifications.[53]

Notes

1. Leo Strauss, *Liberalism Ancient and Modern* (New York: Basic Books, 1968), Preface.
2. See Peter Emberley and Barry Cooper, ed. and trans., *Faith and Political Philosophy: The Correspondence between Leo Strauss and Eric Voegelin, 1934–1964* (University Park: Pennsylvania State University Press, 1993), 59.
3. Leo Strauss, *On Tyranny: Including the Strauss-Kojève Correspondence*, ed. Victor Gourevitch and Michael S. Roth (Chicago, IL: University of Chicago Press, 2000), 314.
4. Leo Strauss, "A Note on Lucretius," in *Natur und Geschichte: Karl Löwith 70, Geburstag*, ed. Hermann Braun and Manfred Riedel (Stuttgart, W. Kohlhammer Verlag, 1967), 322–32.
5. Leo Strauss, "Notes on Lucretius," in *Liberalism Ancient and Modern*, 76–139.
6. Ibid., 91. See also Leo Strauss, *Persecution and the Art of Writing* (Chicago, IL: University of Chicago Press, 1952).
7. Leo Strauss, *Die Religionskritik Spinozas als Grundlage seiner Bibelwissenschaft* (Berlin: Akademie-Verlag, 1930); Leo Strauss, *Spinoza's Crititique of Religion*, trans. E. M. Sinclair (New York: Schocken, 1965).
8. Lucretius, *De rerum natura* ("On the Nature of Things", hereafter *DRN*), 1.62–79.
9. Ibid., 1.80–101.
10. Emberley and Cooper, *Faith and Political Philosophy*, 62.
11. Strauss, "Notes on Lucretius," 79.
12. Ibid., 77.
13. Ibid., 79.
14. Ibid., 80.
15. *DRN*, 3.9–10.
16. Strauss, "Notes on Lucretius," 107.
17. *DRN*, 1.44–49.
18. Ibid., 1.445–82.
19. Ibid., 2.112–41.
20. Strauss, "Notes on Lucretius," 95.
21. *DRN*, 1.943–50.
22. Ibid., 6.1–41.
23. Ibid., 5.21; 6.4.
24. Strauss, "Notes on Lucretius," 104.
25. *DRN*, 2.167–83.
26. *DRN*, 3.787.
27. Strauss, "Notes on Lucretius," 110.
28. Ibid., 116.

29. Ibid., 117.
30. Ibid., 95.
31. Ibid., 94.
32. *DRN*, 2.1023–47.
33. Strauss, "Notes on Lucretius," 102.
34. Ibid., 103.
35. Ibid., 104.
36. Ibid., 122.
37. *DRN*, 5.1161–240.
38. Ibid., 5.1233–35.
39. Ibid., 6.535–607.
40. Strauss, "Notes on Lucretius," 135.
41. Ibid.
42. *DRN*, 6.601–7.
43. Ibid., 3.63–64 (Lucretius's own words).
44. Strauss, "Notes on Lucretius," 105.
45. *DRN*, 2.600–43.
46. Strauss, "Notes on Lucretius," 100.
47. *DRN*, 5.1136–60.
48. Ibid., 5.1151 (Lucretius's own words).
49. Strauss, "Notes on Lucretius," 127.
50. *DRN*, 1.62–79.
51. Emberley and Cooper, *Faith and Political Philosophy*, 62.
52. Ibid.
53. A French first version of this paper, "Notes sur les 'Notes sur Lucrèce' de Leo Strauss," was published in Alain Gigandet, ed., *Lucrèce et la modernité: Le vingtième siècle* (Paris: Armand Colin, 2013). I am grateful to Armand Colin for their permission, and to Warren Montag for his rereading of my English text.

CHAPTER ELEVEN

Reflections of Lucretius in Late Antique and Early Modern Biblical and Scientific Poetry: Providence and the Sublime

PHILIP HARDIE

My topic is a part of a history that goes back to Virgil, that of the reaction of writers and thinkers who adhere to providentialist and transcendental models of reality to the materialist and anti-providentialist poem of Lucretius.[1] As such it might seem to have no place in a book on Lucretius and modernity, if by modernity is understood rationalism, free-thinking, libertinism, and a scientific and anti-deist understanding of the world. There was, of course, a time when modernity was Christianity, and the church fathers' attacks on Epicurean atheism were intended to confirm their readers' belief in the new dispensation. But I shall be dealing with texts that, on the surface at least, are confident that they are speaking from a position of established truth. Questions nevertheless remain. Why do accounts of a biblical creation and world order look to Lucretius's poem on the nature of the universe? Is it the case that these texts safely contain the Lucretian message, or is there a surplus that threatens Christian orthodoxy? What degree of anxiety, or indeed illicit sense of liberation, is involved in imitating Lucretius's gospel of rationalist materialism?

Hexaemeral Poetry

In this section I examine a range of responses to Lucretius in biblical poetry on the creation of the world and the early history of mankind. These range from straightforward opposition to accommodation of various kinds, including the incorporation of a "scientific," non-mythical, account of the development of the world within an overall Christian framework. Modernity, among other things, is the history of Christianity's adaptation to revolutions in science, philosophy, and history. One parallel from our own modern world might be the development of creation science as an attempt to mirror the scientific discourse of big bang theory and evolutionism.

A word of definition: hexaemeron, with the adjective hexa(e)meral, refers to a narrative of the six days of creation in Genesis, whether in prose, as in the hexaemeral homiletic commentaries of Basil and Ambrose, or in poetry. Hexaemeral poetry is a subgenre of didactic or epic.[2] From the beginning of the tradition the biblical and the philosophical could be combined: in Basil's *Hexaemeron* there are elements of Stoicism, a philosophy that, of course, is more compatible with a Christian worldview than is Epicureanism.[3] Conversely, pagan didactic poetry on the origins and nature of the world could easily be fitted to a Christian worldview, notably the cosmogony at the beginning of Ovid's *Metamorphoses*, in which the primeval chaos is given order and form by *deus et melior . . . natura* "god and a better nature" (1.21).[4] Ovid's cosmogony is eclectic, but includes a fair admixture of Lucretian pastiche. Conversely, Genesis commentaries regularly use the Ovidian phrase describing chaos as an *indigesta moles* [a disorganized mass] (*Met.* 1.7).[5]

For an example of the oppositional inversion of the Lucretian model, take the scenes of Genesis in the Temple at Jerusalem in Girolamo Vida's widely read Neo-Latin epic on the life of Christ, the *Christiad* of 1535[6] (1.582–724). The ecphrasis is introduced as

argumentum ingens, senum monimenta dierum,
magna quibus magni compacta est machina mundi,
et ueterum euentus, et prisca ex ordine auorum
facta, haud humanis opus enarrabile uerbis. (583–86)

[A great subject-matter, a memorial of the six days in which the great fabric of the world was constructed, together with the deeds of men of old, and the ancient exploits of the ancestors, shown in order, a work that can scarcely be described in human words.]

senum . . . dierum labels this as a hexaemeron; *machina mundi* is a phrase first found in Lucretius (*De Rerum Natura* (*DRN*) 5.96, but widely current thereafter), but this "machine" is the product neither of natural processes nor of human hands. The "work" of creation and of the following Old Testament history cannot even be fully told in human words. *haud enarrabile* alludes to another epic ecphrasis, the scenes of the providential history of Rome on the Shield of Aeneas in Book 8 of Virgil's *Aeneid* (8.625, *clipei non enarrabile textum* [the shield's indescribable fabric]), a work made by the anthropomorphic hands of the god Vulcan.[7] The Virgilian Shield depicts the construction of a human society, Rome, but also alludes to a natural-philosophical, cosmogonic, allegory of the Homeric Shield of Achilles current in antiquity, an allegory that incorporates allusion to the Empedoclean cosmic principles of Love and Strife. There is a Lucretian connection here, since Empedocles's Love and Strife are emblematized in the tableau of Venus and Mars at the beginning of the *DRN*. That Lucretian scene is itself echoed verbally in Virgil's description, on the Shield of Aeneas, of the she-wolf, in the Cave of Mars, the Lupercal, at the heart of the Rome soon to be founded, lovingly licking into shape her human babies, Romulus and Remus.[8]

Vida's ecphrasis of the scenes in the temple continues with the early biblical history of mankind, culminating in types of the Passion (the Sacrifice of Abraham, Moses and the brazen serpent, and so on). The choice of scenes from Roman history on the Virgilian Shield also works typologically, foreshadowing the ultimate triumph of Augustus. This is history full of meaning, where the abstract relationships between discrete happenings are privileged over the material and sensuous immediacy of events. This is not a conception of history that could find any place within an atomist account of temporal process.

When the ecphrasis comes to the moment of the Fall, the event that makes necessary Christ's self-sacrifice, Vida incorporates his most emphatic imitation of Lucretius, as Adam hides in the trees of Paradise after eating the apple, to avoid the angry gaze of God:[9]

> nec iam coelituum regis grauia ora ferentem.
> namque uidebatur fuluae inter uellera nubis
> horribili super impendens mortalibus ore
> dura redarguere, et saeuas indicere poenas
> pro meritis, quas ille olim, quas omnis ab illo
> progenies lueret lucis uentura sub auras. (1.660–65)

> [no longer able to endure the stern face of the heavenly king. For God's terrifying face seemed to hang over the mortals amidst the fleecy folds of a golden cloud, and give harsh judgment of their guilt and to impose severe punishments in keeping with their deserts, penalties which Adam would pay in future time, and all mankind to come from him into life and light.]

What Adam sees (or seems to see) is the Lucretian face of *Religio* lowering from the skies, the sign of an unending series of punishments for future generations: cf. *DRN* 1.63–65: *religione | quae caput a caeli regionibus osten-debat | horribili super aspectu instans* [religion which showed its head in the regions of the sky, its fearful face standing over mankind]. In Lucretius Epicurus comes to slay this monster and save mankind from endless but empty punishments (*poenae*), self-inflicted by a religion that exacts such horrors as the sacrifice of a daughter (Iphigeneia) by her father.[10] In Vida's version of history salvation will come only through the willing sacrifice of a son who will vanquish the (real) monster Satan.

For an example of the accommodation of Lucretian and biblical accounts of the early history of the world, take the origin of animals.

Lucretius presents a doctrine of the survival of the fittest in a universe where living things are not created to fulfill a purpose or to make a link in the great chain of being, but he does not have a theory of evolution. Different kinds of animals do not evolve from earlier and simpler forms, they just have to appear, but in a way that is in keeping with a materialist account of reality. Lucretius offers a scientific version of the mythological notion of the earth as the mother of living creatures. To the widespread ancient belief in spontaneous generation is added the idea that, by analogy with animals who give birth, when the world was new wombs grew in the body of mother earth, from which animals emerged at their due date (5.793ff.). This produces an image of animals, including humans, bursting out of the ground:

> Therefore I repeat again and again that the earth has deservedly won and keeps the name of mother, since she of herself gave birth to the human race and at a fixed time poured forth every beast that runs wild all over the great mountains. (5.821–24)

This image of animals bursting forth from the earth is picked up in narratives of the biblical creation, for example, in the account of the creation of animals on the sixth day in the late fifth-century *De laudibus Dei* by the Carthaginian Dracontius:

> The sixth day had come forth with a shining sunrise, when mother nature (*natura parens*) brought forth animals from the earth. Young bullocks burst out, foreheads armed with horns, and the heifer follows her wandering bull through the meadows. The flighty deer with its branched horns wanders over the fields, and the swift horse bursts forth, an animal useful in war. The cruel earth brings forth fearsome lions. (1.240–46)[11]

There is a similar account in Milton's *Paradise Lost* 7.449ff.:[12]

> The earth obeyed, and straight
> Opening her fertile womb teemed at a birth
> Innumerous living creatures, perfect forms,
> Limbed and full grown: out of the ground up rose
> As from his lair the wild beast where he wons...
> The grassy clods now calved, now half appeared
> The tawny lion, pawing to get free
> His hinder parts, then springs as broke from bounds (453–57, 463–65)

The effect in Dracontius and Milton is to give a naturalistic color to what is a miraculous and sudden creation, a plausible process of new creatures being born, rather than just being conjured up with a magic wand. The *rapprochement* with the Lucretian account is further eased by the fact that

Lucretius has translated into (quasi-)scientific terms mythical ideas about the spontaneous bounty of the Golden Age. In Milton the scientific specificity of the wombs of Lucretius's earth has gone a long way to turning back into a poetic figure of speech. Where in Lucretius's account the newborn animals come forth as babies that are nourished by a milk-equivalent secreted by the earth, in Milton creatures are miraculously born in their full-grown shape. "Perfect forms" may correct Lucretius's non-providentialist account in which at the beginning of the world many monstrous hybrid forms of animal life were thrown up randomly by the earth, which died out because they were unable to survive.

If life in the biblical Eden was easily assimilable to the prescientific classical myth of the Golden Age, a myth that Lucretius, to some extent, rationalizes in the *DRN*, life after the Fall could more readily be framed within Lucretius's view of a world in which all is not for the best. This is a world in which the development of human society follows a painful path of trial and error within a largely hostile environment, rather than enjoying the free gifts of caring gods or the benefactions of preternaturally endowed "first inventors." This accommodation of a Lucretian account of the progress of civilization within a providentialist framework is already found in the first book of Virgil's *Georgics*, where Jupiter's introduction of privation and hardship into a previously bountiful nature prompts the development of arts and technologies through human trial and error (1.118–46, the so-called theodicy or aetiology of labor).

A modern commentator on Maurice Scève's *Microcosme* (1562), an encyclopedic poem on the Fall and on Adam and Eve's experience after the Fall, notes that "once Adam has been chased out of Paradise and forced to depend on his own resources alone, nothing distinguishes him from primitive man such as represented by modern science, and of whom Scève could find a realistic description in book 5 of the *De Rerum Natura*" (my translation).[13] Scève's ambition is to write a French philosophical poem in the tradition of Dante and Lucretius.

One of Lucretius's strongest arguments against a providentialist world is the fact that *natura rerum* "is encumbered with such great faults" (2.181 *tanta stat praedita culpa* = 5.199). On 2.181 *culpa* Don Fowler notes in his commentary: "The use is not common and many of the Latin examples involve a degree of personification; *culpa* naturally refers to *human* responsibility."[14] Fowler goes on: "Chrysippus' ingenuity, the rhetoric of Seneca and Epictetus, or the piety of the Fathers cannot really convince that this is the best of all possible worlds; it is interesting that the *locus de providentia* gets pushed more and more into one of the punishment of the sinful—flaws exist in the world, but they are *our* fault."[15] In a Christian worldview the defects of the world are the fault not of a semi-personified nature, but of human beings, Adam and Eve. The extended listing of the ways in which nature is faulty at Lucretius 5.200–27 could easily be transferred to an account of the changes in nature consequent to the Fall: a hostile geography (mountains, swamps, forests infested by wild beasts, a treacherous sea, climatic extremes), the need for continual hard work on mankind's part to extract a livelihood from the soil, the constant presence of death in a vale of tears, and the world of which God had told Adam after the Fall: "Cursed is the ground for thy sake...Thorns also and thistles it shall bring thee forth" (Genesis 3:17–18).[16] Compare Lucretius: "What is left for tillage, even that nature by its power would overrun with thorns, unless the force of man resisted it" (5.206–7).

According to Lucretius our world is getting progressively worse, as a result of a natural decline from its early vigor and fertility. Using the same analogy from motherhood in the animal world that he had drawn upon for the wombs in the earth from which the first animals emerged, he presents an image of a mother earth now exhausted by childbearing, and reluctantly bearing fruit despite the labors of farmers and their oxen: "And even now the age is enfeebled and the earth, exhausted by bearing, scarcely produces small animals, she who produced all races and gave birth to the huge bodies of wild beasts" (2.1150–52).

Du Bartas, whose *Sepmaines* (*La Creation du monde ou première sepmaine* and *Seconde sepmaine*) I shall cite in Sylvester's translation, *The Divine Weeks and Works of Guillaume de Saluste Sieur du Bartas*,[17] attributes this state of affairs to our first parents' sin ("the third day of the first weeke"):

> And though through sin, whereby from Heavn'ly state
> Our Parents barr'd us, th'Earth degenerate
> From her first beauty, bearing still upon-her
> Eternall Skarres of her fond Lords dishonour:
> Though with the Worlds age, her weake age decay,
> Though she become less fruitfull every day
> (Much like a Woman with oft-teeming worne,
> Who, with the Babes of her owne body borne,
> Having almost stor'd a whole Towne with people,
> At length becomes barren, and faint, and feeble)
> Yet doth she yeeld matter enough to sing
> And praise the Maker of so rich a Thing. (I.iii.587–98)

This qualified version of the bleak Lucretian doctrine is reinforced by praise of the variety of flowers "in pleasant Spring," with which may be compared the appearance of spring in the procession of the seasons: "Spring and Venus lead the way...Mother Flora scatters flowers before them and fills all things with wonderful colours and scents" (Lucretius 5.737–40).

Another of the late antique hexameral poets, Claudius Marius Victor polemicizes against the Lucretian view of the universe in his *Alethia* (third decade of the fifth century): "For it is not the case that, in the view expressed by a tongue of sacrilegious madness, chance bereft of mind, as it rolled around unconscious atoms, hurled into being this great work of providence" (1.22–24).[18] But Marius Victor does include a version of

Lucretius's account of the discovery of metalworking following the accidental smelting of metal ores in a forest fire (Lucr. 5.1241–80), but with a Christian twist (*Alethia* 2.90–162): the fire was started when Adam threw a stone at the serpent after the expulsion from Eden, so striking the first spark and starting Lucretius's forest fire, leading to the discovery of molten and solidified metals. Marius Victor uses the trial-and-error language of Lucretius: "Suddenly a new thought occurred to them in their astonishment and sharpens their minds, and teaches them to follow up chance their teacher with art" (*Alethia* 2.148–50). But the incident follows a contrite prayer by Adam to God, whose aid in the apparently accidental event is recognized. Du Bartas, however, removes the providential element from his version, in "The Handy-crafts" (II.i.4), 235ff. Adam throws a "knobbie flint" at a wild beast, misses and hits a rock, producing sparks: "This happie chance made Adam leap for glee | And quickly calling his cold company, | In his left hand a shining flint he locks | Which with another in his right he knocks" (245–48).

This cautious framing of Lucretian material is recurrent in Du Bartas. One of the best-known examples is his close adaptation of Lucretius's arguments against the possibility that something could come into being out of nothing, and that anything could vanish into nothing (*Divine Weeks* I.ii.153–96) (cf. Lucretius 1.159–264). But as with the history of civilization, the Lucretian narrative is allowed to kick in only after an un-Lucretian divine intervention: "For All that's made, is made of the First Matter | Which in th'old Nothing made the All-Creator" (1.157–58). At the beginning of the Second Day Du Bartas aligns himself with a Lucretian poetics of truth and disillusionment, attacking poets who lead their young readers astray with the false charms of poetry on love, attributing divinity to "a blind Bowe-Boy...a Dwarfe, a Bastard" (Cupid) (7), and able to "make of an old, foule, frantike Hecuba, | A wondrous fresh, faire, wittie Helena" (3–4). This is the trick played by desire on Lucretius's blind lovers, who bestow beautifying endearments on their misshapen objects of desire (Lucr. 4.1153–70). Du Bartas warns: "For, under th'honey of their learned Workes | A hatefull draught of deadly poison lurkes" (19–20). This is a poisonous version of Lucretius's honeyed cup of wholesome, but, on its own, bitter, instruction (Lucr. 1.936–42). By implication Du Bartas's own honeyed cup will convey health-giving instruction, through a proper reformation of Lucretius's scientific poetry. Later in the same book Du Bartas adapts Lucretius's "atomology," the analogy between the construction of the world through atoms in various combinations and the construction of a text through letters in various combinations, in his account of how "the various Formes, wherewith the face | Of this faire World is so imbellished" (262–63) are all made out of the basic elements:

As sixe sweet Notes, curiously varied
In skilfull Musike, make a hundred kindes
Of Heavenly sounds, that ravish hardest minds,

And with Division of a choise device,
The Hearers soules out at their eares intice:
Or, as of twice twelve Letters, thus transposed,
This World of Words is variously composed;
And of these Words, in divers order sowne,
This sacred Volume that you read, is growne
(Through gracious succour of th'Eternall Deitie)
Rich in discourse, with infinite Varietie. (265–74)

Lucretius's image of the aleatory combination of atoms is converted into the divinely written book of nature. But, for all that, Du Bartas has a feel for the variety and abundance of the natural world that might be called Lucretian—an emphasis on the sensory experience of the world, rather than on the symbolic meanings of the book of nature, in line with the Lucretian foundation of knowledge on the senses, even if this is a sensory world now viewed through the spectacles of faith.[19]

Du Bartas's use of Lucretius is not restricted to isolated episodes or arguments. As we have seen, a complex of Lucretian allusion, drawing on different parts of the *DRN*, runs through the first part of the Second Day of the First Weeke. Another extended Lucretian engagement occurs later in the Second Day when Du Bartas comes to discuss the phenomenon of thunder and lightning, I.ii.677–744:

But harke, what heare I in the Heav'ns? me thinks
The Worlds wall shakes, and his Foundation shrinkes:
It-seemes even now that horrible Persephone
Loosing Meger, Alecto, and Tysiphone,
Wearie of raigning in blacke Erebus,
Transports her Hell between the Heav'n and us. (677–82)

Du Bartas alludes to passages from the lengthy demythologization of the thunderbolt: "In this way also all things appear to quake often from the shock of heavy thunder, and the mighty walls of the capacious world (*capacis moenia mundi*) seem to have been torn asunder and to have sprung apart" (Lucr. 6.121–23); and "Clouds at such times form so dense a mass over the whole sky that we might think that all its darkness had abandoned Acheron and filled up the great vaults of heaven" (Lucr. 6.250–52). And right at the beginning of the *DRN* the thunderbolt is emblematic of the terrors of superstition that do not deter Epicurus from his voyage of discovery through the boundless void: *quem neque fama deum nec fulmina nec minitanti | murmure compressit caelum* (1.68–69) [him neither stories of the gods nor thunderbolts nor heaven with its threatening roar could quell.] Du Bartas follows his terrifying image of the pagan Furies let loose in the skies, with a rationalistic, Lucretian, account of thunder and lightning as caused by hot vapors confined in clouds. An extended simile comparing the rumbling of these fiery vapors to the "hidious roaring" of a caged

lion develops a briefer Lucretian comparison of winds pent up in clouds
to wild beasts roaring in their cages (Lucr. 6.197–98 *magno indignantur
murmure clausi | nubibus in caueisque ferarum more minantur*). But at 781ff.
Du Bartas pulls himself up short:

> But O fond Mortals! Wherefore doo ye strive
> With reach of sence, Gods wonders to retrive? . . .
> I'le not denie, but that, a learned man
> May yeeld some Reason (if he list to scan)
> Of all that moves under Heav'ns hollow Cope;
> But not so sound as can all scruple stop.

Du Bartas then proceeds to reinstate *fama deum*:

> Me thinks I heare, when I doo heare it Thunder,
> The Voice that brings Swaynes up, and Caesars under:
> By that Tower-tearing stroake, I understand
> Th'undaunted strength of the Divine right hand:
> When I behold the Lightning in the Skies,
> Me thinks I see th'Almighties glorious eyes. (793–98)

There follows a list of prodigies, which leads to a direct rebuttal of Epicurus:
these prodigies "'gainst Epicures prophane assertions, show | That 'tis not
Fortune guides this World below" (837–38). Du Bartas thus starts from
the Lucretian move to demystify *religio*, but then reinstates thunder and
lightning as an expression of God's anger. A—or at least this—Christian
poet can only go so far in signing up to a Lucretian rationalist account of
nature. Otherwise Lucretius's defeat of *religio* ["superstition"] may lead to
too radical a removal of the divine from nature.

Abraham Cowley in "To the Royal Society" allows Francis Bacon a
more thorough victory of reason, liberating mankind from its imaginary oppressor, but only by turning Lucretius's *Religio* into the monster
Authority:

> But 'twas Rebellion call'd to fight
> For such a long-oppressed Right.
> Bacon at last, a mighty Man, arose
> Whom a wise King and Nature chose
> Lord Chancellour of both their Lawes,
> And boldly undertook the injur'd Pupils cause.
> Autority, which did a Body boast,
> Though 'twas but Air condens'd, and stalk'd about,
> Like some old Giants more Gigantic Ghost,
> To terrifie the Learned Rout,
> With the plain Magick of true Reasons Light,
> He chac'd out of our sight. (35–46)

Lucretian Sublime Flights

Lucretius, as James Porter has forcibly brought to our attention, plays an important role in the history of the sublime. Porter points out, for example, that Kant's list of the terrifying scenes of nature that evoke the sublime "put us in mind of nothing so much as *De Rerum Natura* 6."[20] The sublime in Lucretius is an aesthetic effect that serves the poet's doctrinal ends. We may, in fact, talk of contrasting sublimities in the *DRN*.[21] On one hand, there is a negative sublimity associated with the terrors of the pre-Epicurean experience of the universe, and of which the undoubtedly sublime (as Edmund Burke noted) monster *Religio* is an emblem. On the other hand, there is a positive sublime, associated with the vision of the Epicurean truth: Epicurus's flight of the mind at the beginning of the *DRN*, and the "epiphany" of the atoms falling endlessly through the boundless void at the beginning of Book 3, are the most striking examples.

In this section I look at what hexaemeral poets do with the sublime Lucretian image of Epicurus's flight of the mind through the void. Here I shall stray beyond the limits of the biblical, following the path that takes us on into the sublime flights of early modern science, the trajectory that leads in a fairly straight line to the sublimities of the big bang and black holes. For Christian poets the temptation of the Lucretian sublime flight brings with it the danger of overreaching, of straying into forbidden realms, entailing the necessity of a proper accommodation between the desire to explore the secrets of the universe and man's place in God's providential order.

As he sets out on his vast poem, Du Bartas expresses a proper moderation of ambition in singing of God's creation:

Climb they that list the battlements of Heav'n:
And with the Whirle-wind of Ambition driv'n,
Beyond the World's walls let those Eagles flie,
And gaze vpon the Sun of Majestie:
Let other-some (whose fainted spirits doo droope)
Downe to the ground their meditations stoope,
And so contemplate on these Workmanships,
That th'Authors praise they in themselves eclipse.
My heedfull Muse, trayned in true Religion,
Devinely-humane keepes the middle Region:
Least, if she should too-high a pitch presume,
Heav'ns glowing flame should melt her waxen plume;
Or, if too-low (neere Earth or Sea) she flagge,
Laden with mists her moisted wings should lagge. (I.i.127–40)

Du Bartas's sustained use here of the story of Daedalus's unheeded advice to his son Icarus to keep to a middle path in his flight, in Ovid's *Ars amatoria* 2 and *Metamorphoses* 8 (which itself owes some debts to Lucretian models) is introduced by an unmistakable reference to Epicurus's flight "Beyond the World's walls." This is the "middle flight" that Milton says that his "adventurous song" will not follow as it "soar[s] | Above the Aonian mount" (*Paradise Lost* 1.13–15),[22] for all that Raphael advises Adam not to be curious for knowledge beyond his human state at the conclusion of Raphael's speech:

> Heaven is for thee too high
> To know what passes there; be lowly wise:
> Think only what concerns thee and thy being;
> Dream not of other worlds, what creatures there
> Live, in what state, condition or degree,
> Contented that thus far hath been revealed
> Not of earth only but of highest heaven. (*Paradise Lost* 8.172–78)

For Andrew Marvell, in "On *Paradise Lost*," Milton's own sublime poetic flight properly matches his subject matter (l. 53: "Thy verse created like thy theme sublime").[23] Marvell praises Milton with allusion both to Epicurus's flight of the mind and to Lucretius's own reaction to the sublime vision of the universe vouchsafed by Epicurus (Lucr. 3.14–30): "At once delight and horror on us seize, | Thou singst with so much gravity and ease; | And above human flight dost soar aloft | With plume so strong, so equal, and so soft" ("On *Paradise Lost*" ll. 35–38).[24]

Du Bartas himself had not been entirely consistent in the matter of flight paths. As he warms to the task of narrating the creation of the heavenly bodies (I.iv.1ff), Du Bartas calls on the Spirit to take him up on the celestial flight of Elijah, which is also a flight of Phaethon that this time will not come to grief: "And with the Load-stone of my conquering Verse, | Above the Poles attract the most perverse." Later Du Bartas celebrates the power of the heaven-born soul of the little world that is man:

> And, though our Soule live as imprison'd here
> In our fraile flesh, or buried (as it were)
> In a dark Tombe; Yet at one flight she flies
> From Calpe t'Imaus, from the Earth to Skies:
> Much swifter then the Chariot of the Sunne...
> She mounts above the Worlds extreamest wall,   851
> Farre, farre beyond all things corporeall;
> Where she beholds her Maker face to face. (I.vi.831–56)

This is an Epicurean flight to a non-Epicurean goal. Marvell's praise of Milton is anticipated by earlier seventeenth-century praise of Du Bartas, for example, in Phineas Fletcher's *The Purple Island*: "And that French

Muses eagle eye and wing | Hath soar'd to heav'n" (1.14.1–2); or in Joseph
Hall: "To Mr Josuah Sylvester, of his Bartas metaphrased":[25]

> One while I finde her, in her nimble flight,
> Cutting the brazen spheares of Heaven bright:
> Thence, straight shee glides, before I bee aware,
> Through the three Regions of the liquid Ayre:
> Thence, rushing downe, through Nature's Closet-dore,
> She ransacks all her Grandame's secret store:
> And, diving to the darkness of the Deep,
> Sees there what Wealth the Waves in Prison keep:
> And, what shee sees above, below, between,
> She showes and sings to others eares and eyne. (II.7–15)

The risk associated with the Lucretian flight is sensed in later versions of
the topic, both in hints of the punishment inflicted on audacious excess,
and in the care taken to subordinate high-flying science to theology. The
first is exemplified in Thomas Gray's praise of Milton in his Pindaric ode
"The Progress of Poesy" (1754):[26]

> Nor second he, that rode sublime
> Upon the seraph-wings of Ecstasy,
> The secrets of the abyss to spy.
> He passed the flaming bounds of place and time:
> The living throne, the sapphire-blaze,
> Where angels tremble while they gaze,
> He saw; but blasted with excess of light,
> Closed his eyes in endless night. (95–102)

"Blasted with excess of light" (alluding to *Paradise Lost* 3.380 [God's
skirts] "Dark with excessive bright") might put us in mind of the fate of
the Giants who attempted to scale the heavens, or of Capaneus, blasted
by Jupiter when he climbed the battlements of Thebes and challenged
Olympus itself (Statius, *Thebaid* 10.837–939), mythological parallels that
were perhaps also in Du Bartas's mind in his opening dismissal of over-
reachers: "Climb they that list the battlements of Heav'n" (I.i.127).
   The second way of handling the Lucretian flight through the void,
by containing it (or attempting to contain it) safely within a Christian
worldview, is exemplified in one of the many poems in praise of Newton
that rework Lucretius's praise of Epicurus,[27] James Thomson's Miltonic
"To the Memory of Sir Isaac Newton" (late 1720s):[28]

>   When instead
> Of shatter'd parcels of this earth usurp'd
> By violence unmanly, and sore deeds   35
> Of cruelty and blood, Nature herself

Stood all subdued by him, and open laid
Her every latent glory to his view.²⁹
All intellectual eye, our solar round
First gazing through, he by the blended power   40
Of Gravitation and Projection saw
The whole in silent harmony revolve.
From unassisted vision hid, the moons

.   .   .   .   .   .

Then breaking hence, he took his ardent flight   57
Through the blue infinite; and every star,
Which the clear concave of a winter's night
Pours on the eye, or astronomic tube,   60
Far stretching, snatches from the dark abyss.

.   .   .   .   .   .

He, first of men, with awful wing pursued   76
The Comet through the long elliptic curve,
As round innumerous worlds he wound his way;
Till, to the forehead of our evening sky
Return'd, the blazing wonder glares anew,   80
And o'er the trembling nations shakes dismay.

For Thomson, it is not Religion, but Nature that is subdued by Newton. Newton's penetrating vision of the nature of things serves instead to reinforce a belief in a supreme supernatural being:

What wonder thence that his devotion swell'd   137
Responsive to his knowledge? For could he,
Whose piercing mental eye diffusive saw
The finish'd university of things,   140
In all its order, magnitude, and parts,
Forbear incessant to adore that power
Who fills, sustains, and actuates the whole?

Postmortem, Newton will return to wander through the "endless worlds," rather like Lycidas translated to a Christian heaven, his immortal soul now granted a closer communion with God and his angels—a comfortable, but perhaps ultimately unsatisfactory, attempt to contain the *uoluptas atque horror* of the Lucretian void, which is now the void of modern science:

The virgin in her bloom   177
Cut off, the joyous youth, and darling child,
These are the tombs that claim the tender tear,
And elegiac song. But Newton calls   180
For other notes of gratulation high,
That now he wanders through those endless worlds³⁰
He here so well descried, and wondering talks,

And hymns their author with his glad compeers.
O Britain's boast! whether with angels thou   185
Sittest in dread discourse, or fellow-bless'd,
Who joy to see the honour of their kind;
Or whether, mounted on cherubic wing,
Thy swift career is with the whirling orbs,
Comparing things with things, in rapture lost,   190
And grateful adoration, for that light
So plenteous ray'd into thy mind below,
From light himself; Oh, look with pity down
On humankind, a frail erroneous race!

The pity in the last two lines is a softer, more Christian, version of Lucretius's pitying scorn for the "wretched minds of men, blind hearts" at *DRN* 2.14 (*o miseras hominum mentis, o pectora caeca*), mediated via Virgil's own more sympathetic version at the beginning of the *Georgics*, 1.41 (addressing Octavian): "With me take pity on the rustics ignorant of the path" (*ignarosque uiae mecum miseratus agrestis*). At the end Thomson imagines Newton "wander[ing] through those endless worlds," but now in angelic company.

Notes

1. For the text of Lucretius, I use the Oxford Classical Text of *De Rerum Natura*, ed. Cyril Bailey, 2nd ed. (Oxford: Oxford University Press, 1922); hereafter abbreviated Lucr. My translations of Lucretius are adapted from those of H. A. J. Munro, trans., *T. Lucreti Cari De rerum natura libri sex*, 4th ed., 3 vols. (Cambridge: Deighton Bell, 1886); other translations are my own.

2. In general, see Frank E. Robbins, *The Hexaemeral Literature: A Study of the Greek and Latin Commentaries on Genesis* (Chicago, IL: Chicago University Press, 1912); J. Martin Evans, *Paradise Lost and the Genesis Tradition* (Oxford: Oxford University Press, 1968).

3. See Karl Gronau, *Poseidonius, eine Quelle für Basilos' Hexahemeros* (Braunschweig, 1912).

4. Ovid, *P. Ovidi Nasonis Metamorphoses*, ed. Richard J. Tarrant (Oxford: Oxford University Press, 2004); hereafter abbreviated *Met.* and cited by book and line number.

5. On the *interpretatio Ovidiana* of Genesis, see Michael Roberts, "Ovid's *Metamorphoses* and the Latin Poets of Late Antiquity," *Arethusa* 35 (2002): 403–15; *indigesta moles* applied to the Genesis story: A. B. Chambers, "Chaos in *Paradise Lost*," *Journal of the History of Ideas* 24 (1963): 61.

6. Marco Girolamo Vida, *Christiad*, ed. and trans. James Gardner (Cambridge, MA, and London: Harvard University Press, 2009).

7. See also Vida, *Christiad*, 1.605 *nec mora uix coeli extuderat septemplicis orbem* [immediately he had forged the circle of the sevenfold heavens] (God creates the heavens) with Virgil, *Aeneid*, 8.448–49 *septenosque orbibus orbis | impediunt* [they bind together the seven circular layers of the shield] (the making of the Shield of Aeneas); 12.925 *clipei*

extremos septemplicis orbis [the outermost circles of the sevenfold shield] (of Turnus). Citations of Virgil's *Aeneid* and *Georgics* are taken from *P. Vergilii Maronis Opera*, ed. R. A. B. Mynors (Oxford: Oxford University Press, 1969).

8. Philip Hardie, *Virgil's Aeneid: Cosmos and Imperium* (Oxford: Oxford University Press, 1986), 360–61.

9. Cf. Genesis 3: 8, *abscondit se Adam et uxor eius a facie Domini Dei in medio ligni paradisi* [Adam and his wife hid themselves from the presence of the Lord God amongst the trees of the garden]; see *Biblia Sacra Vulgata*, ed. Bonifatius Fischer et al., 3rd ed. (Stuttgart: Deutsche Bibelgesellschaft, 1984).

10. Endless *poenae*: see Lucr. 1.111; 3.1014, 1021; 5.1151; 6.72.

11. *Dracontius: Louanges de Dieu, livres I et II*, ed. Claude Moussy and Colette Camus (Paris: Belles Lettres, 1985).

12. On Milton and the hexaemeral tradition, see Mary I. Corcoran, *Milton's Paradise with Reference to the Hexameral Background* (Washington, DC: Catholic University of America Press, 1945). References to *Paradise Lost* are from *The Poems of John Milton*, ed. John Carey and Alastair Fowler (London and New York: Longman, 1968).

13. Enzo Giudici, ed., *Maurice Scève: Microcosme* (Cassino and Paris: Vrin, 1976), 85–88; with *Microcosme* 2.101–4. See also Lucr. 5.925–87 on the life of primitive man. On Lucretius in sixteenth-century France, see Simone Fraisse, *L'Influence de Lucrèce en France au seizième siècle: Une conquête du rationalisme* (Paris: A. G. Nizet, 1962); Philip Ford, "Lucretius in Early Modern France," ed. Stuart Gillespie and Philip Hardie, *The Cambridge Companion to Lucretius* (Cambridge: Cambridge University Press, 2007), 227–41.

14. Don P. Fowler, *Lucretius on Atomic Motion: A Commentary on Lucretius De Rerum Natura 2.1–332* (Oxford: Oxford University Press, 2002), ad loc.

15. Ibid., 261.

16. See Alexandra Walsham, *The Reformation of the Landscape: Religion, Identity, & Memory in Early Modern Britain & Ireland* (Oxford: Oxford University Press, 2011), 379–83 on the physical appearance of earth as a direct consequence of human sinfulness, both the Fall and the Flood; a key text is Thomas Burnet's *Telluris theoria sacra* (London, 1681); English version, *The Sacred Theory of the Earth* (London, 1684).

17. In the edition of Susan Snyder, ed., *The Divine Weeks and Works of Guillaume de Saluste Sieur Du Bartas, translated by Josuah Sylvester*, 2 vols. (Oxford: Oxford University Press, 1979). For the French text, see Urban T. Holmes, John C. Lyons, Robert W. Linker, eds. *The Works of Guillaume de Salluste, Sieur du Bartas*, 3 vols. (Chapel Hill: University of North Carolina Press, 1935–40). On Du Bartas and Lucretius, see V. K. Whitaker, "Du Bartas' Use of Lucretius," *Studies in Philology* 33 (1936): 134–46; J. Kany-Turpin, "Une Reinvention de Lucrèce par Guillaume du Bartas," in *La Littérature et ses avatars: Discredits, deformations et rehabilitations dans l'histoire de la littérature*, ed. Y. Bellenger (Paris: Aux Amateurs de Livres, 1991), 31–39; S. Lamacz, "La Construction du savoir et la réécriture du *De Rerum Natura* dans *La Sepmaine* de Du Bartas," *Bibliothèque d'Humanisme et Renaissance* 64 (2002): 617–38.

18. Stanislas Gamber, *Le Livre de la 'Genèse' dans la poésie latine au cinquième siècle* (Paris, 1899), 62–63. References to Victor are to Claudius Marius Victorius, *Claudii Marii Victorii Alethia*, ed. P. F. Hovingh, Corpus Christianorum, series Latina 128 (Turnholt: Brepols 1960).

19. This is properly stressed by Lamacz, "La Construction."

20. James Porter, "Lucretius and the Sublime," in Gillespie and Hardie, *Cambridge Companion*, 167–84, 178.

21. Contrasting Lucretian sublimities: Philip Hardie, *Lucretian Receptions: History, The Sublime, Knowledge* (Cambridge: Cambridge University Press, 2009), 76.

22. See David Quint, "Fear of Falling: Icarus, Phaethon, and Lucretius in *Paradise Lost*," *Renaissance Quarterly* 57 (2004): 875 for Milton's revision here of Du Bartas. In general on Milton's use of Du Bartas, see George C. Taylor, *Milton's Use of DuBartas* (Cambridge, MA: Harvard University Press, 1934).

23. *The Poems of Andrew Marvell*, ed. Nigel Smith (Harlow: Pearson/Longman, 2003).

24. See Hardie, *Lucretian Receptions*, 278–79.

25. Both passages are cited in Anne L. Prescott, "The Reception of Du Bartas in England," *Studies in the Renaissance* 15 (1968): 155. For the originals, see Giles and Phineas Fletcher, *Poetical Works*, ed. F. S. Boas, 2 vols. (Cambridge: Cambridge University Press, 1908–09); Joseph Hall, "To Mr Josuah Sylvester, of his Bartas Metaphrased," in *Bartas His Devine Weekes and Werkes*, trans. Josuah Sylvester (London, 1608), sig. B5v.

26. *Thomas Gray and William Collins, Poetical Works*, ed. Roger H. Lonsdale (Oxford: Oxford University Press, 1977).

27. Patricia Fara and David Money, "Isaac Newton and Augustan Anglo-Latin Poetry," *Studies in History and Philosophy of Science* 35 (2004): 549–71.

28. *The Complete Poetical Works of James Thomson*, ed. J. Logie Robertson (London: Oxford University Press, 1908).

29. Cf. Lucr. 3.29–30 *quod sic natura tua ui | tam manifesta patens ex omni parte retecta est* [since through your might nature has been revealed, so clearly laid open in every part]; "subdued" might remind us of Lucr. 1.78 *religio pedibus subiecta* [religion subjected underfoot].

30. Cf. Lucr. 1.74: *atque omne immensum peragrauit mente animoque* [and in his mind and soul he wandered through all the boundless void].

BIBLIOGRAPHY

Althusser, Louis. *Philosophy of the Encounter: Later Writings, 1978–1987*, edited by François Matheron and Oliver Corpet. Translated by G. M. Goshgarian. New York: Verso, 2006.

Anderson, Kirsti. *The Geometry of an Art: The History of the Mathematical Theory of Perspective from Alberti to Monge*. New York: Springer, 2007.

Angeli, Anna, and Tiziano Dorandi. "Gli Epicurei e la geometria: Un progetto di geometria anti-euclidea nel Giardino di Epicuro?" In *Lucrezio, la natura e la scienza*, edited by Marco Beretta and Francesco Citti, 1–9. Florence: L. S. Olschki, 2008.

Aristotle. *Nicomachean Ethics*. Translated by W. D. Ross. Oxford: Clarendon Press, 1908.

Aristotle. *Physics*. Translated by R. P. Hardie and R. K. Gaye. In *The Complete Works of Aristotle: The Revised Oxford Translation*, edited by Jonathan Barnes. 2 vols. Princeton, NJ: Princeton University Press, 1984.

Asmis, Elizabeth. "Crates on Poetic Criticism." *Phoenix* 46 (1992): 128–69.

Asmis, Elisabeth. *Epicurus' Scientific Method*. Cornell: Cornell University Press, 1984.

Asmis, Elisabeth. "Epicurean Empiricism." In *The Cambridge Companion to Epicureanism*, edited by James Warren, 84–104. Cambridge: Cambridge University Press, 2009.

Assad, Maria. "Ulyssean Trajectories: A (New) Look at Michel Serres' Topology of Time." In Herzogenrath, *Time and History*, 85–102.

Baker, Eric. "Lucretius and the European Enlightenment." In *The Cambridge Companion to Lucretius*, edited by Stuart Gillespie and Philip Hardie, 274–88. Cambridge: Cambridge University Press, 2007.

Bakker, F. A. *Three Studies in Epicurean Cosmology*. Quaestiones Infinitae: Publications of the Department of Philosophy, Utrecht University. Vol. 64. PhD diss., University of Utrecht, 2010.

Balibar, Etienne. "From Philosophical Anthropology to Social Ontology and Back: What to Do with Marx's Sixth Thesis on Feuerbach?" *Postmodern Culture* 22.3 (2012). Online at *Postmodern Culture* 22:3, May 2012, 10.1353/pmc.2012.0014.

Balibar, Etienne. "Anthropologie philosophique ou Ontologie de la relation? Que faire de la 'VI Thèse sur Feuerbach'?" "Complément." In *La philosophie de Marx*, edited by Etienne Balibar, 193–250. Paris: La Découverte/Poche, 2014.

Balzac, Honoré de. "Brillat-Savarin." In *Biographie universelle ancienne et moderne*, edited by Joseph-François Michaud and Louis-Gabriel Michaud, Vol. 5: 250. Paris: Michaud Frères, 1811–62.

Barnes, Jonathan, ed. *Early Greek Philosophy*. 2nd edition. New York: Penguin Books, 2001.

Bayle, Pierre. *General Dictionary Historical and Critical*. 10 vols. Translated by John Peter Bernard, Thomas Birch, John Lockman, and other hands. London: Roberts, 1738–41.

Bayle, Pierre. *Continuation des pensées diverses*. 2 vols. Amsterdam: Herman Uytwerf, 1722.

Beaune, J.-C., S. Benoit, J. Gayon, J. Roger, and D. Woronoff, eds. *Buffon 88: Actes du Colloque international pour le bicentenaire de la mort de Buffon*. Paris: J. Vrin, 1992.

Bénatouïl, Thomas. "Les critiques épicuriennes de la géométrie." In *Construction: Festschrift for Gerhard Heinzmann*, edited by Pierre-Edouard Bour, Manuel Rebuschi, and Laurent Rollet, 151–62. London: College Publications, 2010.

Bennett, Jane, and William Connolly. "The Crumpled Handkerchief." In Herzogenrath, *Time and History*, 153–71.

Berlin, Isaiah. *Four Essays on Liberty.* Oxford: Oxford University Press, 1969.

Biblia Sacra Vulgata, edited by Bonifatius Fischer et al. 3rd ed. Stuttgart: Deutsche Bibelgesellschaft, 1984.

Bobzien, Suzanne. *Freedom and Determinism in Stoic Philosophy.* Oxford: Oxford University Press, 1999.

Bobzien, Suzanne. "Did Epicurus Discover the Free-Will Problem?" *Oxford Studies in Ancient Philosophy* 19 (2000): 287–337.

Bodnár, Istvan M. "Atomic Independence and Indivisibility." *Oxford Studies in Ancient Philosophy* 16 (1998): 35–61.

Bowie, Andrew. *Aesthetics and Subjectivity from Kant to Nietzsche.* Manchester: Manchester University Press, 1990.

Boulanger, Nicolas Antoine. *Oeuvres de Boullanger.* 8 vols. Paris: Jean Servières, 1792.

Boyer, Carl B., and Uta C. Merzbach. *A History of Mathematics.* 2nd ed. Hoboken, NJ: John Wiley, 1991.

Brandt, Rheinhard. *Die Bestimmung des Menschen bei Kant.* Hamburg: Meiner, 2007.

Brillat-Savarin, Jean-Anthelme. *La Physiologie du goût,* edited by Jean-François Revel. Paris: Flammarion, 1982.

Brown, Alison. *The Return of Lucretius to Renaissance Florence.* Cambridge, MA: Harvard University Press, 2010.

Brown, Robert. *Lucretius on Love and Sex: A Commentary on* De Rerum Natura *4.1030–287, with Prolegomena, Text, and Translation.* Columbia Studies in the Classical Tradition 15. Leiden: Brill, 1987.

Buffon, George Louis Leclerc. *Buffon's Natural History Containing a Theory of the Earth, a General History of Man, of the Brute Creation, and of Vegetables, Minerals, &c.* 10 vols. Translated by James Smith Barr, London: J. S. Barr, 1792.

Buffon, George Louis Leclerc. *Les Époques de la Nature.* 3 vols. Paris: Imprimerie Royale, 1780.

Buffon, George Louis Leclerc. *Histoire Naturelle, générale et particulière, avec la description du Cabinet du Roy.* 15 vols. Paris: Imprimerie du Roi, 1749–57.

Bullard, Paddy. "Edmund Burke among the Poets: Milton, Lucretius and the *Philosophical Enquiry.*" In *The Science of Sensibility: Reading Burke's* Philosophical Enquiry, edited by Koen Vermeir and Michael Funk Deckard, 247–63. New York: Springer, 2012.

Burnet, Thomas. *The Sacred Theory of the Earth.* London, 1684.

Burnet, Thomas. *Telluris theoria sacra.* London, 1681.

Calvino, Italo. *Six Memos for the Next Millennium.* Translated by Patrick Creagh. Cambridge, MA: Harvard University Press, 1988.

Campbell, Gordon L. "Lucretius Reaches the Mainstream." *Classical Review* 59:1 (2009): 115–17.

Castillon, Jean de. *Discours sur l'origine de l'inégalité.* 1756. Reprint, Amsterdam: J. F. Jolly, 2006.

Chaitin, Gregory. "The Limits of Reason." *Scientific American* 294:3 (2006): 74–81.

Chambers, A. B. "Chaos in *Paradise Lost.*" *Journal of the History of Ideas* 24 (1963): 55–84.

Chaney, Joseph. "The Revolution of a Trope: The Rise of the New Science and the Divestment of Rhetoric in the Seventeenth Century." In *Signs of Change: Premodern → Modern → Postmodern,* edited by Stephen Barker, 155–74. New York: State University of New York Press, 1996.

Chappell, V. C. "Locke on the Freedom of the Will." In *Locke's Philosophy: Content and Context,* edited by G. A. J. Rodgers, 101–21. Oxford: Oxford University Press, 1994.

Chappell, V. C. "Locke on the Suspension of Desire." *Locke Studies* 29 (1998): 23–38.

Cicero. *Akademische Abhandlungen Lucullus,* edited and translated by Christoph Schäublin. Hamburg: Felix Meiner Verlag, 1998.

Cicero. *De Natura Deorum, Academica.* Translated by H. Rackham. Cambridge, MA: Harvard University Press, 1933.

Cicero. *On Ends.* Translated by H. Rackham. Cambridge, MA: Harvard University Press, 1914.

Cicero. *Tusculan Disputations.* Translated by J. E. King. Cambridge, MA: Harvard University Press, 1950.

Clayton, Kevin. "Time Folded and Crumpled: Time, History, Self-Organization, and the Methodology of Michel Serres." In Herzogenrath, *Time and History,* 31–49.

Clucas, Stephen. "Liquid History: Serres and Lucretius." In *Mapping Michel Serres,* edited by Niran Abbas, 72–83. Ann Arbor: University of Michigan Press, 2005.

Commager Jr., H. S. "Lucretius's Interpretation of the Plague." In Gale, *Oxford Readings*, 182–98.

Cooper, John. "Plato on Sense-Perception and Knowledge (Theaetetus 184–186)." In *Plato, Vol. 1: Metaphysics and Epistemology*, edited by Gail Fine, 377–83. Oxford: Oxford University Press, 1999.

Cooper, Melinda. "Marx beyond Marx, Marx before Marx: Negri's Lucretian Critique of the Hegelian Marx." In *Reading Negri: Marxism in the Age of Empire*, edited by Pierre Lamarche, Max Rosenkrantz, and David Sherman, 127–49. Chicago, IL: Open Court, 2011.

Corcoran, Mary I. *Milton's Paradise with Reference to the Hexameral Background.* Washington, DC: Catholic University of America Press, 1945.

Costa, C. D. N. *Lucretius De Rerum Natura V.* Oxford: Oxford University Press, 1984.

Crane, Tim. "Is Perception a Propositional Attitude?" *The Philosophical Quarterly* 59 (2009): 452–469.

Creuz, Friedrich Karl Casimir Freyherr von. *Die Gräber: Ein Philosophisches Gedicht in Sechs Gesängen.* Frankfurt: Maynz, 1760.

Creuz, Friedrich Karl Casimir Freyherr von. *Versuch über die Seele.* Frankfurt and Leipzig: Knoch und Esslinger, 1754.

Darmon, Jean-Charles. *Philosophie épicurienne et littérature au XVIIe siècle.* Paris: Presses Universitaires de France, 1998.

De Lacy, Phillip. "Distant Views: The Imagery of Lucretius 2." *Classical Journal* 60 (1964): 49–55.

De Lacy, Phillip. "Distant Views: The Imagery of Lucretius 2." In Gale, *Oxford Readings*, 146–57.

Deleuze, Gilles. "Lucrèce et le naturalisme." *Études philosophiques* 1 (1961): 19–29.

Deleuze, Gilles. "Renverser le platonisme (Les simulacres)." *Revue de Métaphysique et de Morale* 71 (1966): 426–38.

Deleuze, Gilles. *The Logic of Sense.* Translated by Mark Lester and Charles Stivale. New York: Columbia University Press, 1990.

Deleuze, Gilles. *Difference and Repetition.* Translated by Paul Patton. New York: Columbia University Press, 1995.

Deleuze, Gilles. *Expressionism in Philosophy: Spinoza.* Translated by Martin Joughin. New York: Zone Books, 1992.

Derrida, Jacques. "My Chances/Mes Chances: A Rendezvous with Some Epicurean Stereophonies." In *Taking Chances: Derrida, Psychoanalysis, and Literature*, edited by J. Smith and W. Kerrigan, 1–32. Baltimore, MD: Johns Hopkins University Press, 1984.

Diderot, Denis. *Political Writings.* Translated and edited by John Hope Mason and Robert Wokler. Cambridge: Cambridge University Press, 1992.

Diderot, Denis, and Jean d'Alembert. *Encyclopédie, ou Dictionnaire raisonné des sciences, des arts et des métiers.* 1751–57. Reprint [17 vols., plus plates and supplement in 5 vols.], New York: Readex Microprint, 1969.

Diderot, Denis, and Jean le Rond d'Alembert. *Encyclopédie, our Dictionnaire raisonné des sciences, des arts, et des métiers.* 2 vols. Edited by A. Pons. Paris: Flammarion, 1993.

Diels, H., and W. Kranz, eds. *Die Fragmente der Vorsokratiker.* 3 vols. Berlin: Weidmann, 1996.

Dinshaw, Carolyn. *How Soon Is Now? Medieval Texts, Amateur Readers, and the Queerness of Time.* Durham, NC: Duke University Press, 2012.

Diogenes Laertius. *Lives of Eminent Philosophers.* With an English translation by R. D. Hicks. 2 vols. Cambridge, MA: Harvard University Press; London: Wm. Heinemann, 1958–59; Vol. 1, 1959.

Diogenes of Oenoanda. *Diogenes of Oenoanda: The Epicurean Inscription*, edited and translated by Martin Ferguson Smith. La scuola di Epicuro, Supplemento No. 1. Naples: Bibliopolis, 1993.

Dracontius. *Dracontius: Louanges de Dieu, livres I et II*, edited by Claude Moussy and Colette Camus. Paris: Belles Lettres, 1985.

Duchesneau, François. "Haller and the Theories of Buffon and C. F. Wolff on Epigenesis." *History and Philosophy of the Life Sciences* 1 (1979): 65–100.

Dueck, Daniela, and Kai Broderson. *Geography in Classical Antiquity.* Cambridge: Cambridge University Press, 2012.

Edwards, Karen L. *Milton and the Natural World: Science and Poetry in "Paradise Lost."* Cambridge: Cambridge University Press, 1999.

Emberley, Peter, and Barry Cooper, eds. and trans. *Faith and Political Philosophy: The Correspondence between Leo Strauss and Eric Voegelin, 1934–1964.* University Park: Pennsylvania State University Press, 1993.

Engels, Friedrich. *Socialism: Utopian and Scientific.* Translated by Edward Aveling. In *Marx/Engels Selected Works.* Vol. 3, 95–151. Moscow: Progress, 1970.

Epicurus. *Epicuro: Opere,* edited by Graziano Arrighetti. Turin: Einaudi, 1960.

Epicurus. *Epicuro: Opere,* edited by Graziano Arrighetti. 2nd ed. Turin: Einaudi, 1973.

Epicurus, "Letter to Herodotus." In *Lives of Eminent Philosophers.* By Diogenes Laertius. Perseus Digital Library. http://www.perseus.tufts.edu/hopper/text?doc=urn:cts:greekLit:tlg0004.tlg001 .perseus-grc1:10.1

Eusebius. *Eusebius Werke, Band 8: Die Praeparatio evangelica,* edited by K. Mras. *Die griechischen christlichen Schriftsteller.* Vols. 43.1 and 43.2. Berlin: Akademie Verlag, 1954 (43.1), 1956 (43.2).

Evans, J. Martin. *Paradise Lost and the Genesis Tradition.* Oxford: Oxford University Press, 1968.

Evans, James. *The History and Practice of Ancient Astronomy.* New York: Oxford University Press, 1998.

Everson, Stephen. "Epicurus on the Truth of the Senses." In *Epistemology,* edited by Stephen Everson, 161–83. Cambridge: Cambridge University Press, 1990.

Fallon, Stephen M. *Milton among the Philosophers: Poetry and Materialism in Seventeenth-Century England.* Ithaca, NY, and London: Cornell University Press, 1991.

Fara, Patricia, and David Money. "Isaac Newton and Augustan Anglo-Latin Poetry." *Studies in History and Philosophy of Science* 35 (2004): 549–71.

Feuerbach, Ludwig. *Geschichte der neuern Philosophie von Bacon von Verulam bis Benedict Spinoza.* Ansbach, 1833.

Fleischmann, Wolfgang. *Lucretius and English Literature, 1680–1740.* Paris: A. G. Nizet, 1964.

Fleischmann, Wolfgang. "The Debt of the Enlightenment to Lucretius." *Studies on Voltaire and the Eighteenth Century* 15 (1963): 631–43.

Fletcher, Giles, and Phineas. *Poetical Works,* edited by F. S. Boas. 2 vols. Cambridge: Cambridge University Press, 1908–09.

Ford, Philip. "Lucretius in Early Modern France." In Gillespie and Hardie, *Cambridge Companion,* 227–41.

Fowler, Don. *Lucretius on Atomic Motion: A Commentary on De Rerum Natura 2.1–332.* Oxford: Oxford University Press, 2002.

Fowler, Peta. "Lucretian Conclusions." In *Classical Closure: Reading the End in Greek and Latin Literature,* edited by D. H. Roberts, F. M. Dunn, and D. P. Fowler, 112–38. Princeton, NJ: Princeton University Press, 1997.

Fraisse, Simone. *L'Influence de Lucrèce en France au seizième siècle: Une conquête du rationalisme.* Paris: A. G. Nizet, 1962.

Frede, Michael. "Observations on Perception in Plato's Later Dialogues." In *Plato 1: Metaphysics and Epistemology,* edited by Gail Fine, 355–76. Oxford: Oxford University Press, 1999.

Friedländer, Paul. "Pattern of Sound and Atomistic Theory in Lucretius." *The American Journal of Philology* 62:1 (1941): 16–34.

Frischer, Bernard. *The Sculpted Word: Epicureanism and Philosophical Recruitment in Ancient Greece.* Berkeley, 1982; rev. ed. 2006. Accessed April 19, 2013. http://quod.lib.umich.edu/cgi/t/text /text-idx?c=acls;cc=acls;view=toc;idno=heb90022.0001.001

Furley, David. *Two Studies in the Greek Atomists.* Princeton, NJ: Princeton University Press, 1967.

Fusil, C. A. "Lucrèce et les philosophes du XVIIIe siècle." *Revue d 'histoire littéraire de la France* 35 (1928): 194–210.

Fusil, C.A. "Lucrèce et les litterateurs, poètes et artistes du XVIIIe siècle." *Revue d 'histoire littéraire de la France* 37 (1930): 161–76.

Gaisser, Julia H. "The Reception of Classical Texts in the Renaissance." In *The Italian Renaissance in the Twentieth Century,* edited by Allen J. Grieco, Michael Rocke, and Fiorella Gioffredi Superbi, 387–400. Florence: L. S. Olschki, 2002.

Gale, Monica R. *Myth and Poetry in Lucretius.* Cambridge: Cambridge University Press, 1994.

Gale, Monica R., ed. *Oxford Readings in Classical Studies: Lucretius.* Oxford: Oxford University Press, 2007.

Galen. *Three Treatises on the Nature of Science.* Translated and edited by Richard Walzer and Michael Frede. Indianapolis, IN: Hackett, 1985.

Gamber, Stanislas. *Le Livre de la 'Genèse' dans la poésie latine au cinquième siècle*. Paris, 1899.

Garay, Luis J. "Quantum Gravity and Minimum Length." *International Journal of Modern Physics* A10 (1995): 145–66. Accessed September 9, 2011. http://arxiv.org/PS_cache/gr-qc/pdf/9403 /9403008v2.pdf

Gigandet, Alain. *Lucrèce: Atomes, mouvement: Physique et éthique*. Paris: Presses Universitaires de France, 2001.

Gigante, Marcello. *Philodemus in Italy: The Books from Herculaneum*. Translated by Dirk Obbink. Ann Arbor: University of Michigan Press, 1995.

Gillespie, Stuart. *English Translation and Classical Reception: Towards a New Literary History*. Malden, MA: Wiley-Blackwell, 2011.

Gillespie, Stuart. "Lucretius in the English Renaissance." In Gillespie and Hardie, *Cambridge Companion*, 242–53.

Gillespie, Stuart, and Philip Hardie, eds. *The Cambridge Companion to Lucretius*. Cambridge: Cambridge University Press, 2007.

Gillespie, Stuart, and Donald Mackenzie. "Lucretius and the Moderns." In Gillespie and Hardie, *Cambridge Companion to Lucretius*, 306–24.

Gingerich, Owen. "Did Copernicus Owe a Debt to Aristarchus?" *Journal for the History of Astronomy* 16 (1985): 37–42.

Ginzburg, Carlo "The High and the Low: The Theme of Forbidden Knowledge in the Sixteenth and Seventeenth Centuries." In *Myths, Emblems, Clues*. Translated by J. and A. Tedeschi, 60–76. London: Hutchinson Radius, 1990.

Giudici, Enzo, ed. *Maurice Scève. Microcosme*. Cassino and Paris: Vrin, 1976.

Glidden, David K. "'Sensus' and Sense Perception in the 'De Rerum Natura.'" *California Studies in Classical Antiquity* 12 (1979): 155–81.

Goldberg, Jonathan. *The Seeds of Things: Theorizing Sexuality and Materiality in Renaissance Representations*. New York: Fordham University Press, 2009.

Gordon, Cosmo Alexander. *A Bibliography of Lucretius*. Winchester: St. Paul's Bibliographies, 1985.

Graver, Margaret. "The Eye of the Beholder: Perceptual Relativity in Lucretius." *Apeiron* 23 (1990): 91–116.

Gray, Thomas, and William Collins. *Thomas Gray and William Collins, Poetical Works*, edited by Roger H. Lonsdale. Oxford: Oxford University Press, 1977.

Greenblatt, Stephen. "The Answer Man: An Ancient Poem Was Rediscovered—And the World Swerved." *The New Yorker*, August 8, 2011, 28–33.

Greenblatt, Stephen. *The Swerve: How the World Became Modern*. New York: W. W. Norton, 2011.

Gronau, Karl. *Poseidonius, eine Quelle für Basilos' Hexahemeros*. Braunschweig, 1912.

Hall, Joseph. "To Mr Josuah Sylvester, of his Bartas Metaphrased." *Bartas His Devine Weekes and Werkes*. Translated by Josuah Sylvester, sig. B5v. London, 1608.

Haller, Albrecht. *Briefe über die wichtigsten Wahrheiten der Öffenbarung*. Bern: Neue Buchhandlung, 1772.

Haller, Albrecht. *Letters from Baron Haller to His Daughter: On the Truths of the Christian Religion, Translated from the German*. London: John Murray, 1780.

Hardie, Philip. *Lucretian Receptions: History, The Sublime, Knowledge*. Cambridge: Cambridge University Press, 2009.

Hardie, Philip. "Milton and Lucretius." In Hardie, *Lucretian Receptions*, 264–79 (first published in *Milton Quarterly* 29 [1995]: 13–24).

Hardie, Philip. *Virgil's Aeneid: Cosmos and Imperium*. Oxford: Oxford University Press, 1986.

Harris, Jonathan Gil. *Untimely Matter in the Time of Shakespeare*. Philadelphia: University of Pennsylvania Press, 2009.

Heath, Thomas. *Aristarchus: The Ancient Copernicus*. Oxford: Oxford University Press, 1913.

Hegel, G. W. F. *The Science of Logic*. Translated by A. V. Miller. London: Allen & Unwin, 1969.

Herzogenrath, Bernd, ed. *Time and History in Deleuze and Serres*. London: Continuum, 2012.

Hettner, Hermann. *Gesch. der deutschen Literatur im Achtzehnten Jahrhundert*, edited by George Witowski. 4 vols. Leipzig: P. List, 1928.

Hinch, Jim. "Why Stephen Greenblatt Is Wrong—And Why It Matters." *The Los Angeles Review of Books*, December 1, 2012. http://lareviewofbooks.org/review/why-stephen-greenblatt-is -wrong-and-why-it-matters

Hinds, Stephen. "Language at the Breaking Point: Lucretius 1.452." *The Classical Quarterly,* New Series 37:2 (1987): 450–53.

Hodge, M. J. S. "Two Cosmogonies ('Theory of the Earth' and 'Theory of Generation') and the Unity of Buffon's Thought." In *Buffon 88: Actes du Colloque international pour le bicentenaire de la mort de Buffon,* edited by J.-C. Beaune, S. Benoit, J. Gayon, J. Roger, and D. Woronoff, 241–54. Paris: J. Vrin, 1992.

Holford-Strevens, Leofranc. "*Horror vacui* in Lucretian Biography." *Leeds International Classical Studies* 1:1 (2002): 1–23.

Holmes, Brooke. "Daedala Lingua: Crafted Speech in *De Rerum Natura.*" *American Journal of Philology* 126:4 (2005): 527–85.

Holmes, Urban T., John C. Lyons, and Robert W. Linker, eds. *The Works of Guillaume de Salluste, Sieur du Bartas.* 3 vols. Chapel Hill: University of North Carolina Press, 1935–40.

Housman, A. E., ed. *M. Manilii Astronomicon liber secundus,* 2nd ed. Cambridge: Cambridge University Press, 1937.

Huby, Pamela. "The First Discovery of the Freewill Problem." *Philosophy* 42 (1967): 353–62.

Hundert, E. J. *The Enlightenment's Fable: Bernard Mandeville and the Discovery of Society.* Cambridge: Cambridge University Press, 2005.

Hutcheson, Francis. *An Essay on the Nature and Conduct of the Passions and Affections.* 1742. Reprint, Hildesheim: Olms, 1990.

Ingalls, Wayne. "Repetition in Lucretius." *Phoenix* 25:3 (1971): 227–36.

Irwin, T. H. "Who Discovered the Will?" *Philosophical Perspectives* 6 (1992): 453–73.

Iversen, Margaret. "The Discourse of Perspective in the Twentieth Century: Panofsky, Damisch, Lacan." *Oxford Art Journal* 28 (2005): 191–202.

Janko, Richard. "Reconstructing Philodemus, On Poems." In *Philodemus and Poetry,* edited by Dirk Obbink, 69–96. Oxford: Oxford University Press, 1995.

Janko, Richard. *Philodemus, On Poems, Book One.* Oxford: Oxford University Press, 2000.

Janko, Richard. *Philodemus, On Poems, Books 3–4, with the Fragments of Aristotle, On Poets.* Oxford: Oxford University Press, 2010.

Jaucourt, Louis de. "Guerre." In Diderot and D'Alembert, *Encylopédie,* Vol. 2, 157.

Jerome. *Eusebius Werke,* edited by R. Helm. Vol. 7, Die Chronik des Hieronymus. 3rd ed. Die Griechischen Christlichen Schriftsteller der Ersten Jahrhunderte, 47. Berlin: Akademie-Verlag, 1984.

Johnson, Monte, and Catherine Wilson. "Lucretius and the History of Science." In *The Cambridge Companion to Lucretius,* edited by Stuart Gillespie and Philip Hardie, 131–48. Cambridge: Cambridge University Press, 2007.

Johnson, W. R. *Lucretius and the Modern World.* London: Duckworth, 2000.

Jones, Howard. *The Epicurean Tradition.* London: Routledge, 1989.

Jürss, Fritz. *Die epikureische Erkenntnistheorie.* Berlin: Akademie-Verlag, 1991.

Kant, Immanuel. *Conflict of the Faculties.* Translated by Mary J Gregor. New York: Abaris, 1979.

Kant, Immanuel. "Conjectures on the Beginning of Human History." In *Political Writings,* edited by Hans Reiss, translated by H. B. Nisbet, 221–34. Cambridge: Cambridge University Press, 1991.

Kant, Immanuel. *Critique of Judgment.* Translated by Werner S. Pluhar. Indianapolis, IN: Hackett, 1987.

Kant, Immanuel. *Critique of Pure Reason.* Translated by Norman Kemp Smith. New York: Macmillan, 1965.

Kant, Immanuel. *Gesammelte Werke.* Berlin: De Gruyter, 1900–.

Kany-Turpin, J. "Une Réinvention de Lucrèce par Guillaume du Bartas." In *La Littérature et ses avatars: Discrédits, déformations et réhabilitations dans l'histoire de la littérature,* edited by Y. Bellenger, 31–39. Paris: Aux Amateurs de Livres, 1991.

Kavanagh, Thomas M. *Enlightened Pleasures: Eighteenth-Century France and the New Epicureanism.* New Haven, CT, and London: Yale University Press, 2010.

Kennedy, Duncan F. *Rethinking Reality: Lucretius and the Textualization of Nature.* Ann Arbor: University of Michigan Press, 2002.

Konstan, David. "Ancient Atomism and Its Heritage: Minimal Parts." *Ancient Philosophy* 2 (1982): 60–75.

Konstan, David. "Atomism." In *The Oxford Handbook of Epicureanism*, edited by Phillip Mitsis. Oxford: Oxford University Press, forthcoming.

Konstan, David. *Sexual Symmetry: Love in the Ancient Novel and Related Genres*. Princeton, NJ: Princeton University Press, 1994.

Kovel, Joel. "A Materialism Worthy of Nature." *Capitalism Nature Socialism* 12:2 (2001): 73–84.

Kramnick, Jonathan. *Actions and Objects from Hobbes to Richardson*. Stanford, CA: Stanford University Press, 2010.

Lamacz, S. "La Construction du savoir et la réécriture du *De Rerum Natura* dans *La Sepmaine* de Du Bartas." *Bibliothèque d'Humanisme et Renaissance* 64 (2002): 617–38.

Langman, Lauren, and Devorah Kalekin-Fishman, eds. *The Evolution of Alienation: Trauma, Promise, and the Millennium*. London: Rowman & Littlefield, 2006.

Latour, Bruno. "The Enlightenment without the Critique: A Word on Michel Serres' Philosophy." In *Contemporary French Philosophy*, edited by Allen Phillips Griffiths, 83–97. Cambridge: Cambridge University Press, 1987.

Latour, Bruno. *We Have Never Been Modern*. Translated by Catherine Porter. Cambridge, MA: Harvard University Press, 1993.

Lee, Mi-Kyoung. "Antecedents in Early Greek Philosophy." In *The Cambridge Companion to Ancient Scepticism*, edited by Richard Bett, 13–35. Cambridge: Cambridge University Press, 2010.

Leonard, J. 2000. "Milton, Lucretius, and 'The Void Profound of Unessential Night.'" In *Living Texts: Interpreting Milton*, edited by Kristin A. Pruitt and Charles W. Durham, 198–217. Selinsgrove, PA: Susquehanna University Press, 2000.

Lezra, Jacques. *Unspeakable Subjects: The Genealogy of the Event in Early Modern Europe*. Stanford, CA: Stanford University Press, 1997.

Lieb, Michael. *The Dialectics of Creation: Patterns of Birth & Regeneration in Paradise Lost*. Amherst: University of Massachusetts Press, 1969.

Locke, John. *An Essay Concerning Human Understanding*, edited by Peter H. Nidditch. Oxford: Clarendon Press, 1975.

Long, A. A., and D. N. Sedley, eds. and trans. *The Hellenistic Philosophers*. 2 vols. Cambridge: Cambridge University Press, 1987.

Lucretius. *De rerum natura*. Translated by W. H. D. Rouse. Translation revised by Martin Ferguson Smith. Cambridge, MA: Harvard University Press, 1992.

Lucretius. *De Rerum Natura*, edited by Cyril Bailey. 2 vols. Oxford: Oxford University Press, 1922.

Lucretius. *De Rerum Natura*. Books I–VI. Commentary by Cyril Bailey. 3 vols. Oxford: Oxford University Press, 1947.

Lucretius. *De rerum natura libri sex*, edited by H. C. A. Eichstadt. Leipzig: Wolf, 1801.

Lucretius. *De rerum natura libri sex*. The Latin Library. http://www.thelatinlibrary.com/lucretius.html

Lucretius. *Lucreti De rerum natura libri sex*, edited by Cyril Bailey. Oxford: Oxford University Press, 1963.

Lucretius. *Lucretius on the Nature of Things*. Translated by Ian Johnston, 2010. Accessed September 10, 2011. http://records.viu.ca/~johnstoi/lucretius/lucretiusbookoneweb.htm#t21

Lucretius. *On the Nature of Things*. Translated by Anthony M. Esolen. Baltimore, MD: Johns Hopkins University Press, 1995.

Lucretius. *On the Nature of Things*. Translated by Martin Ferguson Smith. Indianapolis, IN: Hackett, 1969.

Lucretius. *T. Lucreti Cari De rerum natura libri sex*. Translated by H. A. J. Munro, 4th ed. 3 vols. Cambridge: Deighton Bell, 1886.

Lucretius. *T. Lucretii Cari De rerum natura libros sex, ad exemplarium mss. fidem recensitos, longe emendatiores reddidit*, edited by Gilbert Wakefield, Richard Bentley, and Roscoe Pound. London: A: Hamilton, 1796.

Lucretius. *Titi Lucreti Cari De Rerum Natura libri sex*, edited and translated by Cyril Bailey. Vol. 1. Oxford: Oxford University Press, 1947.

Luria, S. "Die Infinitesimaltheorie der antiken Atomisten." *Quellen und Studien zur Geschichte der Mathematik* (B: Studien) 2 (1932–33): 154–56.

Lyon, John, and Philip R. Sloan. *From Natural History to the History of Nature*. Notre Dame and London: University of Notre Dame Press, 1981.

Ma, Ming-Quian. "The Past Is no Longer Out-of-Date." *Configurations* 8 (2000): 235–44.

MacDonogh, Giles. *Brillat-Savarin: The Judge and His Stomach*. London: John Murray, 1992.

MacIntyre, A. C. *Three Rival Versions of Moral Inquiry*. Notre Dame: Notre Dame University Press, 1990.

Madigan, Timothy J., and David B. Suits, eds. *Lucretius: His Continuing Influence and Contemporary Relevance*. Rochester, NY: RIT Press, 2011.

Mallette, Karla. "Ahead of the Swerve: From Anachronism to Complexity." In Pugh et al., "Book Review Forum," 359–62.

Marjara, H. *Contemplation of Created Things: Science in 'Paradise Lost'*. Toronto and London: University of Toronto Press, 1992.

Markovits, Francine. *Marx dans le jardin d'Epicure*. Paris: Editions de Minuit, 1974.

Marshall, John. *John Locke: Resistance, Religion, and Responsibility*. Cambridge: Cambridge University Press, 1994.

Martindale, Charles. *Redeeming the Text: Latin Poetry and the Hermeneutics of Reception*. Cambridge: Cambridge University Press, 1993.

Marvell, Andrew. *The Poems of Andrew Marvell*, edited by Nigel Smith. Harlow: Pearson/Longman, 2003.

Martindale, Charles. "Thinking through Reception." In *Classics and the Uses of Reception*, edited by Charles Martindale and Richard Thomas, 1–13. Malden, MA: Blackwell, 2006.

Marx, Karl. "England and Materialist Philosophy." In "Further Selection from the Literary Remains of Karl Marx," edited and translated by Max Beer. *Labour Monthly* (August 1923): 105–13.

Marx, Karl. *The Holy Family*. In *Marx/Engels Collected Works*. Vol. 4. New York: International, 1927.

Marx, Karl. *Marx-Engels Werke*. Berlin: Dietz Verlag, 1962–68.

Marx, Karl. *Notebooks on Epicurean Philosophy*. In *Marx/Engels Collected Works*. Vol. 1. New York: International, 1927.

Marx, Karl. "Theses on Feuerbach." Translated by William Lough. In *Marx/Engels Selected Works*. Vol. 1, 13–15. Moscow: Progress, 1969.

Marx, Karl. *Epikureische Philosophie*. In *Marx-Engels Werke*. Berlin: Dietz Verlag, 1968.

Marx, Karl, Friedrich Engels, and Ferdinand Lassalle. *Die heilige Familie: Aus dem literarischen nachlass*, edited by F. Mehring. Stuttgart: J. H. W. Dietz, 1902.

Meeker, Natania. *Voluptuous Philosophy: Literary Materialism in the French Enlightenment*. New York: Fordham University Press, 2006.

Menn, Stephen. "*The Discourse on the Method* and the Tradition of Intellectual Autobiography." In Miller and Inwood, *Hellenistic and Early Modern Philosophy*, 141–91.

Meyer, S. S. "Fate, Fatalism, and Agency in Stoicism." *Social Philosophy and Policy* 16 (1999): 250–73.

Michael, Fred, and Emily Michael. "Gassendi's Modified Epicureanism and British Moral Philosophy." *History of European Ideas* 21:6 (1995): 743–61.

Michaud, Joseph and Louis. *Biographie universelle ancienne et moderne*. 85 vols. Paris: Michaud Frères, 1811–62.

Miller, Jon, and Brad Inwood, eds. *Hellenistic and Early Modern Philosophy*. Cambridge: Cambridge University Press, 2003.

Milton, John. *The Poems of John Milton*, edited by John Carey and Alastair Fowler. London and New York: Longman, 1968.

Minadeo, Richard. *The Lyre of Science: Form and Meaning in Lucretius' De Rerum Natura*. Detroit, MI: Wayne State University Press, 1969.

Mitsis, Phillip. *Epicurus' Ethical Theory: The Pleasures of Invulnerability*. Ithaca, NY: Cornell University Press, 1988.

Mitsis, Phillip. "Locke's Offices." In Miller and Inwood, *Hellenistic and Early Modern Philosophy*, 45–61.

Mitsis, Phillip. "Locke on Pleasure and Law as Motives." In *Motive*, edited by Iakovos Vasiliou. Oxford: Oxford University Press, forthcoming.

Moreau, Pierre-François. *Lucrèce: L'âme.* Paris: Presses Universitaires de France, 2002.

Morel, Jean. "Recherches sur les Sources du *Discours sur l'Origine de l'Inégalité.*" *Annales de la Société Jean-Jacques Rousseau* 5 (1909): 119–98.

Morel, Pierre-Marie. "Les Communautés humaines." In *Lire Épicure et les épicuriens,* edited by Alain Gigandet and Pierre-Marie Morel, 167–86. Paris: Presses Universitaires de France, 2007.

Murdin, Paul. "Seleucus of Seleucia." In *Encyclopedia of Astronomy and Astrophysics,* edited by Paul Murdin. New York and London: Nature Publishing Group and Institute of Physics Publishing Company, 2001. Accessed April 19, 2013. http://eaa.iop.org

Murray, Oswyn. "Philodemus on the Good King According to Homer." *Journal of Roman Studies* 55 (1965): 161–82.

Murray, Oswyn. "Rileggendo *Il buon re secondo Omero.*" *Cronache ercolanesi* 14 (1984): 157–60.

Nagel, Alexander, and Christopher S. Wood. *Anachronic Renaissance.* New York: Zone Books, 2010.

Nichols, James H. *Epicurean Political Philosophy.* Ithaca, NY: Cornell University Press, 1976.

Nisbet, H. B. "Lucretius in Eighteenth Century Germany." *Modern Language Review* 81 (1986): 97–115.

Nisbet, R. G. M. *Cicero, In L. Calpurnium Pisonem oratio.* Oxford: Oxford University Press, 1961.

Nixon, Cheryl, ed. *Novel Definitions: An Anthology of Commentary on the Novel, 1688–1815.* Toronto: Broadview Press, 2009.

Obbink, Dirk. "Lucretius and the Herculaneum Library." In Gillespie and Hardie, *Cambridge Companion,* 33–40.

Obbink, Dirk, ed. *Philodemus and Poetry.* Oxford: Oxford University Press, 1995.

O'Connor, J. J., and E. F. Robertson. "Aristarchus of Samos." In *The MacTutor History of Mathematics Archive.* St. Andrews: School of Mathematics and Statistics, 1999. Accessed April 19, 2013. http://www-history.mcs.st-and.ac.uk/~history/Biographies/Aristarchus.html

Ovid. *P. Ovidi Nasonis Metamorphoses,* edited by Richard J. Tarrant. Oxford: Oxford University Press, 2004.

Palmer, Ada. *Reading Lucretius in the Renaissance.* Cambridge, MA: Harvard University Press, 2014.

Passannante, Gerard. "Homer Atomized: Francis Bacon and the Matter of Tradition," *English Literary History* 76 (2009): 1015–47.

Passannante, Gerard. *The Lucretian Renaissance: Philology and the Afterlife of Tradition.* Chicago, IL: Chicago University Press, 2011.

Passmore, John. "The Malleability of Man in Eighteenth-Century Thought." In *Aspects of the Eighteenth Century,* edited by E. R. Wasserman, 21–46. Baltimore, MD: Johns Hopkins University Press, 1965.

Philipp, Wolfgang. *Das Werden der Aufklärung in theologiegeschichtlicher Sicht.* Goettingen: Vanderhoeck and Ruprecht, 1957.

Philoponus. *Commentaria in Aristotelem Graeca.* Vols. 16 and 17, edited by Girolamo Vitelli. Berlin: G. Raimer, 1887–88.

Plato. *Plato: Complete Works,* edited by John M. Cooper. Indianapolis, IN: Hackett, 1997.

Plato. *Republic,* edited and translated by Chris Emlyn-Jones and William Preddy. 2 vols. Loeb Classical Library. Cambridge, MA: Harvard University Press, 2013.

Plutarch. *Against the Stoics: On Common Notions.* Translated by Harold Cherniss. In *Plutarch's Moralia,* 621–873. Vol. 13, part 2 of the Loeb Classical Library. Cambridge, MA: Harvard University Press, 1976.

Plutarch. *Moralia,* edited by G. N. Bernardakis. Leipzig: B. G. Teubner, 1893.

Plutarch. *Reply to Colotes in Defense of the Other Philosophers.* In *Plutarch: Moralia.* Vol. 14. Translated by Benedict Einarson and Phillip H. de Lacy, 151–315. Cambridge, MA: Harvard University Press, 1967.

Polignac, Melchior de. *Anti-Lucrèce, sive de Deo et Natura libri novem posthumum.* Paris: Guerin, 1747.

Pollock, Jonathan. *Déclinaisons: Le naturalisme poétique de Lucrèce à Lacan.* Paris: Editions Hermann, 2010.

Pongerville, Jean-Baptiste Sanson de. "Lucretius." *Dictionnaire de la conversation et de la lecture.* Paris: Belin-Mandar, 1832–39.

Porter, James. "Content and Form in Philodemus: The History of an Evasion." In *Philodemus and Poetry*, edited by Dirk Obbink, 97–146. Oxford: Oxford University Press, 1995.

Porter, James. "Lucretius and the Sublime." In Gillespie and Hardie, *Cambridge Companion*, 167–84.

Prescott, Anne L. "The Reception of Du Bartas in England." *Studies in the Renaissance* 15 (1968): 144–73.

Pugh, Tison, Noah Guynn, Peggy McCracken, Patricia Clare Ingham, and Elizabeth Scala, eds. "Book Review Forum: *The Swerve: How the World Became Modern*. By Stephen Greenblatt. W. W. Norton, 2011." Book Review Cluster. *Exemplaria: A Journal of Theory in Medieval and Renaissance Studies* 25:4 (2013): 313–70.

Quint, David. "Fear of Falling: Icarus, Phaethon, and Lucretius in *Paradise Lost*." *Renaissance Quarterly* 57 (2004): 847–81 (revised version in Quint, David. *Inside Paradise Lost*. Princeton, NJ: Princeton University Press, 2014: chapter 3).

Reimarus, Hermann Samuel. *Die vornehmsten Wahrheiten der natürlichen Religion*. Hamburg: Bohn, 1766.

Reimarus, Hermann Samuel. *The Principal Truths of Natural Religion Defended and Illustrated, in Nine Dissertations; wherein the Objections of Lucretius, Buffon, Maupertuis, Rousseau, La Mettrie, and Other Antient and Modern Followers of Epicurus Are Considered, and Their Doctrines Refuted*. Translated by Richard Wynne. London: B. Law, 1766.

Rist, John M. *Epicurus: An Introduction*. Cambridge: Cambridge University Press, 1972.

Robbins, Frank E. *The Hexaemeral Literature: A Study of the Greek and Latin Commentaries on Genesis*. Chicago, IL: Chicago University Press, 1912.

Roberts, Michael. "Ovid's *Metamorphoses* and the Latin Poets of Late Antiquity." *Arethusa* 35 (2002): 403–15.

Robertson, Kellie. "Medieval Materialism: A Manifesto." *Exemplaria* 22:2 (2010): 99–118.

Roger, Jacques. *Buffon: A Life in Natural History*. Translated by Sarah Lucille Bonnefoi. Ithaca, NY: Cornell University Press, 1997.

Royou, Thomas-Maurice. *Le Monde de verre réduit en poudre: Ou Analyse et réfutation des* Époques de la nature *de M. Le Comte de Buffon*. Paris: Mérigot, 1780.

Russo, Elena. *Styles of Enlightenment: Taste, Politics and Authorship in Eighteenth-Century France*. Baltimore, MD: Johns Hopkins University Press, 2007.

Russo, Lucio. *La rivoluzione dimenticata: Il pensiero scientifico greco e la scienza moderna*. 5th ed. Milan: Feltrinelli, 1998 (1st ed. 1996).

Saint-Just, Louis Antoine de. *Oeuvres Complètes*, edited by Anne Kupiec and Miguel Abensour. Paris: Gallimard, 2004.

Sarasohn, Lisa T. *Gassendi's Ethics: Freedom in a Mechanistic Universe*. Ithaca, NY: Cornell University Press, 1996.

Schmitt, Carl. *Frieden oder Pazifismus?: Arbeiten zum Völkerrecht und zur internationalen Politik 1924–1978*, edited by Günter Maschke. Berlin: Duncker & Humblot, 2005.

Schouls, Peter A. *Reasoned Freedom: John Locke and the Enlightenment*. Ithaca, NY: Cornell University Press, 1992.

Schrijvers, P. H. *Horror ac divina voluptas: Études sur la poétique et la poésie de Lucrèce*. Amsterdam: A. M. Hakkert, 1970.

Séchelles, Hérault de. *Voyage à Montbar*. 1801. Reprint, Paris: Aulard, 1890.

Sedley, David. *Creationism and Its Critics in Antiquity*. Berkeley: University of California Press, 2007.

Sedley, David. "Epicureanism in the Roman Republic." In *The Cambridge Companion to Epicureanism*, edited by James Warren, 29–45. Cambridge: Cambridge University Press, 2009.

Sedley, David. *Lucretius and the Transformation of Greek Wisdom*. Cambridge: Cambridge University Press, 1998.

Seneca. *Natural Questions, Books 4–7*. Translated by Thomas H. Corcoran. Cambridge, MA: Harvard University Press, 1972.

Serres, Michel. *The Birth of Physics*. Translated by Jack Hawkes, edited by David Webb. Manchester: Clinamen Press, 2000.

Serres, Michel. *Le contrat naturel*. Paris: F. Mourin, 1990.

Serres, Michel, with Bruno Latour. *Conversations on Science, Culture, and Time.* Translated by Roxanne Lapidus. Ann Arbor: University of Michigan Press, 1995.

Serres, Michel. *Éclaircissements: Cinq entretiens avec Bruno Latour.* Paris: Éditions François Bourin, 1992.

Serres, Michel. *La naissance de la physique dans le texte de Lucrèce: Fleuves et turbulences.* Paris: Éditions de Minuit, 1977.

Serres, Michel. *The Natural Contract.* Translated by Elizabeth MacArthur and William Paulson. Ann Arbor: University of Michigan Press, 1995.

Sextus Empiricus. *Sextus Empiricus: Against the Logicians,* edited and translated by R. Bett. Cambridge: Cambridge University Press, 2005.

Sextus Empiricus. *Sextus Empiricus in Four Volumes.* Translated by R. G. Bury. Vol. 4, *Against the Professors.* Cambridge, MA: Harvard University Press, 1944.

Shakespeare, William. *Hamlet,* edited by Stephen Greenblatt. In *The Norton Shakespeare: Based on the Oxford Edition,* edited by Stephen Greenblatt et al., 1659–759. New York: W. W. Norton, 1997.

Shapin, Steven. *The Scientific Revolution.* Chicago, IL: University of Chicago Press, 1996.

Sheridan, Patricia. *Locke: A Guide for the Perplexed.* New York: Bloomsbury, 2010.

Snyder, Susan, ed. *The Divine Weeks and Works of Guillaume de Saluste Sieur Du Bartas, Translated by Josuah Sylvester,* 2 vols. Oxford: Oxford University Press, 1979.

Sobel, Dava. *Longitude: The True Story of a Lone Genius Who Solved the Greatest Scientific Problem of His Time.* New York: Walker, 1995.

Spalding, Johann Joachim. *Die Bestimmung des Menschen.* 2nd ed. Leipzig: Weidmann, 1768.

Spinoza, Baruch. *Complete Works.* Translated by Samuel Shirley. Indianapolis, IN: Hackett, 2002.

Spinoza, Baruch. *Renati Descartes, Principia Philosophiae,* Spinoza et nous, http://spinozaetnous.org /wiki/Renati_Descartes_Principia_philosophiae

Spinoza, Baruch. *Ethica.* The Latin Library. http://www.thelatinlibrary.com/spinoza.ethica1.html

Strauss, Leo. *Die Religionskritik Spinozas als Grundlage seiner Bibelwissenschaft.* Berlin: Akademie-Verlag, 1930.

Strauss, Leo. *Liberalism Ancient and Modern.* New York: Basic Books, 1968.

Strauss, Leo. "A Note on Lucretius." In *Natur und Geschichte: Karl Löwith zum 70, Geburtstag,* edited by Hermann Braun and Manfred Riedel, 322–32. Stuttgart: W. Kohlhammer Verlag, 1967.

Strauss, Leo. *On Tyranny: Including the Strauss-Kojève Correspondence,* edited by Victor Gourevitch and Michael S. Roth. Chicago, IL: University of Chicago Press, 2000.

Strauss, Leo. *Persecution and the Art of Writing.* Chicago, IL: University of Chicago Press, 1952.

Strauss, Leo. *Spinoza's Critique of Religion.* Translated by E. M. Sinclair. New York: Schocken, 1965.

Striker, Gisela. "Epicurus on the Truth of Sense-Impressions." *Archiv für Geschichte der Philosophie* 59 (1977): 125–42. Reprinted in Striker. *Essays in Hellenistic Epistemology and Ethics,* 77–91. Cambridge: Cambridge University Press, 1996.

Swedberg, Richard, ed. *Max Weber: The Protestant Ethic and the Spirit of Capitalism.* New York: W. W. Norton, 2009.

Taub, Liba. "Cosmology and Meteorology." In *The Cambridge Companion to Epicureanism,* edited by James Warren, 105–24. Cambridge: Cambridge University Press, 2009.

Taylor, C. C. W. "'All Perceptions Are True'." In *Doubt and Dogmatism,* edited by Malcolm Schofield, Jonathan Barnes, and Myles Burnyeat, 105–24. Oxford: Oxford University Press, 1980.

Taylor, C. C. W. *The Atomists: Leucippus and Democritus: A Text and Translation with a Commentary.* Toronto: University of Toronto Press, 1999.

Taylor, George C. *Milton's Use of DuBartas.* Cambridge, MA: Harvard University Press, 1934.

Thomson, James. *The Complete Poetical Works of James Thomson,* edited by J. Logie Robertson. London: Oxford University Press, 1908.

Tompkins, Jane P. *Reader Response Criticism: From Formalism to Post-Structuralism.* Baltimore, MD: Johns Hopkins University Press, 1980.

Toomer, G. J. "Ptolemy." In *Dictionary of Scientific Biography,* edited by C. C. Gillespie. Vol. 11, 186–206. New York: Charles Scribner, 1975.

Townend, Gavin B. "The Fading of Memmius." *The Classical Quarterly,* New Series 28:2 (1978): 267–83.

Tuck, Richard. "The Civil Religion of Thomas Hobbes." In *Political Discourse in Early Modern Britain*, edited by Nicholas Phillipson and Quentin Skinner, 120–39. Cambridge: Cambridge University Press, 1993.

Vander Waerdt, Paul. "Colotes and the Epicurean Refutation of Skepticism." *Greek, Roman and Byzantine Studies* 30 (1989): 225–67.

Victorius, Claudius Marius. *Claudii Marii Victorii Alethia*, edited by P. F. Hovingh. Corpus Christianorum, series Latina 128. Turnholt: Brepols, 1960.

Vida, Marco Girolamo. *Christiad*, edited and translated by James Gardner. Cambridge, MA, and London: Harvard University Press, 2009.

Virgil. *P. Vergilii Maronis Opera,* edited by R. A. B. Mynors. Oxford: Oxford University Press, 1969.

Vogt, Katja Maria. *Belief and Truth: A Skeptic Reading of Plato*. New York: Oxford University Press, 2012.

Volk, Katharina. *Manilius and His Intellectual Background*. Oxford: Oxford University Press, 2009.

Voltaire (François-Marie Arouet). *Philosophical Dictionary*. 3 vols. Translated by J. G. Gurton. London: Hunt, 1824.

Vyverberg, Henry. *Historical Pessimism in the French Enlightenment*. Cambridge, MA: Harvard University Press, 1958.

Wallach, Barbara Price. *Lucretius and the Diatribe against the Fear of Death:* De Rerum Natura *III, 830–1094*. Mnemosyne suppl. 40. Leiden: Brill, 1976.

Walsham, Alexandra. *The Reformation of the Landscape: Religion, Identity, & Memory in Early Modern Britain & Ireland*. Oxford: Oxford University Press, 2011.

Warren, James. "Lucretius and Greek Philosophy." In Gillespie and Hardie, *Cambridge Companion*, 19–32.

Warren, James, ed. *The Cambridge Companion to Epicureanism*. Cambridge: Cambridge University Press, 2009.

Webb, David. "Michel Serres on Lucretius: Atomism, Science, and Ethics." *Angelaki: Journal of the Theoretical Humanities* 11 (2006): 125–36.

Weber, Max. *The Protestant Ethic and the Spirit of Capitalism*. Translated by Talcott Parsons. New York: Charles Scribner's, 1958 (translation originally published 1930).

Whitaker, V. K. "Du Bartas' Use of Lucretius." *Studies in Philology* 33 (1936): 134–46.

Wilkinson, L. P. "Lucretius and the Love-Philtre." *The Classical Review* 63:2 (1949): 47–48.

Williams, Bernard. "The Truth in Relativism." *Proceedings of the Aristotelian Society* 75 (1974–75): 215–28.

Williams, C. J. F. *Philoponus on Aristotle's On Coming-to-be and Perishing 1.6–2.4*. Ithaca, NY: Cornell University Press, 1999.

Williams, Ioan, ed. *Novel and Romance 1700–1800: A Documentary Record*. London: Routledge and Kegan Paul, 1970.

Wilson, Catherine. *Epicureanism at the Origins of Modernity*. Oxford: Oxford University Press, 2008.

Wilson, Catherine. "Political Philosophy in a Lucretian Mode." In *Lucretius and the Early Modern*, edited by David Norbrook, Stephen Harrison, and Philip Hardie. Oxford: Oxford University Press, 2015.

Wood, Christopher. "Reception and the Classics." In *Reception and the Classics: An Interdisciplinary Approach to the Classical Tradition*, edited by William Brockliss, Pramit Chaudhuri, Ayelet H. Lushkov, and Katherine Wasdin, 163–73. Cambridge: Cambridge University Press, 2011.

Wordsworth, William. *William Wordsworth: Last Poems 1821–1850*, edited by Jared Curtis. Ithaca, NY: Cornell University Press, 1999.

Yaffe, Gideon. *Liberty Worth a Name: Locke on Free Agency*. Princeton, NJ: Princeton University Press, 2000.

CONTRIBUTORS

Liza Blake is an Assistant Professor of English at the University of Toronto, and studies the intersection of literature, science, and philosophy in early modernity. She has published in the journals *postmedieval* and *SEL: Studies in English Literature 1500–1900*, and is writing a book called *Early Modern Literary Physics*.

Joseph Farrell is Professor of Classical Studies and the M. Mark and Esther W. Watkins Professor in the Humanities at the University of Pennsylvania. He studies Latin poetry and its reception. Among his books is *Latin Language and Latin Culture from Ancient to Modern Times* (2001).

Alain Gigandet teaches the History of Ancient Philosophy at the Université de Paris-Est Créteil (ex Paris 12). He has published *Fama deum: Lucrèce et les raisons du mythe* (1998), *Lucrèce: Atomes, mouvement* (2001), and *Lire Épicure et les épicuriens* (with P.-M. Morel, 2007), and numerous papers on ancient Epicurean philosophy as well as modern readings of Epicureanism (Montaigne, Diderot, Leopardi, Hegel, Strauss, and Foucault).

Philip Hardie is a Senior Research Fellow at Trinity College, Cambridge, and Honorary Professor of Latin Literature at the University of Cambridge. He is coeditor (with Stuart Gillespie) of *The Cambridge Companion to Lucretius* (2007).

Brooke Holmes is Professor of Classics and Director of the Interdisciplinary Doctoral Program in the Humanities at Princeton University. She is the author of *The Symptom and the Subject: The Emergence of the Physical Body in Ancient Greece* and *Gender: Antiquity and Its Legacy*, as well as coeditor of *Dynamic Reading: Studies in the Reception of Epicureanism*.

Thomas M. Kavanagh teaches at Yale University. His research centers on eighteenth-century literature, culture, and the visual arts. His publications include *Enlightened Pleasures: Eighteenth-Century France and the New Epicureanism* (2010) and *Enlightenment and the Shadows of Chance* (1993). He is currently working on a book-length study of post-Revolutionary pleasures.

David Konstan is Professor of Classics at New York University (NYU). Among his recent books are *The Emotions of the Ancient Greeks: Studies in Aristotle and Classical Literature* (2006), *"A Life Worthy of the Gods": The Materialist Psychology of Epicurus* (2008), *Before Forgiveness: The Origins of a Moral Idea* (2010), and *Beauty: The Fortunes of an Ancient Greek Idea* (2014). He is a past president of the American Philological Association.

Jacques Lezra is Professor of Spanish and Comparative Literature at NYU, and a member of the Departments of English and German. His most recent book is *Wild Materialism: The Ethic of Terror and the Modern Republic* (2010; Spanish translation 2012; Chinese translation 2013). A book on Cervantes, *Contra los fueros de la muerte: El suceso cervantino*, is in press; one titled *On the Nature of Marx's Things* is in preparation.

Phillip Mitsis is the A. S. Onassis Professor of Hellenic Culture and Civilization at NYU, a Senior Affiliate at NYU Abu Dhabi, and Academic Director of the American Institute of Verdi Studies. He works on Greek and Roman epic and on ancient philosophy, especially Hellenistic philosophy, and its influence on later philosophers such as Gassendi, Locke, Hume, and Kant. His most recent book is *L'Éthique d'Épicure* (trans. A. Gigandet 2014).

Warren Montag is the Brown Family Professor of Literature at Occidental College in Los Angeles. His most recent book is *The Other Adam Smith* (2014).

Katja Maria Vogt is Professor of Philosophy at Columbia University. She specializes in ancient philosophy, ethics, and normative epistemology. Vogt is interested in questions that figure in both ancient and contemporary discussions: What are values? What kind of values are knowledge and truth? What does it mean to want one's life to go well?

Catherine Wilson is Anniversary Professor of Philosophy at the University of York (United Kingdom) and Visiting Distinguished Professor of Philosophy at the Graduate Center, City University of New York. Her most recent book was *Epicureanism at the Origins of Modernity* (2008/2011). Her *Very Short Introduction to Epicureanism* is scheduled to appear in December 2015 from Oxford University Press.

INDEX

CPSIA information can be obtained
at www.ICGtesting.com
Printed in the USA
LVOW04s1624150216

475201LV00008B/99/P